BRITAIN AND THE MAASTRICHT NEGOTIATIONS

ST ANTONY'S SERIES
*General Editors: Alex Pravda (1993–97), Eugene Rogan (1997–), both
Fellows of St Antony's College, Oxford*

Recent titles include:

Mark Brzezinski
THE STRUGGLE FOR CONSTITUTIONALISM IN POLAND

Peter Carey (*editor*)
BURMA

Stephanie Po-yin Chung
CHINESE BUSINESS GROUPS IN HONG KONG AND POLITICAL
CHANGE IN SOUTH CHINA, 1900–25

Ralf Dahrendorf
AFTER 1989

Alex Danchev
ON SPECIALNESS

Roland Dannreuther
THE SOVIET UNION AND THE PLO

Noreena Hertz
RUSSIAN BUSINESS RELATIONSHIPS IN THE WAKE OF REFORM

Iftikhar H. Malik
STATE AND CIVIL SOCIETY IN PAKISTAN

Steven McGuire
AIRBUS INDUSTRIE

Yossi Shain and Aharon Klieman (*editors*)
DEMOCRACY

William J. Tompson
KHRUSHCHEV

Marguerite Wells
JAPANESE HUMOUR

Yongjin Zhang and Rouben Azizian (*editors*)
ETHNIC CHALLENGES BEYOND BORDERS

St Antony's Series
Series Standing Order ISBN 0–333–71109–2
(*outside North America only*)

You can receive future titles in this series as they are published by placing a standing order.
Please contact your bookseller or, in case of difficulty, write to us at the address below with
your name and address, the title of the series and the ISBN quoted above.

Customer Services Department, Macmillan Distribution Ltd
Houndmills, Basingstoke, Hampshire RG21 6XS, England

Britain and the Maastricht Negotiations

Anthony Forster
Lecturer in Politics
University of Nottingham

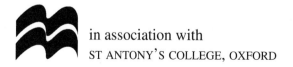

in association with
ST ANTONY'S COLLEGE, OXFORD

First published in Great Britain 1999 by
MACMILLAN PRESS LTD
Houndmills, Basingstoke, Hampshire RG21 6XS and London
Companies and representatives throughout the world

A catalogue record for this book is available from the British Library.

ISBN 0–333–73170–0

 First published in the United States of America 1999 by
ST. MARTIN'S PRESS, INC.,
Scholarly and Reference Division,
175 Fifth Avenue, New York, N.Y. 10010

ISBN 0–312–21848–6

Library of Congress Cataloging-in-Publication Data
Forster, Anthony, 1964–
Britain and the Maastricht negotiations / Anthony Forster.
p.   cm. — (St Antony's series)
Includes bibliographical references and index.
ISBN 0–312–21848–6 (cloth)
1. European Union—Great Britain.   I. Title.   II. Series.
HC240.25.G7F67   1999
337.41—dc21
                                                            98–42267
                                                                  CIP

This book is printed on paper suitable for recycling and made from fully managed and sustained forest sources.

10   9   8   7   6   5   4   3   2   1
08   07   06   05   04   03   02   01   00   99

Printed and bound in Great Britain by
Antony Rowe Ltd, Chippenham, Wiltshire

To V.J.C

Contents

Acknowledgements

In researching this subject and preparing my doctorate for publication, I owe a considerable debt of gratitude to a number of people. I would like to thank my supervisor William Wallace for his support throughout. From start to finish his insights, guidance and encouragement made the research a pleasure to undertake. William continues to inspire a whole generation of scholars and I would like to express my thanks to him. I would also like to thank Anne Deighton, Geoffrey Edwards, Anand Menon and Vincent Wright for their valuable advice at crucial moments.

I am grateful to the politicians, officials and those involved in the policy-making process who agreed to be interviewed for this research. I would further like to thank Alasdair Blair, Andrew Crockett, Debra France, Maurice Fraser, David Hadley, Christopher Taylor and Anthony Teasdale who read the whole manuscript or parts of it. I am responsible for both matters of interpretation and argument, but I am grateful to them for their critical advice.

The research was funded by the Economic and Social Research Council, but I would also like to acknowledge financial support from St Hugh's College, Oxford, the Institut d'Etudes Européennes, Université Libre de Bruxelles, where I held a Weiner Anspach visiting research fellowship, and the Western European Union Institute for Security Studies, Paris.

My greatest thanks are to Victoria Child who has never flinched from challenging my assumptions and unpicking my arguments. Her intellectual honesty and rigour has provided me with a debt of gratitude I can never hope to repay. This book is dedicated to her.

Introduction

This book seeks to explain the British government's position in the negotiation of the 1992 Treaty on European Union (TEU). Popularly known as the Maastricht Treaty, this represented the most important development in European integration since the Treaty of Rome. Not only did it establish a European Union, but it also made a commitment to a single currency, a common foreign and defence policy and European citizenship.[1] The negotiations for the Treaty took place over the course of a year, between December 1990 and December 1991, and were composed of two distinct elements, an Intergovernmental Conference on Economic and Monetary Union (IGC-EMU) and an Intergovernmental Conference on Political Union (IGC-PU), both of which culminated in the Maastricht European Council in December 1991 and from which the Treaty takes its name.[2]

The controversy these complex negotiations generated in Britain remains a major factor in the current debate concerning Britain's European policies. Indeed, opposition to the commitment to political union and a single currency included in the Maastricht agenda has provided an important rallying point for those who continue to oppose moves towards closer European integration. In exploring the domestic controversy occasioned by the negotiation of the Treaty, the book sheds light on the wider British attitude towards Europe, and in particular the image of Britain as an awkward partner in its dealings with the European Community (EC).[3] One aspect of the 'awkward partner' school is the argument that London finds it hard to make deals, is resistant to the linkage of issues and is poor at building coalitions in the Council of Ministers. The negotiations of 1990 to 1991 offer an ideal testing ground for this argument and the depiction of London as 'obstructionist and bloody minded' and unskilled in the art of compromise.[4]

But the importance of explaining the British position extends further, since it is widely agreed that one cannot understand the shape of the Treaty without understanding the role of Britain in the negotiations.[5] The prism of British policy therefore provides insights into the Treaty negotiations as a whole, and so into the process of European integration itself. This is because the Maastricht negotiations marked a turning-point in the integration project. As Helen and William Wallace argue, solutions adopted at the Maastricht European Council explicitly broke the 'Community method' whereby all Member States needed to agree the same measures, and substituted in its place selective involvement in key policy areas.[6] Why and how Britain contributed to this process is a crucial element in explaining the change.

The existing empirical literature on the negotiations is divided into four categories. First, there are the *histoires engagées* written by participants.[7] Second, there is the cluster of publications that outline the general shape of the Treaty and its potential effect on Community/Union decision-making and competences.[8] Third, there is a handful of British studies examining Britain's general relationship with Europe and the British negotiating position in the IGC-PU.[9] Finally, a number of sectoral studies addresses the outcome of particular dossiers in the negotiations.[10] Existing works, however, generally suffer from being published too soon after the negotiations, and fail to examine the motivations of the British government fully.[11]

The central argument of this book is that the British government's position and achievements in the 1990–1 IGCs can only be understood by close reference to the domestic political context. A leading theme is that 'men make their own history, but not just as they please'.[12] The book thus takes issue with the argument that systemic factors are the sole key to explaining the outcome of the TEU.[13] It is true that the coincidence of a series of remarkable international events centred on the collapse of Communism shaped the immediate context and parallel nature of the IGCs on EMU and political union. But these events did not directly affect the content of the IGCs, which were concerned with an existing West European agenda and took little direct account of the implications of changes in Central and Eastern Europe. In this sense Maastricht was a backward-looking treaty.

The British influence on the course and outcome of the negotiations was determined most directly by the domestic circumstances of John Major's government. Above all, the Prime Minister was motivated by the need to hold the Conservative Party together in the aftermath of Mrs Thatcher's downfall, and this consideration in all its various aspects had a direct bearing on both the timing and a great deal of the content of the policies John Major pursued in the IGCs. The reasons why party unity had such an impact, related not only to the adversarial, first-past-the-post nature of the British political system. It also stemmed from the long history of British failure at the governmental and popular levels to come to grips with the implications of membership of the EC and Britain's declining world position.

The origins and international context of the IGCs are explored in the second half of this Introduction, while the domestic background to the negotiations is discussed in Chapter 1. The subsequent chapters then provide a detailed analysis of British aims and achievements in the four key areas of debate: Economic and Monetary Union, social policy, defence and foreign policy, and institutional reform, in particular the enhancement of the powers of the European Parliament (EP). Chapter 6 considers the overall balance-sheet of British successes and failures at the two IGCs and analyses the common themes in British actions across the dossiers. The Conclusion reflects on the overall balance of the Treaty, and its implications for both Britain and the European integration project as a whole.[14]

In pursuing these objectives, the book draws on secondary literature of an empirical and a theoretical nature. However, in terms of the availability of primary material, scholars obviously face a difficult task. All public records, departmental and Cabinet papers remain officially classified and unavailable under the thirty-year rule. In addition, the intergovernmental negotiations were conducted in private and many Presidency documents were not published. Nevertheless, a wide range of information is available at the national and European level.

In Britain, official publications, reports from Parliamentary Select Committees and parliamentary debates, the government press service and Conservative Central Office were all useful sources of information on the government's negotiating position. Much use was also made of the work of the House of Lords European Communities Committee, which placed in the public domain material based on evidence from government officials, ministers, Members of the European Parliament (MEPs) and European politicians during the IGC negotiations.

The growing number of former ministers' memoirs has filled in an important part of the missing Cabinet dimension,[15] while the press-cuttings service of the Royal Institute of International Affairs, and the Western European Union, provided a comprehensive screening of the quality British and European press and so gave important insights into the nature of the domestic debate.

All this information was supplemented by interviews with national and European officials, Members of Parliament (MPs), MEPs and others involved in the preparation of policy (listed in Appendix 1). It has been commented that interview information 'can be the kiss of death to objectivity'.[16] Certainly the quality of evidence varied with the seniority and vantage-point of the interviewee, with few participants playing a part in all aspects of the policy-making process and a number of interviewees jealous of their own reputations and keen to write their place in history. Moreover, although many were willing to be quoted, some made an interview conditional on anonymity in the text. Care was therefore taken to interview as wide a range of national and European officials and politicians as possible, and to include information from relevant interest groups. Wherever possible, information was also verified against evidence presented in the secondary literature and, in particular, in the works authored by people directly involved in the IGC-EMU and IGC-PU negotiations.

European sources also provided a rich source of primary material. Much to the irritation of the British government – and contrary to an agreement between the member governments – many national submissions to the IGCs were leaked and a number reproduced in *Europe Documents*. Written evidence also included official Commission, EP and Council and Presidency documents, including the various draft texts of the Treaty produced by the Luxembourg and Dutch Presidencies of the Council of Ministers. Much use was also made of *Agence Europe*, and in particular its well-informed commentary on the conduct of specific meetings, often including reports of the comments by each of the personal representatives. Clearly, without full access to departmental records, there are limitations which remain. However, so many of the negotiations were conducted in an informal manner, over the telephone or in forums where detailed records of conversations were not kept, that many of the participants note the official record may not be as useful as some might suppose. Indeed, the Foreign and Commonwealth Office (FCO) abandoned an attempt to write an official history of the Maastricht negotiations because the documentary evidence was patchy and left a wholly inaccurate view of the dynamics of the negotiations.[17]

THE INTERNATIONAL CONTEXT

Both the IGCs of 1990 to 1991 were a response to shifts in international political economy and world politics. Their origins, however, can be traced back to the Single European Act (SEA) of 1987, and these origins had a large impact on the terms and spirit in which they were conducted. Delegations brought with them to the negotiating table not only specifically national views of how the EC should develop but also the baggage of previous disputes and controversies unresolved by the SEA.

The SEA came into effect in June 1987 and had as its principal aim the introduction of a Single Market by 1 January 1993. It was seen by many in Britain as a victory for the neo-liberal instincts of Margaret Thatcher and as a means to steer the Community away from social and monetary issues.[18] It was therefore perceived in London as a defeat for the more federalist-minded Member States, and the maximalist EP, which had approved a *Draft Treaty Establishing the European Union* in 1984.[19]

However, this perception was not wholly accurate, since the SEA was in reality a compromise between 'those Member States wishing to advance more rapidly and those more reticent.'[20] Monetary Union was presented by the more ambitious as a logical accompaniment to the Single Market, and in June 1988 these Member States succeeded in establishing the Delors Monetary Committee to examine Economic and Monetary Union (EMU). Despite outright condemnation by Mrs Thatcher, together with more measured German reservations, the Madrid European Council in June 1989 recommended a three-stage approach to EMU. The Strasbourg European Council in December 1989 agreed that an IGC-EMU should be convened in December 1990 with the express purpose of amending the Treaties of Rome to create the specific mechanisms for a single currency. Thereafter, the German government, alongside the Belgian and Italian governments and the EP, was active in pressing for the IGC to be widened to consider other institutional and procedural changes to accompany moves towards a single currency.

It was not until December 1989, however, that acceptance of the need for an extensive review of the Treaties of Rome, and so of the institutional arrangements and policy competences of the EC, became widespread.[21] The disintegration of the Communist system in Eastern Europe and rapid German unification in October 1990 were the key catalysts leading to the political union negotiations. These momentous international events had two particular effects. First, the regimes of Central and Eastern Europe turned to the EC for assistance in their transformation to democracies and free-market economies.[22] Second, and more important for the internal development of the EC, the speed of German unification and the potential economic and political influence of a united Germany in both West and Eastern Europe unnerved the political class in all Member States and raised the spectre of a new 'German problem.'[23]

Prompted by these developments, many governments abandoned their scepticism concerning the need for closer political integration. Mrs Thatcher had argued that there was already a full agenda and the focus should be completing the Single Market, signing association agreements with the Visegrad countries and bringing the Uruguay Round of trade talks to a successful conclusion.[24] Instead, at the Dublin European Council in June 1990, it was agreed to convene a second IGC to consider a wide range of institutional and procedural changes to the Treaty of Rome.[25] This second IGC, termed the IGC-PU, was to run from 10 December 1990 to 11 December 1991 in parallel with the IGC-EMU. The two IGCs would culminate in the Maastricht European Council, at which heads of government would conduct final discussions prior to agreeing a treaty amendment, to be ratified and come into effect on 1 January 1993.

There was a striking difference between the IGC-EMU and the IGC-PU. The IGC-EMU had as its core agenda the creation of a single currency, and many of the fundamental premises upon which EMU was based had been explored in the two years prior to the formal launch of the IGC-EMU. Indeed much of the preparatory work had been completed leaving a narrow (but important) cluster of issues to be resolved. But the political union negotiations by contrast had no pre-agreed core objective much beyond a number of institutional proposals which the Belgian government put forward in March 1990.[26] Mitterrand and Kohl subsequently linked these proposals to the objective of creating an undefined 'European Union,'[27] but in the absence of any detailed proposals their aim was 'more of a guiding star than a road map.'[28] Even by the time of the Rome European Council in December 1990 there was no hint of what this 'European Union' might be or of what changes were necessary to achieve it.[29]

The IGC-PU was not then the product of a controlled and orderly process. On a number of key issues underlying differences between the EC's Member States were unresolved, and this left them more vulnerable to the vagaries of events. Indeed the whole of the negotiations were dogged by the absence of any agreement on what the objectives behind the rhetoric really were.[30] The agenda for the IGC-PU was therefore limited to what can best be described as a 'wish list' for the negotiating teams to tackle.[31] By the time of the Rome Summit this included the possibility of enhancing the powers of the EP and

Commission, developing a foreign and security policy, developing social, economic and civil rights, extending the EC's competences and institutional changes to the working methods of the Council.[32]

The context of the negotiation was further affected by two key factors. First, there was a delay between the decision to hold the IGCs and their formal launch. Whereas the mood of June 1990 was optimistic, the intervening six months saw a perceptible change in attitudes.[33] In that time the invasion of Kuwait by Iraq and the need to coordinate their response became the overriding preoccupation of European leaders. Anxiety also emerged over economic and political instability in the east. The rapid strides towards German unification gave rise to concern over the high economic cost of assimilating East Germany into the Federal Republic and its implications for the rest of the EC, especially plans for Economic and Monetary Union. At the same time the EC seemed set to clash with the United States at the Brussels meeting for the Uruguay Round, scheduled for mid-December 1990. Nor was the general mood helped by an economic downturn in Europe. The spectre of deep recession made a number of governments hesitate to support binding commitments to specific types of monetary and fiscal policies and to accept pre-arranged targets as a precondition of monetary union.

The second factor shaping the context of the negotiations was policy overload. At the beginning of 1991, the Luxembourg Presidency was preoccupied with the Soviet aggression in the Baltic States and the launch of Operation Desert Storm into Kuwait.[34] The aftermath of the recapture of Kuwait was a similarly demanding period for the Luxembourg Presidency, and an emergency European Council meeting called at the beginning of April 1991 to review progress in the IGC-PU had instead to be devoted to the issue of Kurdish safe-havens in northern Iraq.[35]

While events in the Baltic States and the Gulf thus slowed down the initial stages of the IGC-PU and to some extent the IGC-EMU, the main distraction during the second half of 1991 was the disintegration of Yugoslavia. When the crisis broke out in June 1991, many of the most sensitive issues in the IGC-PU had not yet been resolved and there was still no consensus on the overall structure of the treaty. The Yugoslavian problem meant that the Dutch Presidency, the Troika and the personal representatives were preoccupied with drafting resolutions, re-establishing a ceasefire in Croatia and then deploying EC peace monitors. The problems for negotiators were further exacerbated by a fourth exceptional event, the Soviet *putsch* on 19 August

1991 and the eventual collapse of the Soviet Union in December. These issues further delayed the reconvening of the IGC-PU, for example, preventing it from meeting at working-group level between the end of June and the end of September 1991, a period of 43 working days.

The overload caused by these international developments had two particular consequences for the context and course of the IGCs. First, it encouraged the view among participants that 'no agreement would have been worse than an imperfect one.'[36] Indeed, prior to the Maastricht European Council, the Dutch Foreign Minister suggested that the summiteers were 'condemned to succeed', and Kohl highlighted the pressure they felt themselves to be under with his comment that to fail would be to miss out on 'the chance of a generation.'[37] Senior British negotiators did not escape this pressure.[38] Of particular concern to them was the fear that, if treaty revisions were not agreed, European Community enlargement would be set back irrevocably.[39]

Second, the sheer scale of policy overload led to an atmosphere in which treaty drafts and compromises tended to be put forward with the minimum of discussion and preparation within delegations, let alone between them. For example, on 24 September 1991, a mere 12 weeks before the Maastricht European Council, Piet Dankert, the Dutch European Minister, tabled a new draft treaty which he had not cleared with his Prime Minister or Foreign Minister. They had been preoccupied with the Yugoslav crisis and with the near collapse of the Dutch governing coalition. The draft was in fact rejected on 30 September 1991 by 10 of the 12 foreign ministers. While only Belgium and the Netherlands formally supported the text, the irony was that four other governments – Germany, Italy, Spain and Greece – were openly sympathetic to its aims. Indeed, they rejected it simply because it was tabled too late in the IGC-PU and in their view made it impossible to conclude the negotiations by December 1991.[40]

It is true that a busy Community agenda for political leaders and national officials is in itself so routine as to be unremarkable.[41] What made it noteworthy during 1990 to 1991 was the magnitude of the issues at stake both within the conference chamber and outside it. With no consensus as to what one important strand of the negotiations – the IGC-PU – should actually be about, and feeling themselves nevertheless under intense pressure to produce an agreement, policymakers were prone to expedients, to impatience and to errors. It is thus of the utmost importance to bear in mind the human character of the negotiators, where factors such as personality and ability to understand a complex dossier could play a pivotal role.

THE STRUCTURE OF THE IGCS

While the context of the negotiations was shaped most immediately by international events, and the way those events influenced the options and behaviour of the participants, the negotiations were not without formal structures. Although the length of the IGCs was exceptional in comparison with the SEA negotiations, the negotiations took place within a well-established if specialized framework of rules and procedures.[42]

IGC-PU

In organizational terms the IGC-PU took place at three different levels: personal representatives, foreign ministers and heads of state and government. The personal representatives were appointed by each government. In Britain's case, Sir John Kerr, the British ambassador to the EC, was also the British personal representative to the IGC-PU, with David Hadley the senior official in the European Secretariat of the Cabinet Office Kerr's deputy. For a number of reasons some other governments, notably France, Denmark and Italy chose not to 'double-hat' their EC ambassadors. The personal representatives were responsible for the routine negotiations and generally met on a weekly basis, in a forum clearly distinct from the Committee of Permanent Representatives (COREPER) meetings, which dealt with other EC business. Any issue that could not be resolved by the personal representatives, or which was deemed sufficiently contentious to require political authority, was passed up to the foreign ministers who met once a month in the margins of the Foreign Affairs Council and in two specially convened 'conclaves' towards the end of the negotiations. The British representatives at the foreign ministers' level were the Foreign Secretary, Douglas Hurd, and his European Minister Tristan Garel-Jones. It was the informal remit of the foreign ministers to make national sticking-points clear, launch detailed policy initiatives to break any deadlock and give the negotiations added political momentum. In reality, however, it was only on foreign and security policy issues that the foreign ministers actually pushed the negotiations forward.

Nominally they discussed the other main issues, but many foreign ministers' meetings were a re-run of the personal representatives' meetings, with one official noting that most minsters simply read out scripts prepared by their officials. It was only at the two pre-Maastricht conclaves that the foreign ministers addressed issues other than foreign and security policy. The Heads of State and Government considered IGC issues at the Luxembourg and Maastricht European Councils and at a specially convened emergency European Council in the spring of 1991. The Heads of State and Government were responsible for taking stock of the negotiations at the half-way point and for negotiating the final package deal at the Maastricht European Council in December 1991.

Luxembourg and the Netherlands each held the Council Presidency for six months and had overall responsibility for managing the negotiations at the three levels. They chaired the European Councils, along with monthly foreign ministers' meetings and weekly meetings of personal representatives. The presidencies were responsible for choosing the agenda, setting the priorities, preparing the draft treaty texts, accepting or rejecting treaty amendments and for presenting the final text to the heads of government. There were three further groupings that supported the Luxembourg and Dutch presidencies in their tasks. First, there was the 'Friends of the Presidency Group', which acted as a clearing house for ideas before they were formally tabled in the personal representatives' meetings.

Second, there was a 'drafting group' comprised of senior officials in the Council of Ministers Secretariat and Commission, whose task was to assist the Presidency in the rather specialized task of drafting treaty articles. This group usually met immediately after the personal representatives' weekly meeting. In fact, the Commission had a right to attend the IGCs and table proposals, and Jacques Delors withdrew Commission officials from the drafting group because he felt the Commission could exercize greater influence in the IGC meetings by being unencumbered by this particular function.[43]

Third and finally, the Luxembourg Presidency drew together officials from Belgium, France and Germany at an informal level to provide an inner group of 'committed' participants to test its ideas and to pre-bargain issues before they were formally tabled at personal representatives' meetings. Interestingly, the Dutch, who might have been expected to be part of such an inner core as a member of the BENELUX grouping, but also as the next presidency, were excluded on the grounds that they were too close to the British and might contaminate pre-bargaining. The organization and responsibilities of the IGC-PU are outlined in Table 1.

Table 1: Organization and Responsibilities in the IGC-PU

Level	Personalities participating	Type of meeting	Number of meetings	Function	Other forums for meeting
Official (Low)	Personal Representatives	Working Sessions	28	Identifying problems and areas of agreement	COREPER 42 meetings
Political (Medium)	Foreign Ministers	a. European Cooperation	a. 2	Launching political initiatives	a. NATO 2 meetings
	or Deputy Foreign Ministers	b. General Affairs Council	b. 2	Solving issues that require political input	b. WEU 8 meetings
	or Ministers for European Affairs	c. IGC-PU	c. 12	Examining areas where progress is slow	c. Margins of the European Council 4 meetings
Political (High)	Heads of State and Government	European Council a. Regular sessions	a. 2	Taking stock	a. NATO 2 meetings
		b. Extra-ordinary sessions	b. 2	Package deals	b. Group of 7 1 meeting

IGC-EMU

While the fundamentals were the same, the IGC-EMU was organized on a slightly different basis. First, there were different personal representatives drawn from treasury and finance ministries. In the case of the UK, Sir Nigel Wicks, the second Permanent Secretary at the Treasury, led the British team while his number two in the meetings was Sir John Kerr.[44] Second, at the intermediate level between the personal representatives and the Heads of State and Government, there were the finance ministers, where the British representative was the Chancellor, Norman Lamont. In addition, the Committee of Central Bank Governors (CCBG) examined the more technical aspects on behalf of the finance ministers.

On the question of the link between the Political Union and EMU negotiations, the two were undoubtedly connected, not least by the German insistence that they were only willing to endorse EMU if it were accompanied by a strengthening of the democracy of the system, particularly enhancing the powers of the European Parliament. For example, in December 1990, Kohl argued that there could be no EMU without progress in Political Union and, in March 1991, he reminded his own countrymen that Political Union and EMU were 'politically and practically linked'.[45] But in public pronouncements British political leaders chose to see the two IGCs as separate, with ministers countering German claims that the two processes were dependent on each other. Moreover, while both IGCs ran in parallel, there appeared little overlap between them until the Maastricht European Council when the two strands were then combined into one treaty for the purposes of ratification.[46] But in private British ministers and officials saw the basic Maastricht bargain in terms of a deal between Germany and France: German acquiescence in EMU in return for French acquiescence in something called political union, all underpinned by a longer-term commitment on the part of both Germany and France to act as the motor of European integration.

THE NEGOTIATIONS

The final consideration shaping the context of the negotiations of 1990 to 1991 was the internal dynamics of the two conferences themselves. In a set of negotiations as complicated as these, networks of bilateral and multilateral alliances were crucial building-blocks of consensus. Coalitions changed as the discussion within particular dossiers ebbed and flowed, and allies on one question might well be implacably opposed on another, apparently closely related one. Often governments launched shared initiatives but aimed them at different objectives. This dynamic is well illustrated by the discussions which took place over the proposed structure of the Union which the Treaty was designed to inaugurate.

At the outset of the negotiations, two broad coalitions could be identified. The Belgian and Dutch governments saw the IGC-PU as an opportunity to codify many existing practices and to integrate a number of sub-systems of the EC into one framework.[47] In this they were supported by the Commission and the EP, both keen to increase their participation in home affairs and foreign and security policy and both of which submitted proposals to the IGC-PU.[48] This coalition was opposed by a loose bilateral alliance between France and Britain, who despite being opposed on many other issues were both fearful of a treaty structure which would constrain their independence and bring sensitive issues inside the EC framework.

To resolve this matter the Luxembourg Presidency on 17 April 1991 presented a draft treaty which made a distinction between Community and European Union competences. Instead of the single set of procedures and institutions which existed for the EC, the EU would have three clearly distinct pillars. The first pillar would be essentially economic. It would be based on supranational procedures and institutions and would principally use majority voting. The second pillar would be concerned with foreign and security policy (CFSP), and the third with justice and home affairs (JHA) issues. Both the second and third pillars would use a more intergovernmental set of procedural mechanisms based on unanimity.[49] While this structure was broadly in line with London's aims, the government was wary of any links between the first pillar and the intergovernmental second and third pillars. It therefore signalled its opposition to the draft treaty within days of its publication.[50]

A majority of Member States led by Germany was also opposed to the Luxembourg draft but for different reasons. Faced with a demand for the pillared structure to be withdrawn,[51] the Presidency substantially revised its proposals, presenting a second draft treaty on 18 June 1991.[52] This reaffirmed that the Union would have a single institutional framework and strengthened the EC pillar as the central element of the Union, supplemented by the two other intergovernmental pillars. This was designed to reassure the integrationists in two ways. First, it made a commitment to a federal goal for the Union, and included an undertaking to review the structure in 1996 with a view to *communautarising* the two intergovernmental pillars. Second, it made clear that the *acquis communautaire* would not be undermined by the new intergovernmental pillars but would in fact be further developed.[53] This draft came under attack as the basis for the continuation of negotiations at the Luxembourg European Council on 28 to 29 June 1991,[54] a meeting which was, however, completely overshadowed by the despatch of the Troika to Yugoslavia.[55]

The lack of progress made in the IGC-PU made during the first half of 1991 was mirrored by the slow progress of the IGC-EMU. Here, the key stumbling-block was the question of when a European Central Bank (ECB) should be created and what powers it should have. The major protagonists were France (with support from the European Commission), which considered that an ECB should be created as early as possible to supervise the development of the European Currency Unit (ECU) into a single currency, and Germany, which opposed this. In May 1991 the Luxembourg Presidency presented a draft treaty on Economic and Monetary Union to break the deadlock. This proposed that Stage Two of EMU should have modest objectives, with the Committee of Central Bank Governors coordinating monetary policy. The draft therefore left the creation of a European Central Bank to the end of Stage Three. The Luxembourg European Council at the end of June took stock of developments in both IGCs but, as mentioned, was preoccupied with the Yugoslav crisis. It was thus left to the Dutch Presidency to move the debate forward in both IGCs.

After some delay, Piet Dankert, the European Minister, circulated a new draft treaty on 24 September.[56] This removed the three-pillared structure and the term 'European Union', referring only to the EC. Instead, it proposed the limited but uniform extension of the competences of the EC and its supranational institutions, while reaffirming the federal vocation of the Community. London was at the forefront of coordinating opposition to this text which ran counter to its preference for intergovernmental rather than supranational cooperation.[57] The draft was accordingly withdrawn on 30 September, termed Black Monday in Dutch diplomatic circles.[58] A similar fate befell the first Dutch redraft of the EMU articles. At a meeting at the beginning of September the Dutch finance minister circulated a new EMU draft which proposed a two-speed process to EMU in which any six members that met the conditions for a single currency could establish a ECB and a single currency.[59] This was opposed by those Member States that feared they would not be included in the first wave, namely Greece, Ireland, Italy, Portugal and Spain, with Britain and Denmark opposed for different reasons.[60]

However, though the draft was abandoned it did generate agreement that Member States should move to Stage Three of EMU by consensus, with no country forced to join or able to veto the process. This led to a complete formal draft on 28 October 1991 which codified progress by including protocols on the European System of Central Banks (ESCB) and European Monetary Institute (EMI) and declarations on the role of the ECOFIN (Finance Ministers) Council. The draft also concentrated minds on the outstanding differences and, following two meetings in November and one in early December, the problem issues were whittled down to three. These three issues, which were now passed to the European Council for consideration were: the procedure for the transition to the third stage; how to handle British and Danish reticence to commit themselves to a single currency; and social cohesion.

The penultimate Political Union draft text was tabled on 8 November and was essentially based on the second Luxembourg draft with several important modifications.[61] It bound the CFSP and JHA pillars more tightly into the procedures adopted by the EC pillar, ensuring that there were at least linkages between the different pillars, and it restated the federal vocation of the EC. It also included an article allowing the Council at some future stage to transform the intergovernmental pillars into more *communautaire* structures through *passerelles*. To London, while preferable to the first Dutch draft, it still presented a number of problems concerning the nature of the intergovernmental pillars.

At the Maastricht European Council on 9–10 December 1991 three institutional issues remained unresolved: the extent of the links between the intergovernmental and supranational pillars; the federal vocation of the Union; and the nature of any future review clause. At Maastricht, Ruud Lubbers, President of the European Council, offered Major a compromise deal on these issues.[62] He proposed an intergovernmental structure for the Union and, given the difficulties the federal goal presented for Britain, Denmark and Ireland, agreed to drop it in return for a commitment to review the treaty structure in 1996, with a view to incorporating more supranational elements into JHA and CFSP. By and large this compromise was accepted and incorporated in the final treaty, albeit with a general rather than a specific review clause to re-examine the effectiveness of the second and third pillars.[63] On EMU final details were resolved, with the notable addition of an irrevocable commitment to introduce a single currency in 1999, even if there was not a majority that supported the move in 1997.

Thus the Maastricht European Council decisions were the product of 12 months of intense preparatory, at times even exploratory, negotiations in which battle lines and tensions as well as areas of consensus had already emerged. No head of government approached Maastricht with an open mind or a *tabula rasa*. It was also the case that there were no clearly defined alliances: the Franco-German axis broke down early in the negotiations, in part because there was no agreement on what political union meant, and in part because of disagreements over EMU, where France was keen on a swift move to a single currency and less keen on an independent European Central Bank. Likewise, Christian Democrat party leaders were deeply divided, with the German Chancellor breaking ranks on a number of issues, while consensus was also lacking among Socialist leaders.

In these negotiations, coalitions depended on the issues at stake and even then were subject to change depending on international and domestic considerations. Nevertheless, from a British perspective it cannot be denied that attitudes and actions of certain of their partners tended to matter more than others. These key participants were most often France and Germany, although on certain issues Denmark, the Netherlands, Ireland and Portugal were no less important in securing British objectives. The next chapter now turns to the question of those objectives, and the influences shaping them.

NOTES

1. For the full text see *Treaty on European Union*, Luxembourg, Office for Official Publications of the European Communities, 1992.
2. Strictly speaking the majority of the Maastricht meeting was not a European Council but the IGC meeting at Heads of State and Government level.
3. See Stephen George (ed.), *Britain and the European Community*, Oxford, Clarendon Press, 1992.
4. Jim Buller, 'Britain as an Awkward Partner: Reassessing Britain's Relations with the EU', *Politics*, vol. 15, no. 1, 1995, pp. 33–42, p. 36.
5. Finn Laursen, 'Explaining the Intergovernmental Conference on Political Union', in Finn Laursen and Sophie van Hoonacker (eds), *The Intergovernmental Conference on Political Union*, Maastricht, European Institute of Public Administration, 1992, pp. 229–48; Philippe de Schoutheete, 'The Treaty of Maastricht and its Significance for Third Countries', *Österreichische Zeitschrift Für Politikwissenschaft*, 1992/3, pp. 247–97.
6. Helen Wallace and William Wallace, *Flying Together in a Larger and More Diverse European Union*, The Hague, Netherlands Scientific Council for Government Policy, W87, June 1995, pp. 75–7.
7. Joseph Weyland and Marc Eyskens, 'Les conférences intergouvernementales avant le conseil Européen de Maastricht', paper presented to the Institut d'Etudes Européennes, 8 November 1991, Université Libre de Bruxelles, D/1991/2672/24; Philippe de Schoutheete, 'Réflexions sur le

Traité de Maastricht', *Annales de Droit de Louvain*, vol. 1, 1993, pp. 73–90; Richard Corbett, 'The Intergovernmental Conference on Political Union', *Journal of Common Market Studies*, vol. XXX, no. 3, September 1992; Yves Doutriaux, *Le Traité sur L'Union Européene*, Paris, Armand Collin, 1992; Jim Cloos, Euston Reinesch, Daniel Vinges, Jim Weyland (eds), *Le Traité de Maastricht: genèse, analyse, commentaires*, Bruxelles, Émile Bruylant, 1993; Jim Weyland, 'Strategies and Perspectives of the Luxembourg Presidency', in Emil Kirchner and Andrew Tsagkari (eds), *The EC Council Presidency: the Dutch and Luxembourg Presidencies*, London, UCAES, 1993. For those who had special access to the Commission during this period and wrote detailed accounts, see: Charles Grant, *Delors: Inside the House that Jacques Built*, London, Nicholas Brealey, 1994; and George Ross, *Jacques Delors and European Integration*, Cambridge, Polity Press, 1995. Two recent Ph.D. theses addressing the Maastricht negotiations are: Carlos J. Closa Montero, 'The Creation of the European Political Union', Ph.D. thesis, Hull University, 1993; Alasdair Blair, 'The UK and the Negotiation of the Maastricht Treaty: 1990–1991', Ph.D. thesis, Leicester University, 1997.

8.   Andrew Duff, John Pinder and Roy Pryce (eds), *Maastricht and Beyond*, London, Routledge, 1994; Juliet Lodge (ed.), *The European Community and the Challenge of the Future*, London, Pinter, 2nd ed., 1993; Loukas Tsoukalis, *The New European Economy*, Oxford, Oxford University Press, 2nd ed., 1993, pp. 46–69; Desmond Dinan, *Ever Closer Union?*, London, Macmillan, 1994, pp. 157–83; Glenda Rosenthal and Alan Cafruny (eds), *The State of the European Community: the Maastricht Debates and Beyond*, vol. 2, London, Lynne Reiner/Longman, 1993.

9.   John Young, *Britain and European Unity 1945–1992*, London, Macmillan, 1993, pp. 156–64; Stephen George, *An Awkward Partner*, Oxford, Oxford University Press, 2nd ed., 1994, pp. 231–54; William Wallace, 'Foreign Policy', in Dennis Kavanagh and Anthony Seldon (eds), *The Major Effect*, London, Macmillan, 1994, pp. 283–300.

10.   Peter Lange, 'Maastricht and the Social Protocol: why did they do it?', *Politics and Society*, vol. 21, no. 1, March 1993, pp. 5–36.

11.   Two notable exceptions are Robert Wester, 'United Kingdom', in Laursen and van Hoonacker, *The Intergovernmental Conference on Political Union*, op. cit., pp. 189–204, and Stephen George, *An Awkward Partner*, op. cit., especially 'A Major Change of Direction?', pp. 231–54.

12.   Quoted in David McLellan, *Karl Marx, Selected Writings*, Oxford, Oxford University Press, 1977, p. 300.

13.   See Finn Laursen, 'Explaining the Intergovernmental Conference', op. cit., p. 241; for a similar argument see also David Andrews, 'The Global Origins of the Maastricht Treaty on EMU', in Rosenthal and Cafruny, *State of the European Community*, pp. 107–42.

14.   Theoretical issues are explicitly addressed in Anthony Forster, 'Britain and the Negotiation of the Maastricht Treaty: a Critique of Liberal Intergovernmentalism', *Journal of Common Market Studies*, vol. 36, no. 3, Autumn 1998, pp. 347–68.

15. Norman Tebbit, *Unfinished Business*, London, Wiedenfeld and Nicholson, 1991; two volumes of Mrs Thatcher's memoirs, *The Downing Street Years*, London, Harper Collins, 1993; *The Path to Power*, London, Harper Collins, 1995; Nicholas Ridley, *'My Style of Government': the Thatcher Years*, London, Fontana, 1992; Nigel Lawson, *The View from No. 11*, London, Bantam Press, 1992; Ken Baker, *The Turbulent Years: My Life in Politics*, London, Faber and Faber, 1993; Geoffrey Howe, *Conflict of Loyalty*, London, Macmillan, 1994. See also Sarah Hogg and Jonathan Hill, *Too Close to Call: Power and Politics*, London, Little, Brown and Company, 1995.

16. Anthony Seldon, 'The Cabinet Office and Coordination, 1979–87', in R. A. W. Rhodes and Patrick Dunleavy (eds), *Prime Minister, Cabinet and Core Executive*, London, Macmillan, 1995, pp. 125–48, p. 126. See also Michael Lee, 'The Ethos of the Cabinet Office: a Comment on the Testimony of Officials', in the same volume, pp. 149–57, p. 149.

17. Author's interview. This task was undertaken by the FCO's Research and Analysis Department. Out of office, Douglas Hurd asked for an official history of the Yugoslav crisis to be compiled by Geoffrey Murrell, a former diplomat, in order to counter the allegation of a link between the negotiation of the Maastricht Treaty and the Yugoslav crisis. For a further discussion of this issue see Chapter 7.

18. See Andrew Moravcsik, 'Negotiating the Single Act: National Interests and Conventional Statecraft in the European Community', *Working Papers*, #21, Centre for European Studies, Harvard University, 1991, p. 28.

19. 'Draft Treaty Establishing the European Union', *Official Journal*, no. C.77, 19 March 1984.

20. Corbett, 'The Intergovernmental Conference on Political Union', op. cit., p. 272.

21. See European Council Rome, 14/15 December 1990, *Presidency Conclusions*, SN 424/1/90, (OR.F) REV 1, p. 6.

22. Karel de Gucht and Stephen Keukeleire, 'The European Security Architecture: the Role of the European Community in Shaping a New European Geopolitical Landscape', *Studia Diplomatica*, vol. XLIV, no. 6, 1992, pp. 29–118.

23. Author's interview with Sir John Kerr and Philippe de Schoutheete.

24. Speaking note, Dublin European Council, dated 28 April 1990, unpublished. For the communiqué see Presidency Conclusions in *Europe Documents*, 22 April 1990. See also David Usborne, 'Political Union Now a Step Closer', *The Bulletin*, 3 May 1990, Brussels, Ackroyd, p. 16.

25. For the communiqué see Presidency Conclusions in *Europe Documents*, July 1990.

26. The Belgian memorandum is reproduced in *Europe Documents*, 1608, 29 March 1990. For the importance of the Belgian memorandum see the unpublished paper by Christian Franck and Wide d'Estamael, 'La Belgique et L'Europe Communautaire: du memo Belge au traité de Maastricht'; see also de Schoutheete, 'The Treaty of Maastricht', op. cit., pp. 247–60.

27. The letter sent by President Mitterrand and Chancellor Kohl to the

Irish Presidency on 19 April 1990 is reproduced in *Agence Europe*, 20 April 1990.

28. Isabelle Hilton, 'Europe's Guiding Stars', *Independent*, 27 April 1990.

29. The Commission President publicly declared his scepticism about the IGC-PU, and feared that lack of preparation and the absence of any agreed objectives might jeopardize the outcome of the EMU negotiations, which Delors considered of greater importance. See Corbett, 'The Intergovernmental Conference on Political Union', op. cit., p. 274.

30. This marked out the IGC-PU strand of the Maastricht negotiations from the SEA negotiations which had been 'classical' negotiations in the sense that they had as a clear objective the construction of a Single Market. Philippe de Schoutheete argues that the launch of the IGC-PU without any substantial Franco-German agreement on the major policy issues paralysed the IGC for many months and contributed to its chaotic organization and outcome. 'The Maastricht Treaty', paper delivered to the seminar series *Europe after Maastricht*, St Antony's College, Oxford, March 1992.

31. The details of the working paper drawn up by the Personal Representatives can be found in 'Preparation of the Intergovernmental Conference on Political Union: the Presidency's Assessment', *Europe Documents*, no. 1666, 6 December 1990.

32. 'European Council Presidency Conclusions', Rome, 14–15 December 1990, *Agence Europe*, 16 December 1990.

33. This point is further discussed by Loukas Tsoukalis, *The New European Economy*, Oxford, Oxford University Press, 2nd ed., 1993, p. 70.

34. Author's interviews. See the comments made by Delors quoted in *Agence Europe*, 24/25 June 1991, p. 3.

35. See *Keesing's Contemporary Archive*, 8 April 1991, 38154.

36. Hans van den Broek quoted in 'Europe of the 21st or 19th Century', *Agence Europe*, 11 October 1991.

37. Ronald van der Krol, 'Lubbers Warns on Revival of Pessimism', *Financial Times*, 3 December 1991; Kohl in *Süddeutsch Zeitung*, quoted in *Guardian*, 22 November 1991; see also Bagehot, 'Pre Maastricht Tension', *Economist*, 7 December 1991, p. 38.

38. Author's interview with Sir John Kerr.

39. Several senior British negotiators noted the importance of a statement in the Maastricht European Council Communiqué committing the Member States to consider the issue of enlargement.

40. *Agence Europe*, 2 October 1991.

41. Emile Kirchner, *Decision Making in the European Community*, Manchester, Manchester University Press, 1992, pp. 71–89.

42. For the general differences between routine and constitutional bargaining see Charles Pentland, *International Theory and Europe Integration*, London, Faber & Faber, 1973, p. 134.

43. Only at the conclaves and the Maastricht European Council, where Delors was personally present to argue his points, did the Commission make headway on some relatively minor issues. Author's interview with David Hadley. For a discussion of the various sub-groups of the IGCs see Alasdair M. Blair, 'The UK and the Negotiation of the Maastricht

Treaty 1990–1991', Ph.D. Leicester University, 1997.

44.   Kerr had only been acceptable to the Treasury because he had spent some time there and been Lawson's principal private secretary. Pressure of work made it impossible for Kerr to attend all the IGC-EMU meetings, especially in their latter stages.

45.   *Agence Europe*, 14 March 1991; see also *Agence Europe*, 13/14 May, 8 June and 3 October 1991.

46.   See de Schoutheete, 'The Treaty of Maastricht', op. cit., p. 248; Desmond Dinan, *Ever Closer Union?*, op. cit., p. 169.

47.   For a description of the various sub-systems see Philippe de Schoutheete, 'The European Community and its Sub-Systems', in Wallace, *The Dynamics of European Integration*, op. cit., pp. 106–24.

48.   For the Commission proposals see *Bulletin of the European Communities*, supplement 1991/2, Brussels, Luxembourg Office for Official Publications of the European Communities, 1991. For the European Parliament's range of proposals see *1993: The New Treaties, European Parliament Proposals*, Luxembourg 1991, pp. 66–209.

49.   For the text see 'Draft Treaty Articles with a View to Achieving a Political Union', *Europe Documents*, no. 1709/10, 3 May 1991. See also 'The Union Makers', *Economist*, 9 November 1991, p. 30.

50.   'Political Disunion', *Economist*, 20 April 1991, p. 46.

51.   *Agence Europe*, 5 June 1991; Joe Rogaly, 'Cutting the Mustard', *Financial Times*, 7 June 1991.

52.   For the text see 'Draft Treaty on the Union', *Europe Documents*, 1722/1723, 5 July 1991.

53.   See *Financial Times*, leader, 'A Vision of Europe', 20 June 1991; see also *Agence Europe*, 10 July 1991.

54.   'European Council Presidency Conclusions' and 'Draft Treaty on European Union', *Europe Documents*, no. 1722/23, 5 July 1991.

55.   *Agence Europe*, 30 June 1991; 'A Busy Five Minutes', *Economist*, 6 July 1991, p. 49.

56.   For the text see 'Dutch Draft Treaty', *Europe Documents*, 1733/34, 3 October 1991.

57.   Ivo Dawnay, 'Major says the Dutch Plan Could Ruin EC Accord', *Financial Times*, 27 September 1991.

58.   See David Gardiner, 'Dutch to Reassess Political Union Plan', *Financial Times*, 1 October 1991; 'Les Douze réjettent le projet de traité neerlandais sur l'union politique', *Le Monde*, 2 October 1991.

59.   *Agence Europe*, 15 September 1991.

60.   Dinan, *Ever Closer Union?*, op. cit., p. 176.

61.   For the text see 'Draft Union Treaty', *Europe Documents*, 1746/1747, 20 November 1991.

62.   David Buchan and David Gardiner, 'Major to be Offered Trade-off', *Financial Times*, 27 November 1991.

63.   *Agence Europe*, 11 December 1991. The *passerelle* was retained for JHA (Article K.9) but only exercisable through unanimity of Member States and national ratification.

1 The Origins of British Policy

The British government's handling of the Maastricht negotiations of 1990 to 1991 must be understood most immediately in the context of the divisions within the Conservative Party following the downfall of Mrs Thatcher. These divisions presented John Major, the incoming prime minister, with two distinct yet interlinked sets of problems. The first was the challenge of managing fractious backbenchers and ministers on a day-to-day basis. The second was the question of the ideological direction of the Party in the absence of a leader who had dominated the political agenda for over a decade. These problems were exacerbated by the knowledge that a general election would have to take place in 1992. In addition to this, however, the Major government was further constrained by the historical weight of previous policy towards Europe. Indeed, as this chapter suggests, any British government would have found it difficult to engage in formal treaty negotiations that had as their explicit aim the creation of a single currency and a political union.

THE HISTORICAL CONTEXT OF BRITISH EUROPEAN POLICY

The broad parameters of John Major's European policy were those established by the historical background of British thinking on Europe. There are two aspects to this. The first is the British preoccupation with sovereignty and with external territorial integrity.[1] Those seeking to explain this preoccupation have pointed to a constitutional doctrine which merges political and legal sovereignty, popular loyalty to the institution of the monarchy and even to the continuity of British institutions which have not comprehensively and disastrously failed as have those of other European countries.[2]

It has been further argued that the British (or more accurately English) attachment to sovereignty is used as shorthand for the way in which the political elite and the mass of the population define themselves as being separate from their continental counterparts. They regard themselves as Anglo-Saxon and Atlanticist rather than Latin and European. Moreover, they view the Second World War as setting Britain apart from the Continent both historically and morally. There is an important sense in which European integration has been seen by successive British governments as a means by which their partners can atone for their actions during the War. Thus the idea of integration has never carried a particularly positive resonance for Britain itself.[3] As Roy Denman argues, however, the notion of losing sovereignty also has practical connotations, with the political elite being concerned at the prospect of the erosion of executive power at Westminster, and using the spectre of rule by foreign bureaucrats to ram this message home to the public.[4]

The second aspect of the historical context of Britain's European policy has been London's global view of its responsibilities and its unwillingness to confine its foreign and economic policies to Western Europe. Britain's role in the United Nations Security Council and the acquisition and maintenance of nuclear weapons were part of a wider set of great power symbols of Britain's role in the world.[5] In economic terms, the reserve-currency role of sterling, economic links with the Commonwealth and Britain's membership of the Group of Seven all drew Britain away from the EC and towards a more global perspective on its interests. The pivot of this international dimension of post-war British foreign policy is the so called 'special relationship' with the United States. This was based upon the shared experience of the War and a common language and common interests as the world's two reserve currencies. It was also inspired by the British belief that they were in a unique position to exert influence over the 'new' superpower.[6]

The consequence of the British preoccupation with sovereignty, so far as her involvement in the integration project is concerned, has been a preference for intergovernmental rather than supranational procedures and processes. In the period between 1945 and 1961, for instance, Britain was actively involved in the creation of intergovernmental bodies such as the Organisation for European Economic Co-operation (OEEC) and the Transatlantic Alliance. But it rejected the Schuman Plan which led to the European Coal and Steel Community (ECSC), the Pleven Plan to create a European Defence Community (EDC), and the two Treaties of Rome establishing the European Economic Communities (EEC).

However, the most important result of the British attachment to notions of sovereignty and reluctance to limit foreign and economic policies to Western Europe has been the lack of a clearly articulated

European policy. Indeed, Churchill's declaration that Britain's interests lay in the intersection of three great circles of influence – the relationship with the USA, the Commonwealth and Europe – has rightly been called 'the last explicit conceptual framework for British foreign policy'.[7] It was the end of Empire, replaced only with an unsatisfactory Commonwealth, and the decline in Britain's economic circumstances, which eventually led to Harold Macmillan's application to join the EEC in 1961. This was followed by repeated applications until membership was finally achieved in 1973.[8]

Membership of the EC was thus a tactical and not strategic change. It was 'adopted one might almost say when all other expedients had failed' and principally out of a fear – which exists to this day – of the consequences of being excluded from a potentially important international forum.[9] The British elites' political commitment to the process of closer European integration was based on weak foundations, which has hindered government's ability to give up its own freedom of manoeuvre for the sake of remaining engaged in the integration process.

Alan Milward convincingly argues that no national government within the original Six Member States has ever been completely committed to the process of European integration, and that most still manage to pursue their own national interests.[10] Once in the European Community, however, British policies appeared not to recognize this possibility. Instead, Britain applied herself to the negative task of impeding any further progress towards closer supranational European integration.[11] A favourite tactic was emphasis of the need for enlargement in the hope that a wider Community would be less likely to deepen its supranational integration.[12]

The problem of the lack of a clearly articulated European policy was exacerbated by the failure of the supporters of entry into the EC to conduct a full and open debate about the issues involved. In what Christopher Hill calls 'a convenient schizophrenia', advocates of EC membership have glossed over the implications to British sovereignty of involvement in the EC and preferred to emphasize the economic and political benefits.[13] In December 1962 Macmillan postponed publishing a legal report on the loss of sovereignty that entry would imply, and justified the first membership application on the grounds that Community membership was the only way to preserve Britain's economic prosperity and great-power status.[14] In the period between the first application and Britain's eventual accession, moreover, it became apparent that the implications for sovereignty would be dramatic. In

1964, for instance, the European Court of Justice (ECJ) established that EC law took precedence over national law, yet the 1971 government White Paper argued that membership of the EC would in no way undermine 'essential national sovereignty' of Westminster'.[15]

Given the historical British fixation with sovereignty and with extra-European questions, ultimately British governments were not prepared fully to admit the consequences of EC membership because they had no desire, as Stephen George has put it, 'to abandon the old discourse of nation for a new discourse of Europe'.[16] More specifically, however, the muffled debate was also a result of the divisions which the European question created in the political parties. While most parties across Western Europe are to some extent divided on Europe, in Britain the nature of the adversarial system, combined with an electoral system which disproportionately rewards the winning party in Parliament, makes the problem acute.[17] Political leaders are encouraged to talk in generalities in order to conceal divisions within their own parties.

A further explanation provided by John Young for Britain's failure to formulate a clear European policy was London's inability to play by the rules of the game in Brussels, its unease with alien decision-making procedures and the continuous nature of negotiations in the EC.[18] As a number of scholars argue, this is due in part to the British policy-making process itself. British input into Community negotiations occurs through a narrow channel of communications from London to Brussels, with the European Secretariat in the Cabinet Office performing a co-ordinating role.[19] Once policy has been formulated, the Permanent Representative in Brussels receives tight guidelines from London on objectives and tactics and is seen to have little room for manoeuvre in comparison with many other permanent representatives.[20]

These procedures mean that London is either first in the *melée* with an unbending position, or reactive and the last to come in on a deal. The negotiating process in the EC, however, is largely comprised of the formulation of coalitions to achieve agreement, a process to which London's approach is highly ill-suited.[21] Ministerial autonomy limited by collective responsibility and poor links between government, business and trade unions also conspire against a more consensual style of negotiating.[22] This means that British negotiators are less open 'to the compromises that come naturally to colleagues who have emerged from proportional voting systems and coalition governments'.[23] Britain has thus acquired a poor reputation as an awkward partner which further impedes her ability to find allies and to be cut in on a deal.[24]

Another explanation for the difficulty all British governments have in ceding powers to the European Community level is that British constitutional practice is based on the chance to elect a new government, campaigning on a philosophy and a specific programme and normally promising to repeal or modify its predecessor's actions or implement new policies. There is no comparable process now or in the foreseeable future, in relation to functions and competences ceded to the European Community.

In this context, treaty-amending negotiations present a particular set of problems. William Wallace notes that British governments have been happy to encourage the transformation of economic markets to maintain Britain's informal sovereignty and the influence (albeit declining) that it wields in the global economy.[25] This not only avoids parliamentary scrutiny, but it also reinforces executive dominance over the direction of policy-making and allows the government of the day to hide from awkward domestic forces.[26] The opposite, however, is true of formal treaties requiring ratification.[27] Formal treaties, often with ambitious objectives, challenge the pragmatic self-image of British policy-making, with an instinctive rejection of rhetorical declarations which do not spell out detailed commitments.[28] Thus Britain is a reluctant participant in treaty negotiations.[29]

THE PARTY MANAGEMENT DIMENSION

Consideration of the domestic historical background to British policy in the IGCs of 1990 to 1991 must, however, take particular account of the troubled relationship between the Conservative Party and Europe. This Conservative dimension is important not solely because the IGC negotiations were conducted by a Conservative government, but because the history of Conservative policies and divisions on Europe created a very particular set of circumstances in 1990 to 1991.

The Conservative Party had been no exception in avoiding detailed discussion of the implications of EC membership, and when Edward Heath finally took Britain into the Community he relied on internal party discipline as a substitute for winning backbenchers round to his position.[30] The 41 Conservative members who opposed the government in October 1971 nevertheless remained active in their opposition to the government after formal accession to the EC. In the period after

British accession, moreover, the European issue quickly became a running sore for the party as it became apparent that European policy had ramifications for policies on economic and social welfare, the balance of priorities in foreign policy and, ultimately, the constitution.[31]

Europe thus became an evermore divisive issue for the Conservative Party, separating free traders from protectionists, unionists from those who supported constitutional reform, and the supporters of a 'blue sea' maritime strategy from those who were 'land based' continentalists. Above all, under Mrs Thatcher's leadership the issue of Europe opened ever wider the cleavage within the modern Conservative Party concerning the role of the state in the economy.[32] Supporters of economic liberalism at home championed the Anglo-Saxon model and opposed what they saw as the 'corporatist' policies of the EC and member governments. Finally, Europe emerged as the key issue in the debate over the future direction of the party, when Michael Heseltine challenged Margaret Thatcher's leadership and used the European issue to symbolize his vision of a more interventionist future.[33]

John Major's election as party leader following the overthrow of Mrs Thatcher seemed, however, to offer the ideal opportunity to heal the divisions crystallized by the debate over the European question. He had a reputation as a natural chairman, preferring to mediate between differing positions within the Cabinet – a key consideration when Mrs Thatcher's autocratic style had figured so large in her downfall.[34] However, in practice John Major's task was far more difficult than might initially have been supposed. Political insiders referred to 'the political bomb-site' left by Margaret Thatcher's defeat – and the pressing need to rebuild shattered party unity.[35] In addition, Major's own power base in the Party was weak. Although Major was Mrs Thatcher's preferred candidate to succeed her,[36] the right wing of the Party remained unsure of his 'Thatcherite credentials' and was uncertain whether the overthrow of Mrs Thatcher was a renunciation of her policies or a transfer to a new generation of Thatcherites. The right wing of the party, therefore, saw the new Prime Minister as a leader on probation, and was prepared to look to Mrs Thatcher if Major was felt to be deviating from her policies.[37] This was indeed an attitude she was keen to encourage, readily emphasizing her own skills as a 'back seat driver'.[38]

In practical terms, Major was also constrained by the front bench inherited from his predecessor and the fact that the Cabinet had been reshuffled five times in the year preceding his election. Eight major departments had incumbent ministers of 13 months' standing or less, while with one exception the longest serving ministers had only been in post 16 months.[39] Indeed, after the last reshuffle Mrs Thatcher had taken the unusual step of announcing there would be no further changes before the general election. Major could not therefore make widespread Cabinet changes without undermining the credibility of his government. A further consideration impeding his ability to assert his identity on the government was the need to include the leaders of important factions in the Cabinet, in part because he wanted a 'Cabinet of all the talents' but also because of the damage senior colleagues could do on the back benches unconstrained by collective responsibility.[40]

Coupled with this was the problem of the overall 'balance' of the Cabinet. Ironically, Mrs Thatcher's Cabinets had never been 'packed' with her supporters and most members of her last Cabinet were closer in their views to Heseltine than herself. Indeed, throughout her tenure in office, Mrs Thatcher preferred to rely on a small circle of ministers and, increasingly, advisors who shared her ideological convictions, along with 'believers' on the back benches.[41] As part of this strategy she entrusted key economic departments to like-minded ministers and confined membership of the Cabinet economic sub-committees to her own supporters.[42] These had already been extensively reshuffled, further restricting the new Prime Minister's scope for making new appointments.[43]

Finding himself with very little room for manoeuvre, Major confirmed Douglas Hurd's position at the Foreign and Commonwealth Office. Deciding on a Cabinet role for Michael Heseltine was more difficult, however, and Major eventually settled on the post of Environment Secretary, with a specific remit to find a replacement to the Community Charge.[44] Chris Patten, a well-respected figure on the Christian Democrat and pro-European wing of the party, was appointed Party Chairman with responsibility for preparing for the 1992 election. Norman Lamont, a Eurosceptic who 'had presented his credentials in a speech to the Bruges Group' during the leadership campaign was promoted from being John Major's number two at the Treasury to the position of Chancellor.[45] As the Financial Secretary, Lamont was the natural choice to lead Major's leadership campaign from the Treasury which he did ably. Lamont was therefore promoted partly out of loyalty and partly *faute de mieux*, in the absence of any other contender for the post with Treasury experience.[46]

At the same time a significant grouping of 'young Turk' Thatcherites were kept in their jobs. Most notable among the

Thatcherites was Michael Howard at the Department of Employment and Peter Lilley in the Department of Trade and Industry. Lilley was the more junior, but to the chagrin of Howard leap-frogged over him to win the senior post after the resignation of Nicholas Ridley in July 1990.[47] Both Cabinet minsters headed departments with junior ministers drawn from the No Turning Back Group, a parliamentary faction committed to a Thatcherite and anti-integrationist agenda.

In short, John Major had to work with a Cabinet in which the economic departments and Cabinet sub-committees remained in the hands of the right wing, although the overall balance had shifted slightly further towards the pro-European Christian Democratic wing of the party. All of this was highly important for explaining why Howard and Lilley – the self-styled 'representatives' of the ideological right in the Cabinet – were so important to John Major, with an important subtext the struggle between Howard and Lilley to become the standard bearer of the right in a Cabinet significantly to the left of the parliamentary party.

Major was also constrained by the need to take account of the opinions of Conservative Party backbenchers.[48] Not only had previous handling of European policy left the party deeply factionalized, but a number of institutional changes under Mrs Thatcher had increased the importance of backbenchers. The leader was increasingly seen by backbenchers (and Cabinet colleagues) less as a 'freeholder' and more as a 'leaseholder' of the office. While the leader might seek to unite the party behind his or her policies, this support could no longer be assumed.[49] Moreover, the re-organization of the select committee system in the House of Commons allowed recalcitrant backbenchers normally deprived of the favours dispensed from the Whips' Office an alternative route of career progression. Back-bench influence was further strengthened by the ineffectiveness of Labour's opposition and the large Conservative Party majorities in 1983 and 1987.

Of particular importance, however, was the increased independence of the local constituency associations from Central Office, coupled with the need for re-selection by the local constituency association. This strengthened the hold of the constituencies over their MPs and ensured that MPs paid close attention to the opinions of local party activists and constituency officers.[50] Moreover, following years of Conservative Party division over the European question, the position now was that grass-roots activists in the local associations were generally hostile to moves towards closer European integration – more so in fact than the government itself.[51] An MP supported by such activists thus had a powerful base from which to resist pressure exerted by the Whips' Office.

Increasingly, too, there was a culture of dissent among Conservative backbenchers which gained momentum in the period after 1987, and which was highlighted most clearly by the Community Charge rebellion, the ramifications of which continued throughout the first 16 months of John Major's premiership as Heseltine struggled to find an acceptable alternative tax.[52] On the issue of Europe, the culture of dissent was compounded by a widening gap between ministers who routinely travelled to Brussels, becoming increasingly familiar with EC procedures and personnel, and government supporters viewing the EC from the distance of Westminster.[53] It was certainly true that Major could hope that, in the run-up to a general election, MPs' instinct for self-preservation would prevent them from jeopardizing party unity. There were after all 70 MPs in marginal seats. The problem was, however, that these marginal seats were held by a disproportionately high number of right wingers. There was thus a strong possibility that right wingers in marginal seats would place their own survival before that of the party and be seduced by Mrs Thatcher's preference for fighting the next general election on an anti-integrationist platform. In so doing they would dictate the terms of Party unity.

THE IDEOLOGICAL CONTEXT

John Major's scope to formulate a negotiating position for the IGCs of 1990 to 1991 was also heavily influenced by the ideological legacy of Mrs Thatcher, and above all by the *volte face* which had occurred in her thinking over Europe. Thatcher's implementation of free-market and monetarist principles in the domestic arena had inevitable consequences for Britain's relations with Europe. In addition, however, Europe was during the 1980s a touchstone of Thatcher's thinking, figuring prominently in her quest for a world role for Britain and desire to 'export' her policies.

Initially, moreover, these ambitions seemed to be paying off, with the 1992 project for a single market suggesting that London was winning the arguments in Brussels even if it was not setting the agenda there.[54] While annoyed by the way in which the Single European Act negotiations had been conducted, Mrs Thatcher was generally pleased with the outcome of the IGC, with its principal aim of creating a single market by 1992. She felt – or at least argued – that no vital interest had been surrendered concerning the British veto, that she had made relatively few compromises as regards 'wording', and that the SEA would signal the limits to be placed on Economic and Monetary Union.[55]

The problem was that, whilst the SEA was packaged and sold as 'Thatcherism on a European scale', this quickly gave way to a feeling that the SEA had actually involved very important concessions. This disillusionment came partly because the Thatcherite interpretation of the SEA had been an illusion. Other Member States had signed for different reasons and Mrs Thatcher's suspicions were aroused as other governments successfully exploited this. Thatcher's disillusionment also had its roots in the actions of the Commission, which extended its competences into new areas by choosing popular causes which had the support of pressure groups in member countries. In addition the Prime Minister felt that the Commission was consistently 'misemploying' Treaty articles that specified majority voting on issues which the British government considered should be decided by unanimity.[56]

Thus after 1987, Thatcher felt that the European agenda was slipping away from Britain back to a Franco-German leadership bloc.[57] The launch of the Delors Committee under the German Presidency to examine further moves towards economic and monetary union, followed by the Commission's launch, with French support, of the Social Charter, reinforced these concerns.[58] Growing disenchantment culminated in one of the great 'set piece speeches of Thatcherism' at Bruges in September 1988,[59] which transformed the European agenda in Britain, and further undermined the cohesion of the Conservative Party on the European issue.[60] From representing an opportunity to export Thatcherism, Europe was now depicted as a threat to it, socialist, corporatist and authoritarian, while Britain was wedded to conservative policies, the free market and economic liberalism.

Whilst Mrs Thatcher's pro-European stance had antagonized the right wing who were her most ardent supporters, her *volte face* signposted by the Bruges speech now delighted them. The Bruges Group was quickly founded to pursue the new European agenda outlined by Thatcher, and it soon became one of the most active and well-resourced lobbies on the intellectual right, with a parliamentary wing, 'The Friends of Bruges', and a turnover of £100 0000 per annum.[61] Bolstered by this, Mrs Thatcher used the platform outlined at Bruges as the basis for her 1989 European election campaign and as a trial run for the next general election.[62] Believing that she had the support of the rank and file in the constituencies and with the economic outlook unpromising, she saw populist anti-Europeanism as her winning electoral strategy.

Thatcher's anti-European strategy was largely unsuccessful and in the June 1989 European election the Conservatives were roundly defeated, losing 10 of their 44 seats in the EP.[63] This was seen by Mrs Thatcher as a temporary setback and did not prevent her from continuing to argue for this point of view, and it was true that it did appeal to a certain strand of voter and party opinion. There was, however, a growing recognition elsewhere in the party that it was a stance which divided the Cabinet and parliamentary party and would never prove a winning electoral strategy.[64] In ideological terms, Thatcher thus bequeathed to Major a poisoned chalice, for she left him not only a divided party but also a failed policy. The task of devising an alternative strategy was accordingly a highly delicate, though necessary one.

CRAFTING A STRATEGY

On becoming Prime Minister, John Major's attention was not focussed on the approaching IGCs, but on the British response to Iraq's invasion of Kuwait. Mrs Thatcher had been the first to urge a robust response from the international community. By the time John Major became the Prime Minister the process of building a coalition and deploying military forces to the Gulf had gathered momentum. At the domestic level, the key issue was finding a solution to the Community Charge. This required a great deal of personal attention from John Major, and close cooperation between the Department of Environment and the Treasury. Michael Heseltine was assigned the task of identifying a solution and Norman Lamont was given a personal brief from the Prime Minister to find the resources to announce a 'transitional relief scheme' reducing the Community Charge by half in the March 1991 budget.[65] During the first six months of his premiership, Major was also heavily engaged in a general review of government policy. He was under enormous pressure from his party and the press to come up with his own big idea that would define 'Majorism' and set out a clear course for his government to follow. Having had no opportunity to develop his thinking from the comfort of the opposition benches, this process started in late January 1991 and culminated in the Citizen's Charter initiative launched in Southport on 23 March 1991.[66]

Given all these domestic preoccupations, Major turned to the pro-Europeanism of Chris Patten and the experienced diplomacy of Douglas Hurd for the construction of his strategy for the negotiation of the IGCs.[67] The strategy these two ministers developed was composed of two key elements. The first was a *rapprochement* between the British government and its European partners, under-pinned by a close relationship with Germany.[68] The second element was a more subtle diplomacy based on building strategic alliances with governments which shared Britain's view on a particular issue, whatever the wider differences.

Thatcher had opposed a unified Germany in a more integrated Europe,[69] and was contemptuous of the French strategy of supporting German unification in return for concessions in the IGC-PU negotiations.[70] Unencumbered by such rigid attitudes on the German question,[71] Patten and Hurd by contrast regarded Germany as the most important ally to win in the negotiations.[72] In addition to this there was also a common interest between London and Bonn based on their shared centre-right ideological perspective, a common desire to tie America into the security structures of Western Europe and an enthusiasm for the extension of Community membership to the East.

At the core of the new strategy of *rapprochement* with Germany was a closer relationship between John Major and Helmut Kohl.[73] Through a close personal rapport with the German Chancellor, Major particularly hoped to exploit German concerns about the Delors plan for a single currency.[74] As John Young notes, this shift in policy offended the French.[75] This was, however, regarded as a small price to pay if Germany could be used to deflect the French from deeper European integration and their principle goal of EMU. Major therefore orchestrated an occasion in March 1991 to make a keynote speech in Bonn redressing the damage caused at Bruges, and publicly committing Britain to be at 'the very heart of Europe'.[76] The purpose of this speech was thus principally to communicate a change in tone and to move the debate away from Mrs Thatcher's crude anti-Europeanism onto a new and more positive footing.[77] The extent to which this was a change in style rather than a change in substance would be put to the test in the IGC negotiations.

The second strand of the Hurd-Patten strategy was the construc-tion of a wider coalition of support for London's position through careful diplomacy. Building on the Catholic and Christian Democratic links Chris Patten had established in Europe while he was head of the Conservative Research Department, the new Party Chairman was quick to foster support in the European Parliament in Strasbourg. An approach was made for Conservative MEPs to join the Christian Democratic centre-right group, the European Peoples' Party. The hope behind this move was that it would lead to John Major attending Christian Democratic leaders' meetings prior to each European Council.[78] It was at these meetings that many of the major deals were pre-bargained between the five Christian Democrat heads of government, and attendance would do much to remedy the problems associated with Britain's long-standing inability to exploit EC coalition-building procedures.[79]

Considerable efforts were also made between the resignation of Mrs Thatcher on 9 November and the start of the IGC on 10 December 'to break out of the diplomatic isolation which British policy-makers found themselves in'.[80] Not only did ministers try to avoid positions which marginalized the government in routine work, but efforts were also made to shape IGC policy initiatives with potential allies in mind.[81] To this end the government submitted a limited number of proposals concerning economic and monetary union, foreign, defence, justice and home affairs issues, which showed a degree of movement away from the tough stance of Mrs Thatcher.[82] Likewise, once the negotiations were underway there was a greater willingness under Major's premiership to make 'unholy alliances' to secure British objectives as and when necessary.[83]

The diplomatic strand of the Hurd-Patten strategy was also reflected by the choice of the negotiating teams assembled for the IGCs. For the IGC-EMU, the Chancellor, Norman Lamont, the second Permanent Under-Secretary at the Treasury, Sir Nigel Wicks, and the British EC Ambassador, Sir John Kerr, were obvious choices. The relationship between Major and Lamont was not a particularly strong one, and by contrast Major's relationship with Wicks was close having worked with him in the Treasury. From the outset the Prime Minister was keen to maintain a close watching brief on developments, his previous position as Chancellor and personal involvement in launching the hard ECU plan giving him a particular interest in these negotiations.

The IGC-PU team was more difficult to select, and the choice of the key players – Douglas Hurd, Tristan Garel-Jones and John Kerr – was as much about domestic and party management affairs as it was about managing the IGCs in Brussels.[84] Hurd brought not only his tremendous diplomatic skills to the IGC negotiating table but also the bonus that he was well respected on both wings of the party. Such was the trust between the new Prime Minister and his Foreign Secretary that Hurd was given the task of chairing the Cabinet committee that dealt with the Maastricht negotiations – a task his Cabinet colleagues considered a supreme mark of respect – and an act inconceivable under Margaret Thatcher. Hurd was 'a conservative in the classic sense who saw politics as a matter of incremental adjustment to external events'.[85] He was solid and reliable with excellent presentational skills and possessed an air of 'irresistible reassurance'.[86] The contrast with his Minister for Europe, Garel-Jones, who was responsible for the more immediate conduct of the negotiations, could not have been more pronounced, both in appearance and temperament. Garel-Jones was schooled by nine years in the Whips' Office, and over the Thatcher years had built up a considerable reputation as a 'political fixer'.

Garel-Jones had played the role of king-maker in the downfall of Mrs Thatcher, based on his pivotal position between the Whips' Office, the Cabinet and the backbenchers. He was regarded as having the sharpest political antennae in the parliamentary party and an intimate knowledge of what might be acceptable to the majority of backbench opinion. More important, he knew what pressure could be brought to bear on those who remained recalcitrant.[87] In all these areas he perfectly complemented the more patrician and diplomatic qualities of Douglas Hurd. His fluency in Spanish further encouraged hopes of closer links with Madrid. The politicians were supported by Sir John Kerr in Brussels, noted for being a quick-witted and seasoned ambassador. To many insiders Kerr combined three qualities: he was very knowledgeable about EC policy-making, he was cunning and he was widely regarded as one of the best 'wordsmiths' in the FCO.[88]

Amongst themselves the team recognized the need to be positive in the IGC negotiations if they were to be successful, to seek areas of agreement where possible and to nurture support from other Member States in order to avoid unpalatable Treaty clauses, but they shared no particular European idealism.[89] The negotiating team was also fully aware of the domestic difficulties, the limited negotiating space on sensitive issues and, ultimately, the primacy of the domestic political context.[90] The key point was that the strategy developed by Hurd and Patten was designed both to induce concessions from Britain's negotiating partners and to minimize domestic tensions that it might generate.[91]

THE BRITISH GOVERNMENT'S POSITION IN THE IGCS

In terms of the specific British objectives at the IGCs, it has been widely argued by both participants and scholars that the British government had no objectives in the IGCs and that it merely wanted to prevent things from happening.[92] It is certainly true that each proposal was given what Douglas Hurd referred to at the time as 'the proof reading treatment'. That is to say British negotiators continually asked what proposals really meant, how they fitted into existing policies and how much they cost.[93] In this way the British government hoped to whittle down the proposals of its more ambitious partners into a more modest set of amendments to the Treaty of Rome.[94]

However, the British were not sitting at the IGCs simply 'as wreckers'. Putting forward a detailed account of the government's position to the two Parliamentary Select Committees and in a set-piece House of Commons debate, the Foreign Secretary made clear that the government did have a limited set of proposals of its own, as well as a clear sense of the proposals it would resist.[95] It was true that no government White Paper was produced on the subject of the negotiations, but there were strategic and tactical reasons behind this. At the strategic level it avoided giving hostages to fortune in what was to be a long and open-ended negotiation, and at the tactical level it meant that the government could conceal its 'bottom line' both from its negotiating partners, from the fractious Conservative Party and even from the government as a whole.[96]

British preferences in the four key subject areas of the negotiations of 1990 to 1991 are delineated in the chapters which follow. Nevertheless, and despite the fact that negotiating positions were amended as the negotiations progressed, three guiding principles can be identified as underpinning them. Based on the long-standing British preference for intergovernmental cooperation, the first objective concerned the institutional structure of the EC, and in particular the notion of giving new competences to the EC and developing extant but dormant competences such as public health, training and culture. London explicitly wanted to ensure that both legislation and the strategic direction of closer integration should ultimately be decided by the Member States themselves and not by the EC's supranational institutions.[97] As London saw it, weak central institutions and a more intergovernmental kind of integration would better serve the interests of the bigger countries in general and Britain in particular.[98]

London's second guiding principle was a generalized preference for preventing a multi-speed Europe in areas on which the Twelve had agreed to make common policies.[99] Both Douglas Hurd and John Major thought that a multi-speed Community was bad for Britain's interests since it was intrinsically divisive. It also had the considerable disadvantage of removing the obligation to reach agreement together, as debate switched to increasingly exclusive tiers which inevitably marginalized the more cautious Member States.[100]

A third negotiating aim was to incorporate a *modus operandi* into the Community's work, to the effect that it should handle only issues which the Member States could not handle themselves, irrespective of competences already incorporated into the Treaty of Rome.[101] To achieve this the British government wanted a method of deciding whether a problem was best handled at the international level through the Community framework or through cooperation between governments.[102] Incorporating the principle of subsidiarity into the Treaty was also a key German objective, though there was some disagreement with the British over the specific detail of the subsidiarity principle, and the government doubted the effectiveness of making it justiciable, but these issues were left open for the negotiations.[103]

Given these three broad aims, it was not surprising that London wanted to prevent automatic moves to incorporate new areas into the competence of the supranational institutions and existing law of the Community. Here, London had in mind cooperation between police forces on judicial issues, terrorism, drug trafficking and foreign and security policy, all areas in which *ad hoc* intergovernmental procedures outside the Community method had hitherto been used. It was London's view that moves towards greater cooperation should not only preserve but also enhance the autonomy of governments. This had the added advantage of not relegating Britain to the second tier of a multi-speed Community.[104]

As regards issues already dealt with by the EC through the 'Community method', the question of extending majority voting touched a very raw nerve since in the British debate the national veto was intimately linked to the sovereignty debate. Moreover, Mrs Thatcher was thought to have yielded the principle of majority voting in her negotiation of the SEA.[105] London questioned the automatic need to extend majority voting within the Council of Ministers (beyond Single Market measures) since this watered down national autonomy.[106] The government also wanted to limit the legislative powers of the EP and opposed any extension of existing co-operation powers, the ability of the EP to veto Council actions, plus any EP claim to initiate legislation.[107] In non-legislative roles London had ideas about developing the scrutiny powers of the EP as a watchdog of the Community's finances to include anti-fraud measures and about giving it greater control over the Commission. However, so far as London was concerned, if governments remained the main participants and were accountable to their national parliaments, the democratic deficit did not exist.[108] London's preference was therefore for developing a greater but undisclosed role for national parliaments.[109]

The government's view of the role of the ECJ was at best ambivalent. On the one hand its aim was to limit any future extension of the policy reach of the Court in general. On the other hand, and unsurprisingly given its own self-perception as being good at implementing Community legislation, the government wanted the ECJ to have the power to fine Member States for non-implementation of EC legislation, and not just of Single Market measures but any obligation under the EC pillar.[110]

The government was equally committed to a list of changes that it wanted to obstruct, and here Schoutheete is right to suggest that the British government was more committed to preventing things happening than to securing its own proposals. It did not want the EC to develop a defence and security identity which it considered to be the role of NATO.[111] Nor did it want the Community to develop a social dimension further, an industrial policy or even an environmental policy. All these it considered would either reduce competition, add costs to businesses, or indirectly increase Britain's already high financial contribution to the EC. These formed the general objectives of the British government.

CONCLUSION

In the broadest terms, John Major's negotiating position at Maastricht was informed by Britain's historical reluctance to grasp the nettle of the European issue. John Major also inherited a fragile Conservative Party that was deeply factionalized, ideologically disorientated and more difficult to manage than it had ever been. Many of its divisions moreover centred around the pivotal issue of Europe. In these circumstances, the negotiations to create a European Union threatened to split the party completely. John Major's difficulties were further compounded by the task of preparing for the next general election and this cast a long shadow over his first 16 months in office. Indeed, political insiders write of this period in terms of a series of 'electoral windows' opening and then closing,[112] which in turn directly affected the way the European issue and negotiating strategy were handled by the government.

Major's overriding priority was thus to reunite the Conservative Party and hold it together through the general election.[113] While he was beholden to no faction, and his image as a unifier was in some respects an asset, it also stoked fears on the political right of the party, which suspected a backsliding from the path marked out by Mrs Thatcher. The right were also distrustful of the new managerial style of leadership and a number of his Cabinet ministers reportedly considered that John Major lacked 'political backbone' and might need 'firming up'.[114] Further complicating this situation, Major inherited a left-of-centre Cabinet which nevertheless contained an important if small grouping of Thatcherite representatives who were entrenched in the economic departments.

While unburdened by his own distinctive political philosophy, the ideological inheritance of Mrs Thatcher prevented Major from making a whole-hearted commitment to Europe without splitting the party. The Patten-Hurd strategy was not an attempt to create an intellectually respectable basis for British relations with the EC. The structure of British politics acted against this, as did the political crisis in the Conservative Party. Given the necessity of an election by May 1992, and the deep divisions between pro- and anti-Europeans in the Conservative Party, the government had little interest in educating the people or backbenchers about European policy.

This then was the mix of historical, institutional and partisan factors within the domestic arena. Most immediately, Major had to juggle the management of a pro-European Cabinet which contained a powerful kernel of anti-European ministers, with his need to nurture back-bench support for his negotiating position. At the same time, he hoped to use the IGC negotiations to boost the government's domestic image, and his own role as an international statesman. This would both consolidate his position in the party and provide a powerful weapon in the looming general election campaign. At worst, Major's aim was to quarantine EC issues from the domestic political arena and so minimize the dangers to party unity and his own prospects of re-election.

NOTES

1. See William Wallace, 'What Price Independence? Sovereignty and Interdependence in British Politics', *International Affairs*, vol. 62, no. 3, 1986, pp. 367–89, p. 387. See also Vernon Bogdanor, 'The Myth of Sovereignty', in Michael Elliott and Richard Holmes (eds), *1688–1988: Time for a New Constitution*, London, Macmillan, 1988, pp. 81–102.
2. A. V. Dicey, *Introduction to the Study of the Law of the Constitution*, London, Macmillan, 9th ed., 1939; F. S. Northedge, 'Britain and the EEC: Past and Present', in Roy Jenkins (ed.), *Britain and the EEC*, Manchester University Press, 1988, p. 26; Bulmer, 'Britain and European Integration', in George, *Britain and the EC*, op. cit., p. 9.
3. William Wallace, 'Foreign Policy and National Identity in the United Kingdom', *International Affairs*, vol. 67, 1991, pp. 651–80, p. 651; Wallace, 'What Price Interdependence?', op. cit., p. 380, p. 383; see also Helen Wallace, 'Britain out on a Limb?' *Political Quarterly*, vol. 166, no. 1, 1995, pp. 46–58, p. 47.
4. Roy Denman, *Missed Chances*, London, Cassell, 1996, p. 295.
5. John Young, *Britain and European Unity*, op. cit., pp. 171–2.
6. Wallace, 'What Price Independence?', op. cit., p. 370.
7. Christopher Tugendhat and William Wallace, *Options for British Foreign Policy in the 1990s*, London, Pinter, 1988, p. 88.
8. Young, *Britain and European Unity*, op. cit., p. 174.
9. Northedge, 'Britain and the EEC: Past and Present', op. cit., p. 26.
10. Alan Milward, et al., *The Frontier of National Sovereignty: History and Theory 1945–92*, London, Routledge, 1992; *The Reconstruction of Western Europe*, London, Routledge, 1992.
11. Wallace, 'What Price Interdependence?', op. cit., p. 368.
12. See Helen Wallace, *The Challenge of Diversity*, London, Routledge for RIIA, 1985.
13. Christopher Hill, 'Britain: a Convenient Schizophrenia', in Christopher Hill (ed.), *National Foreign Policies and European Political Co-operation*, London, Allen and Unwin/RIIA, 1983.
14. Alistair Horne, *Macmillan: 1957–86*, London, Macmillan, 1989, pp. 256–60.
15. *The United Kingdom and the European Communities*, cmnd 4715, July 971, p. 8.
16. Stephen George, 'A Reply to Buller', *Politics*, vol. 15, no. 1, 1995, pp. 43–7.
17. See for instance Christopher Lord, *British Entry to the European Community under the Heath Government of 1970–74*, Aldershot, Dartmouth, 1993, p. 99 & p. 142.
18. See for example Young, *Britain and European Unity*, op. cit., p. 180.
19. For the role of the Cabinet Office see Peter Hennessy, *Cabinet*, Oxford, Oxford University Press, 1986, ch. 2 and Peter Hennessy, *Whitehall*, London, Fontana, 1988, pp. 292–343. For the role of the European Secretariat see Anthony Seldon, 'The Cabinet Office and Coordination 1979–87', *Public Administration*, vol. 68, no. 1, spring, 1990, pp. 103–21.
20. The Permanent Representative does of course play a role in advising

on these guidelines as a member of OPD (E). For a further discussion of policy formulation see Geoffrey Edwards, 'Central Government', in George, *Britain and the European Community*, op. cit., pp. 64–90, p. 72.

21.   See Les Metcalf and Edwardo Goñi Zapico, *Action or Reaction: the Role of National Administrations in European Policy-Making*, London, Sage, 1991; Edwards, 'Central Government', op. cit., p. 67.

22.   Helen Wallace, 'Negotiations and Coalition Formation in the European Community', *Government and Opposition*, vol. 20, no. 4, 1985, pp. 453–72, p. 456.

23.   *Economist*, 14 December 1991, p. 39; see also Brigid Laffan, *Integration and Co-operation in Europe*, London, Routledge, 1992, p. 193.

24.   Michael Clarke, 'The Policy-Making Process', in Michael Smith, Steve Smith and Barry White, *British Foreign Policy*, London, Unwin Hyman, 1988, p. 367.

25.   Wallace, 'What Price Interdependence?', op. cit., p. 367.

26.   See for instance Alan Butt Philip, 'Westminster versus Brussels', in Jolyon Howarth and John Maclean (eds), *Europeans on Europe*, London, Macmillan, 1992, p. 188.

27.   Wallace, 'What Price Interdependence?', op. cit., p. 367.

28.   William Wallace, 'British Foreign Policy after the Cold War', *International Affairs*, vol. 68, no. 3, July 1992, p. 442.

29.   Laffan, *Integration and Cooperation in Europe*, op. cit., p. 195.

30.   Thatcher, *Path to Power*, op. cit., p. 209; Lord, *British Entry to the European Community*, op. cit., pp. 129–46.

31.   David Baker, Andrew Gamble and Steve Ludlam, 'Whips or Scorpions? The Maastricht Vote and the Conservative Party', *Parliamentary Affairs*, vol. 46, no. 2, April 1993, pp. 147–66.

32.   Nigel Ashford, 'The European Economic Community', in Zig Layton-Henry (ed.), *Conservative Party Politics*, London, Macmillan, 1980, pp. 95–125, p. 124.

33.   See Heseltine's two 'Europe manifestos', *Where There's a Will*, London, Hutchinson, 1987, and *The Challenge of Europe: Can Britain Win?*, London, Wiedenfeld and Nicholson, 1989.

34.   Ranelagh, *Thatcher's People*, London, Fontana, 1992, pp. 298–300. For the difference in style between Thatcher and Major see the comments made by Sir Charles Powell quoted in P. Junor, *The Major Enigma*, London, Michael Joseph, 1993, pp. 209–10.

35.   Hogg and Hill, *Too Close to Call*, op. cit., p. 8.

36.   In the second round of the leadership election Major secured 185 votes, with 187 MPs preferring Hurd or Heseltine. For the absence of an ideological power base see Paul Whiteley, Patrick Seyd, Jeremy Richardson and Paul Bissell, 'Thatcherism and the Conservative Party', *Political Studies*, vol. 42, no. 2, June 1994, pp. 185–203.

37.   In particular Thatcherite sympathizers serving on the staff of the *Sunday Telegraph* and *Spectator*. See David Mckie, 'Nightmare on Norm Street', in Helen Margetts and George Smyth (eds), *Turning Japanese?*, London, Lawrence and Wishart, 1994, pp. 128–42, p. 136. For the doubts on the right wing of the party see Teresa Gorman, *The*

Bastards: Dirty Tricks and the Challenge to Europe, London, Pan Books, 1993, p. 13.

38. 'Watch with Mother', *Economist*, 21 March 1991, p. 29.
39. The exception was Lord Mackay who held the post of Lord Chancellor.
40. Hogg and Hill, *Too Close to Call*, op. cit., p. 8. For Major's fear of the influence ex-ministers could wield on the backbenchers see Major's off the record remarks to Michael Brunson, quoted in full in Junor, *Major Enigma*, op. cit., pp. 304–5.
41. Norton, 'Factions and Tendencies in the Conservative Party', in Margetts and Smyth (eds), *Turning Japanese?*, op. cit., p. 95.
42. James, *British Cabinet Government*, op. cit., p. 108. Howe, *Conflict of Loyalty*, op. cit., p. 630.
43. Hogg and Hill, *Too Close to Call*, op. cit., p. 12.
44. James, *British Cabinet Government*, op. cit., p. 106. There is evidence that Major colluded with Hurd during the leadership campaign in return for Hurd remaining Foreign Secretary. See Junor, *Major Enigma*, op. cit., p. 203. For an excellent discussion of the time-consuming nature of Heseltine's task see David Butler, Andrew Adonis and Tony Travers, *Failure in British Government: the Politics of the Poll Tax*, Oxford, Oxford University Press, 1994, pp. 170–83.
45. Philip Stephens, *Politics and the Pound: the Tories, the Economy and Europe*, London, Macmillan, 1997, p. 187.
46. Hogg and Hill, *Too Close to Call*, op. cit., p. 9.
47. Author's interview.
48. For the dependence of the party leader on the parliamentary party see Philip Norton, '"The Lady's Not For Turning" but what about the rest? Margaret Thatcher and the Conservative Party', *Parliamentary Affairs*, vol. 43, no. 1, January 1990, pp. 41–58, p. 45.
49. David Baker, Andrew Gamble and Steve Ludlam, 'The Parliamentary Siege of Maastricht 1993: Conservative Divisions and British Ratification', *Parliamentary Affairs*, vol. 47, no. 1, January 1994, pp. 37–60.
50. Norton, '"The Lady's Not For Turning"', op. cit., p. 43.
51. See Thatcher, *The Downing Street Years*, op. cit., pp. 830–1. The importance of party activists was not their failure to vote for the party but rather the multiplier effect they had in winning votes at election time. See John Aldrich, 'A Downsian Spatial Model with Party Activism', *American Political Science Review*, vol. 77, 1983, pp. 974–90.
52. Gorman, *Bastards*, p. 30. Butler, Adonis and Travers, *Failure in British Government*, op. cit., p. 174.
53. For the lower level of Europeanization of backbenchers, see Bagehot, 'The New Ruling Class', *Economist*, 23 November 1991, p. 48.
54. See the comments by Mrs Thatcher in *The Downing Street Years*, op. cit., p. 547.
55. Lawson warned Mrs Thatcher about the significance of the Treaty text concerning EMU and counselled against signing the SEA. Indeed Article 102A specifically envisages further policy developments entailing Treaty changes. See Lawson, *The View from No. 11*, op. cit., pp. 893–4. In supporting the SEA, Mrs Thatcher subsequently acknowl-

edged that she had ignored the views of many on the right wing of the party. Thatcher, *The Downing Street Years*, op. cit., p. 556.

56. Author's interviews. Thatcher, *The Downing Street Years*, op. cit., p. 743.
57. Thatcher's recollections of the period after 1987 are of a profound shift in the kind of Europe that was taking shape based on a Franco-German bloc with its own agenda. See ibid., p. 727.
58. Howe, *Conflict of Loyalty*, op. cit., p. 533.
59. Thatcher, *The Downing Street Years*, op. cit., pp. 742–6. For a full text see Lawrence Freedman (ed.), *Europe Transformed: Documents on the End of the Cold War*, London, Triservice Press, 1990, pp. 267–74.
60. Shirley Letwin, *Anatomy of Thatcherism*, London, Fontana, 1992, p. 301.
61. Its membership had a considerable overlap with the No Turning Back Group, set up in 1985 by 13 MPs, including John Redwood, Peter Lilley, Michael Portillo, Edward Leigh, Michael Forsyth, Francis Maude, Neil Hamilton and Alan Howarth. All were ministers in the first Major administration. NTB had a more general aim to stiffen Mrs Thatcher's resolve to pursue radical policies, which included a more sceptical stance on Europe. See Gorman, *Bastards*, op. cit., pp. 12–13. The funding of the Bruges Group reportedly came from Lord Forte, Sir James Goldsmith and Lord King.
62. Lawson, *The View from No. 11*, op. cit., p. 922. See also Thatcher, *The Downing Street Years*, op. cit., p. 831.
63. See, for instance, David Reynolds, *Britannia Overruled*, London, Longman, 1991, p. 275.
64. For her perception of grass-roots support, see Thatcher, *The Downing Street Years*, op. cit., p. 831; for back-bench support, see p. 833.
65. Hogg and Hill, *Too Close to Call*, op. cit., p. 58.
66. Ibid., p. 94.
67. 'My Friend Chris', *Economist*, 20 April 1991; Michael Binyon, 'Farewell to an Admirable Fixer', *The Times*, 28 March 1991.
68. Young, *Britain and European Unity*, 1945–92, op. cit., p. 162.
69. 'What the PM Learnt about the Germans', *Independent on Sunday*, 15 July 1990; see also Nigel Lawson's comments on Thatcher's crude anti-German sentiments in *The View from No. 11*, op. cit., p. 900.
70. Some have argued that an actual back-room deal took place between the French and the Germans linking EMU with the outcome of the Two Plus Four Talks. See, for instance, George Valence, 'L'Engrenage Européenne', *L'Express*, 19 October 1990, p. 19.
71. In this respect Major and his generation were the product of a wide-ranging post-war effort to network British and West German political and administrative elites, of which the annual Königswinter conference was the best-known example. See 'Turning to Germany', *The Times*, 9 March 1991.
72. Hogg and Hill, *Too Close to Call*, op. cit., p. 76.
73. Ibid., p. 147.
74. Hogg and Hill note with some amusement that in the run up to Maastricht John Major had to tactfully refuse Kohl's well-meant offer

to 'explain Europe' to Tory MPs. Hogg and Hill, *Too Close to Call*, op. cit., p. 147.

75. Young, *Britain and European Unity, 1945–92*, op. cit., p. 162. See also Ruth Dudley-Edwards, *True Brits: Inside the Foreign Office*, London, BBC Books, 1994, p. 155.

76. See John Major, 'The Evolution of Europe', *Conservative Party News*, 11 March 1991, pp. 13–14. For an 'insider's' account of this speech see Hogg and Hill, *Too Close to Call*, op. cit., pp. 76–9.

77. Author's interview with Sir John Kerr.

78. In fact the negotiations took over two years to conclude and, when they did, only resulted in a partial merger of the British Conservative group and did not lead to the Conservative Party Leader's attendance at pre-summit EPP meetings.

79. Author's interview with Sir Christopher Prout MEP and Michael Welsh MEP. George Brock, 'Tories Poised to Rejoin Alliance', *The Times*, 12 March 1991.

80. Author's interview with Sir John Kerr.

81. See George Brock, 'EC Leaders in Quandary as Mr Enigma Goes to Luxembourg', *The Times*, 8 April 1991.

82. Margaret Thatcher claims she was surprised at the speed with which her stance was reversed. See *The Path to Power*, op. cit., p. 475.

83. Author's interview with a senior British negotiator. See also editorial, 'Corridor Diplomacy', *The Times*, 1 July 1991.

84. Author's interview with Michael Welsh MEP, and Bill Cash MP.

85. Wallace, 'British Foreign Policy after the Cold War', op. cit., p. 287.

86. *Europe after Maastricht*, Foreign Affairs Committee, Second Report Vol. II, House of Commons, Session 1991–2, 223–II.

87. For an account of the political acumen of Garel-Jones see Bruce Anderson, *John Major: the Making of a Prime Minister*, London, Fourth Estate, 1991, pp. 318–19; Gorman, *Bastards*, op. cit., pp. 164–5.

88. John Major used to refer to him as Machiavelli when he worked with him in the FCO. See Anderson, London, Chapmans, *John Major*, op. cit., p. 127; John Dickie, *Inside the Foreign Office*, pp. 278–9. For Garel-Jones' view see Dudley-Edwards, *True Brits*, op. cit., p. 151.

89. Author's interview with Sir John Kerr.

90. Author's interviews.

91. Hogg and Hill, *Too Close to Call*, op. cit., p. 79.

92. Philippe de Schoutheete, paper delivered to the Institut d'Etudes Européennes of the Université Libre de Bruxelles, Brussels ULB D/1992/2672/27. John Pinder, 'Vital Tasks for the Dutch Presidency', in Alfred Pijpers (ed.), *The European Community at the Crossroads*, London, Martinus Nijhoff, 1991, pp. 25–34, p.27; Stephen George, 'The British Government and the Maastricht Agreements', in Rosenthal and Cafruny, *State of the European Community*, vol. 2, pp. 177–92.

93. Douglas Hurd, evidence to the Foreign Affairs Committee, *European Council Luxembourg*, 12 June 1991, House of Commons Paper 77–ii, session 1991–2, col. 1020. The speech by Douglas Hurd to North Shropshire Conservative Association was reported in Robin Oakley, 'Hurd Pledge on United Europe', *The Times*, 3 June 1991.

94. Douglas Hurd, *Parl. Deb. HC*, 26 June 1991, col. 1020.
95. Douglas Hurd, evidence to the Foreign Affairs Committee, *European Council Rome*, 14–15 December, House of Commons Paper 77-1; col. 90.
96. Hurd had proposed the government publish an outline of its submissions in autumn 1990 as part of a broader statement on government's European policy, but this idea was rejected by the Cabinet. The routine parliamentary debate on 6 December 1990 prior to the European Council was a poor substitute in this respect. However, UKREP did formally make submissions on 30 September 1990, which were substantially reworked after the change in leadership. Author's interviews. See also the evidence of Douglas Hurd to the Foreign Affairs Select Committee, *European Council Rome*, December 1990, op. cit., col. 7, pp. 4–5.
97. See the evidence of Douglas Hurd to the House of Lords Select Committee on the European Communities, *Economic and Monetary Union and Political Union*, 27th Report, session 1989–90, House of Lords paper 88–II, col. 992, p. 209; see also Hurd's comments in the House of Commons debate, *Parl. Deb. HC*, 12 June 1991, col. 1021.
98. Douglas Hurd, evidence to the Foreign Affairs Committee, *European Council Luxembourg*, op. cit., col. 67, pp. 23–4.
99. See the evidence of Douglas Hurd to the House of Lords Select Committee on the European Communities, *Economic and Monetary Union and Political Union*, op. cit., col. 1019; contrast this with John Major's subsequent exaltation of the virtue of a multi-speed Europe on his return from Maastricht, *Parl. Deb. HC*, 18 December 1991, col. 283.
100. See the evidence of Douglas Hurd to the Foreign Affairs Committee, 12 June 1991, op. cit., col. 1021; and of John Major to the Treasury and Civil Service Committee, *European Monetary Union*, Wednesday 25 July 1990, House of Lords Paper 620, col. 7, p. 2.
101. See the comments made by Francis Maude to the House of Commons Select Committee on European Legislation, *Minutes of Evidence*, 18 July 1990, House of Commons Paper 188–III, 1989–90, cols 6–8; see also John Major's speech to the House of Commons, *Parl. Deb. HC*, 20 November 1991, cols 269–81.
102. For a wider discussion of this issue see Marc Wilke and Helen Wallace, 'Subsidiarity: Approaches to Power-sharing in the European Community', *RIIA Discussion Paper* no. 27, Royal Institute for International Affairs, 1990.
103. For a further discussion of the difficulty of making subsidiarity justiciable see the House of Commons Foreign Affairs Committee, Second Report, *The Operation of the Single European Act*, House of Commons Paper 446–i, session 1989–90, cols 94–100, pp. 31–2; see also 'Editorial Comments', *Common Market Law Review*, XXVII, 2, 1990, pp. 181–4; and Vald Constantinesco, 'Subsidiaritaet: Zentrales Verfassunsprinzip fuer die Politische Union', *Integration*, 4/90, Bonn, 1990, pp. 165–78.
104. Douglas Hurd, *Parl. Deb. HC*, 174, 11 June 1990, col. 23. These aims were repeated by the Prime Minister in 1991. See John Major, *Parl. Deb. HC*, 20 November 1991, op. cit., col. 275.
105. Bogdanor, 'Myth of Sovereignty', op. cit., p. 81.

106. See the evidence of Douglas Hurd, *Economic and Monetary Union and Political Union*, op. cit., col. 997, p. 210.
107. Ibid., col. 1004, p. 213.
108. Douglas Hurd to the House of Lords Select Committee, *Economic and Monetary Union and Political Union*, op. cit., col. 1006, p. 212. See also Ivor Owen, 'Thatcher Defends Stance on Closer Ties to Europe', *Financial Times*, 27 September 1991.
109. Echoing this debate in January 1991, the House of Commons debated the need to establish two new committees for the scrutiny of EC legislation. See *Parl. Deb. HC*, 22 January 1991.
110. Evidence of Douglas Hurd to House of Lords Select Committee, *Economic and Monetary Union and Political Union*, op. cit., col. 1001. See also evidence of Garel-Jones to the Foreign Affairs Select Committee, *European Council Maastricht*, House of Commons Paper 35–1, col. 39, p. 10.
111. Evidence of Douglas Hurd to House of Lords Select Committee, *Economic and Monetary Union and Political Union*, op. cit., col. 23.
112. Hogg and Hill, *Too Close to Call*, op. cit., pp. 81–2.
113. Anderson, *John Major*, op. cit., p. 386.
114. Author's interviews. Ibid., p. 360.

2 Economic and Monetary Union

Although the issue of Economic and Monetary Union was a core component of the final Maastricht Treaty, the intergovernmental debates on the question differed in two key respects from the rest of the Treaty negotiations. First, unlike the political union negotiations, the IGC on EMU did have an agreed agenda. This was based on the comprehensive report on monetary union submitted by the Delors Committee in April 1989. Second, again in contrast with the political union negotiations, the Commission, and more specifically Jacques Delors, played a central role in the IGC-EMU, actively brokering deals between government negotiators, drafting Treaty articles and providing specialist support for the Luxembourg and Netherlands presidencies.[1]

What also distinguished the EMU debates from most of the other Treaty negotiations was the extent to which Britain was from the beginning isolated from the bulk of its partners on the issue. The British were particularly reluctant to contemplate the possibility of EMU, first and foremost because it raised hugely difficult questions about national sovereignty and the supremacy of the Westminster Parliament, but also economic questions concerning the lack of convergence between the British and continental countries. As this chapter demonstrates, however, the confusion, mutual suspicion and disunity in the Conservative Party over moves towards a single currency from 1987 onwards ensured that the British government had to manage the negotiations at two levels, with their own party and the other EC governments.

The British approach to, and achievements in, the EMU dossier must therefore be understood in the context of the pre-history of the issue and the fact that John Major never established firm control over his own party and so never had a firm base from which to negotiate with other governments. British inattention and pre-occupation with other issues and an underestimation of the serious intent of other governments to create a single currency wrong footed the government. This led to a bungled diplomatic strategy to regain the initiative, which left British negotiators fighting a defensive rear-guard action. British reluctance to make a commitment to participate in the final stage of monetary union ultimately left the government a marginal participant in the negotiations. Ultimately it was forced to concede that other EC countries could use the institutions of the European Union to introduce and run a single currency, and its influence limited to securing a right of exclusion from this process.

THE BACKGROUND

The idea of monetary union can be traced back to Jean Monnet's Action Committee for Europe which proposed monetary union as early as 1961. Member State governments committed themselves to a single currency in the Werner Report in 1970, which set out the steps necessary to achieve Economic and Monetary Union. In 1972, immediately prior to the European Community's first enlargement, the six founding Member States committed themselves to the goal of EMU by 1980.[2] When Britain joined the Community in January 1973, it accepted this commitment as part of the *acquis communautaire* – the body of law, conventions and declarations that governed the EC. The oil crisis, followed by a lengthy economic recession and above all the collapse of the Bretton Woods system and the generalized floating of currencies, temporarily put paid to these aspirations, since the Werner Report was obviously a wholly inadequate prescription in the new situation. However, one legacy of this commitment was the introduction of the European Monetary System and subsequently the Exchange Rate Mechanism, though Britain chose to stand aside from the latter.[3]

The issue of EMU resurfaced again in November 1985 during the Single European Act negotiations. Jacques Delors proposed that EMU be included as a Treaty objective, a recommendation which went well beyond previous non-binding resolutions and declarations concerning EMU.[4] With German support the goal of EMU was eventually removed from the main Treaty, but included in the preamble. Although deeply opposed to EMU, Mrs Thatcher was at the time happy enough with the SEA, believing that 'EMU now meant economic and monetary co-operation, not moving towards a single currency'.[5] Other heads of government, however, took a different line, interpreting the SEA as paving the way towards a European Central Bank and single currency, and continued to press for further progress on this issue.

In April 1987, before the SEA had even been ratified, the Padoa-Schioppa Report sponsored by the European Commission argued that 'monetary policy coordination would have to be significantly strengthened if freedom of capital movements and exchange rate discipline are to survive and coexist'.[6] Mitterrand, Kohl and Delors each added to the mounting pressure for movement towards the goal of EMU. All had different motivations, however.

So far as the French government was concerned, it was becoming increasingly apparent that the Bundesbank was playing the dominant role in the Exchange Rate Mechanism. From the perspective of the French political elite, control of monetary policy had already been lost; the only way to recapture a share of the control was to create a single currency managed by a European Central Bank. For Chancellor Kohl, Economic and Monetary Union would irrevocably anchor Germany to West Europe, provided that a single currency was as anti-inflationary as the Deutschmark. So far as the European Commission was concerned, EMU was something of a federalist holy grail.[7] The Commission President Jacques Delors' hope was that Economic and Monetary Union would make the integration process irreversible, but also mark 'a major new pooling of sovereignty and a huge step towards integration'.[8] In turn, this would require even greater Commission influence and responsibilities in policy sectors which many governments had stubbornly resisted as supranational interference.

In June 1988, this led to the German Presidency proposing that a committee of experts be set up to explore the best means of creating a European Central Bank. Again, as in 1985, the British government was reticent about such a move, but with few allies and given that as a future member of the EC Britain had in 1972 agreed 'to move irrevocably [towards] Economic and Monetary Union' Mrs Thatcher considered that 'there was no point picking a quarrel which we would have lost'.[9]

Thatcher was vehemently opposed to EMU, and sufficiently disturbed by the growing pressure towards this goal to make it a key element of her Bruges speech of September 1988.[10] Yet she was surprisingly relaxed about the remit of the committee and the appointment of Delors to chair it.[11] Part of the explanation lies in the fact that Mrs Thatcher thought that she had won two significant concessions. First, she had secured the appointment to the committee of Central Bank Governors rather than academic experts. The former, she believed, 'not only possessed the expertise required but could be relied upon to keep their feet on the ground'.[12] Second, she had succeeded in having all reference to a European Central Bank removed from the committee's remit.[13]

A further reason for Thatcher's continued complacency was the presence on the committee of Robin Leigh Pemberton, the Bank of England Governor. In particular, she hoped that an alliance between Leigh Pemberton and Karl-Otto Pöhl, the President of the Bundesbank, who was known to be sceptical, 'would prevent the emergence of a report which would give momentum to EMU'.[14] In fact Leigh Pemberton took a somewhat detached approach to his role in the Delors Committee. He considered that his task was not to reflect on whether EMU should take place or not, but simply to address the mechanics of how an effective single currency might be created. In addition, when Pöhl proved 'a broken reed' unwilling to oppose EMU, Leigh Pemberton failed to hold out for a minority report to reflect the position of the British government on EMU.[15] Since he was appointed to the committee in a personal capacity, Leigh Pemberton was sensitive to the charge that he might be perceived as taking orders from the government. In part, Leigh Pemberton, a pro-European himself, 'who was temperamentally sympathetic to the idea of a single currency', genuinely considered the report a legitimate means to achieve a single currency, though he privately doubted much would come of it.[16] When it came to the final report Leigh Pemberton was also sufficiently anxious about the impact of recalcitrance on his personal credibility among the closed group of central bankers that he chose not to oppose it.[17]

Contrary to Mrs Thatcher's expectations, the final report published in April 1989 therefore provided a blueprint for monetary union, and featured complete currency convertibility, liberalization of capital flows, integration of financial markets and the irrevocable fixing of exchange rates leading to a single currency. Three stages were outlined for the achievement of monetary union.[18] These were: first, a strengthening of existing procedures for linking currencies; second, integration between states through a new treaty; and third, the irrevocable locking of exchange rates to produce a single currency managed by a European Central Bank. But the report also left a number of key issues to be decided, notably the nature and timing of the transition stages to monetary union and whether convergence criteria were necessary preconditions for joining a single currency.[19]

Despite warnings from several leading ministers in her government, Mrs Thatcher had thus badly misjudged the growing determination of her partners to proceed towards monetary union.[20] She had been convinced that the Delors Committee would quickly kick the issue of monetary union into the long grass, although Nigel Lawson, her Chancellor, had counselled otherwise.[21] It was certainly difficult to know what the UK might have done to deflect the outcome given the others' objectives, though as an opponent of EMU Pöhl subsequently judged it a mistake to have taken part in the Delors Committee.[22] What is clear is that the report increased the pressure on the British government to concede to the majority will on the question of EMU. What made Britain's subsequent response to these challenges more difficult, however, was the way in which the issue of EMU was increasingly aggravating tensions at the domestic level.

THE DOMESTIC CONTEXT

Three sets of domestic problems were attached to the issue of EMU. The first problem was the attack on national sovereignty which a single currency was perceived as representing. As discussed in the preceding chapter, successive governments had failed to come to terms with the diminution of national sovereignty which involvement in the European integration project entailed. Moreover, they had failed to educate the public on this question. Given this stance, the issue of a single currency was thus especially threatening, since what was being proposed was the removal of an outward and visible sign of continued British independence, the pound sterling. The symbolism of a single currency was hence so extreme that it was difficult for the political elite to discuss it in a rational way, far less engage a totally unprepared public in such a discussion.

Notwithstanding the questions which EMU raised about national sovereignty, the second factor which complicated domestic discussion of the issue was the economic merits of a single currency. The economic pros and cons of the EMU were perceived as highly inconclusive, in that long-term benefits might be forthcoming, but there were significant risks if the project did not proceed according to an agreed plan. The problem was compounded by the confused signals coming from the business community. Business groups were generally positive about ERM membership because it was seen as a means to lower interest rates and ensure exchange rate stability. However, there were clear divisions over a single currency, and as many leading industrialists were against EMU as were in favour of it.

The third factor impeding a reasoned discussion of the issue of EMU was the way in which it had by the late 1980s become a central part of the policy and personality clashes which characterized Mrs

Thatcher's last administration. Interestingly, however, the bone of contention between Thatcher on the one hand and Lawson and Howe on the other was not the issue of EMU, to which all were opposed. The argument centred round the question of British membership of the Exchange Rate Mechanism. Lawson was keen that Britain should join the ERM but was resolutely opposed by Mrs Thatcher who preferred the counsel of her special advisor on economic matters, Alan Walters.[23] Their attention distracted by the issue of the ERM, policy-makers continued to avoid confronting major questions posed by EMU for national sovereignty and Britain's future relationship with Europe.

As a direct consequence of Mrs Thatcher's failure to join the ERM, between 1987 and 1989, Nigel Lawson concluded that an anti-inflationary policy could not simply rest on the control of domestic money supply and pursued a policy that became known as shadowing the Deutschmark, an exchange-rate based monetary policy which implied linking British levels of interest rate to corresponding German levels.[24] This policy led Lawson to argue that ERM membership was good in its own right: it was a logical implication of shadowing the Deutschmark and would be an important anti-inflationary discipline.[25] Thus the setting of a date to join the ERM would establish the good faith of British policy statements since 1985 that Britain would join 'when the time was right'. The Foreign Secretary, Geoffrey Howe, was less implacably opposed to the principle of EMU, and regarded ERM membership principally as a step which could deliver diplomatic gains. Britain could no longer halt momentum towards EMU, but by participating in Stage One of the Delors Report, the government might as a minimum slow down progress towards Stages Two and Three and might even secure EMU along lines acceptable to the British government.[26]

It was because Mrs Thatcher was preoccupied by her arguments with Lawson and Howe over the ERM, that she acquiesced in June 1989 in the Madrid European Council's endorsement of the Delors Report on EMU. Both ministers had threatened to resign if Thatcher refused to take a more active line in setting out the terms and conditions of British membership of the ERM, and she was obliged to bow to these demands at Madrid.[27] But although the British debate was centred around the question of the ERM and not EMU, the Delors Report – and Britain's acceptance of it – meant that the two issues were now explicitly linked. The inescapable fact was that ERM membership was a key component of Stage One of the Delors Report and so of EMU.

Distracted though Mrs Thatcher had been by her disagreements with her two senior ministers, the significance of what she had done became apparent to her during the Madrid European Council. Realizing that the British government would now have to make a significant effort either to derail the impending EMU negotiations completely or to steer them towards an acceptable position, Mrs Thatcher announced that Britain had shifted its stance on EMU and would soon put forward its own plans for monetary union. The extent of her improvisation was indicated by subsequent reports that the Permanent Under-Secretary narrowly avoided crashing his car into a tree when he heard the news on his car radio, so surprised was he to hear that the Treasury had been working on a plan.[28]

The policy which emerged from Thatcher's realization of the need to involve the government seriously in the EMU debate centred around the notion of competing currencies. The core of this plan was that Central Banks would compete inside the framework of the ERM. Competition would be achieved by removing all barriers to the use in any one country of the currency of other Member States. With complete interchangeability and no legal impediments, 'good currencies would eventually drive out the bad' and the EC might eventually find itself with a single currency freely chosen by the people.[29] The plan was thus premised on the belief that monetary union might in effect be achieved by removing exchange rate controls, the creation of a single financial market and capital and labour mobility, and removing all obstacles to the cross border use of all EC currencies: thus the formal imposition of a single currency would not be necessary.[30]

At the strategic level the plan was a response to the growing need for the British government to engage in the EMU debate. There was still a great deal of complacency behind it for, while it was acknowledged that the plan would not deflect those governments that wanted to go ahead with EMU, it was felt that it would at least provide a platform to which the other Member States could return if EMU failed. Moreover, the chief influence shaping the plan was domestic issues, particularly internal government politics. Above all, Nigel Lawson regarded the plan as a means of persuading the Prime Minister to accept his long-standing goal of membership of the ERM for sterling. The plan therefore set out a specific commitment that Britain would join the ERM when the Madrid conditions were met, and made it difficult for Mrs Thatcher to renege on her Madrid commitment that sterling join the ERM 'when the time was right'.[31]

Hardly surprisingly in view of these motivations, this British attempt to regain the initiative was not well received. Finance ministers gathered at the ECOFIN meeting in September 1989 regarded it as a 'Trojan Horse' because it opposed permanently fixed exchange rates and it argued for an evolutionary approach to a single currency which held out no guarantee of achieving monetary union at all.[32] The Bundesbank opposed the competing currencies idea since it might challenge the dominance of the Deutschmark and threatened to expose Germany to the consequences of others' irresponsible monetary policies. Others, particularly the French, feared that it would enshrine the Deutschmark as the most competitive and so dominant currency. In the absence of any support, the plan was therefore still-born; the resignation of Nigel Lawson, ironically one week before the scheme was formally unveiled, was the final 'nail in its coffin'.

As the IGC-EMU drew closer, Britain was thus still no closer to a clear policy which would derail the project of EMU. Instead, it had allowed its continuing preoccupation with the issue of ERM membership to distract it from the bigger picture of which the ERM was merely a part. The bottom line was that the government was increasingly short of inspiration as to how to proceed. When Lawson's successor John Major looked for alternatives to the defunct competing currencies scheme, it was telling that he should turn to non-government figures for ideas. And the idea on which he focussed was the 'hard ECU' proposal conceived by Paul Richards of Samuel Montagu, and developed by the European Committee of the British Invisible Exports Council (BIEC).[33] The Committee membership was drawn from City representatives, Bank of England and Treasury officials and chaired by Sir Michael Butler, a former UK ambassador to the EC, who took on the responsibility of promoting the hard ECU plan to Mrs Thatcher.[34]

There were some similarities between the hard ECU and the competing currencies plan: all existing currencies would compete with each other and a new currency would compete with existing currencies.[35] The hard ECU plan was also a market-led route to a single currency, in contrast to the Delors Report proposal for an administered approach to a single currency. However, the distinctive feature of the hard ECU plan was that a new currency should be introduced which would be, by virtue of its management, as anti-inflationary as the strongest existing EC currency and which would be guaranteed never to devalue against any other EC currency.[36] It would circulate alongside national currencies but not necessarily replace them. A European System of Central Banks would manage the ECU through a new institution, the European Monetary Fund. This would be counter-inflationary, preserve national cooperation on a pragmatic and informal basis and provide sanctions against lax monetary action on the part of member governments. The real interest of the hard ECU proposal, however, lies in the motivations behind it and how they shifted over time.

Although the government seems to have regarded the proposal – at least initially – as a means of distracting its partners from the goal of EMU, City members of the BIEC who developed the proposal believed that a single currency could be the ultimate result of the scheme.[37] Mrs Thatcher was sufficiently worried by the latter possibility that she continued to cast about for alternative proposals. She therefore commissioned two papers, one from her closest confidante Nicholas Ridley, the Secretary of State for Trade and Industry, and the other from the Treasury and FCO to examine a proposal put forward by Alan Walters for an alternative system of linking currencies to an objective reference standard.[38] And while she did finally capitulate to pressure from John Major to launch the scheme as official government policy,[39] Thatcher continued to be wary of it, denying in her report on the Dublin European Council, for instance, that the hard ECU could develop into a single currency.[40]

Further complicating the picture was the fact that John Major, the chief sponsor of the hard ECU scheme, had privately come round to the idea of conceding the principle of EMU by April 1990, two months before the official launch of the policy. Moreover, he was by April 1990 also privately doubtful as to the viability of the hard ECU proposal, believing that it might have to be abandoned in favour of an option clause in the final treaty agreed on EMU.[41] This was a highly significant development because it denoted a departure from the official government line of adamant opposition to a two-speed Europe. There were also doubts inside the Bank of England about the political viability of the hard ECU plan and about some of its technical features.[42]

The irony was, however, that Major was to continue with the official policy of the hard ECU well into the IGC negotiations themselves. While the hard ECU certainly had merit as a market-led approach to monetary union, the most plausible explanation for the continuance of the hard ECU lies in the party benefits which the ambivalence of the hard ECU proposal brought with it.[43] It was a position around which to unite the party since it could be presented to Eurosceptics on the one hand as a means to frustrate the EMU project without appearing anti-European, and to Euro-enthusiasts on the other hand as a step on the way to Britain herself joining a single currency. Certainly the scheme held little attraction for Britain's partners, as Karl-Otto Pöhl made clear two weeks after the plan had been launched. In a speech to the Institute of Economic Affairs, Pöhl announced that there would be no support forthcoming from the Bundesbank, not least because a hard ECU would create a serious and destabilizing rival currency to the Deutschmark.[44]

Domestically convenient as the hard ECU proposal might be, however, the lack of enthusiasm with which it was greeted abroad meant that Britain still needed to demonstrate that she was approaching the IGC-EMU in a positive frame of mind. Faced also with growing demands for agreement on key aspects of EMU before the opening of the IGC, the British government announced on 5 October 1990 that sterling would join the ERM. Although long urged by business leaders and greeted by a wave of euphoria, this was seen principally as a means to regain control of interest rates which by then had increased to 15 per cent, the highest for eight years. But it was also hoped that sterling's membership would indicate that Britain would make a constructive contribution at the IGC. Thatcher had been opposed to the move, but growing isolation in her own Cabinet, exacerbated by the resignation of her staunchest ally Nicholas Ridley over derogatory remarks about Germany and EMU, and the possibility of losing her new Chancellor and Foreign Secretary eventually forced her to concede.[45]

In fact, the diplomatic dividends of sterling's entry into the ERM were negligible, not least because of the way in which entry was managed. The Chancellor and Prime Minister set the exchange rate without any discussion with other EC partners – or indeed with the Bank of England – and simply announced that sterling would join on 8 October 1990 at a rate of DM 2.95 much to the annoyance of the Bundesbank who argued that Britain's partners had a right to have been consulted.[46] To soften the blow to Mrs Thatcher's own supporters, this announcement was accompanied by an immediate 1 per cent cut in interest rates from 15 per cent to 14 per cent which in the exchange markets also 'cast a shadow' over the decision to join.[47] Thus it was only the resignation of Mrs Thatcher, one month later, which offered a strategic opportunity to refocus the British approach to the IGC.

The trigger that led to a leadership election was the resignation of the Deputy Prime Minister, Sir Geoffrey Howe, over Mrs Thatcher's approach to the single currency issue. Howe argued that Mrs Thatcher had undermined the notion that the hard ECU plan 'could given time evolve into a single currency'. In particular, Thatcher had remarked that she didn't think many people would want to use the hard ECU even as a common currency let alone a single currency. As the Deputy Prime Minister remarked 'how on earth are the Chancellor and the Governor of the Bank of England ... to be taken seriously as participants in the debate against that sort of background noise'.[48] Howe's call for others to consider their own response led to the replacement of the Prime Minister by John Major. It generated relief from other heads of government at the European Council and at least opened up the possibility of a shift in the British position from Mrs Thatcher's threat to use the veto over EMU to a position which did not rule in or out any one solution absolutely.

However, by the start of the IGC-EMU the situation was problematic for Britain. First and foremost, Britain had failed to 'undermine the will of other states to move to Stage 3'.[49] All the other member governments were by now clear that EMU necessitated a single currency and a central monetary institution.[50] Second, the economic advantages and disadvantages remained highly uncertain for the UK. In the long term, benefits could be valuable if the project went well, but there would be significant risks from failure. These were economic risks other governments appeared willing to subordinate to the political goal of a single currency, but the British government simply did not share these political motivations. The uncertainties were anyway larger for a 'peripheral' economy like that of the UK than for the core of states, between whom economic integration had gone further.

Third, and arguably even more damaging, was the fact that the British position appeared deeply confused. Having for so long held out against EMU, members of the government, including John Major himself, were now increasingly reconciled to conceding the principle that EMU should go ahead. Yet they were still unclear as to whether or how Britain should participate in EMU. Moreover, the government had failed to educate its own backbenchers, far less the public, as to how its thinking had developed, and it clung instead to the cloak of the hard ECU policy, with its uncertain implications.

The British government had also made significant concessions in the immediate run-up to the convening of the IGC-EMU, which increased the pressure on all participants to reach a clear agreement. In June 1990, Mrs Thatcher had agreed a second IGC to consider political union and accepted that ratification of a single treaty should be completed by December 1992, coinciding with the completion of the Single Market. This laid out a very clear timetable for the IGC, a timetable which not only put pressure on the British government to reach an agreement, but ensured that the Treaty negotiations would be linked with the approaching general election which had to be held by May 1992.[51]

Other governments had also agreed that the second stage of monetary union would start in January 1994, putting further pressure on the participants to agree on the exact nature of both the second and third stages of monetary union even before the IGC had commenced. It should also be noted that there was by December 1990 a detailed agenda based on the Delors Report, draft statutes for the European System of Central Banks and a Commission draft of the Treaty articles necessary to create EMU, and other national proposals notably from France and Germany.[52] The prospects for Britain scuppering an agreement or even of securing a minimal agreement fine-tuned to her own concerns were therefore remote.

DEFINING EMU OBJECTIVES

By the start of the IGC-EMU, ministers were aware they would have to work hard to undo the legacy of distrust built up over London's European policy. The situation was not helped by the fact that London remained officially wedded to the hard ECU plan, which except for some support from the Spanish representative was in the eyes of its other partners by now fatally discredited by Mrs Thatcher's comments. Even inside Whitehall and the Bank of England there were growing doubts concerning the utility of the plan. Meetings to sell the hard ECU plan, in national capitals, had left some Bank of England officials with the overriding impression that whatever the technical merits of the plan the agenda had moved on, and yet another idea from a 'foot dragger' was not only unwelcome, but would also further diminish British influence in the negotiations. There was also some irritation that Bank officials had to invest time in putting across the hard ECU plan which by this time appeared 'rather hopeless'.[53]

Officials in the FCO, particularly Sir John Kerr and Michael Jay, were more sanguine, suggesting that even though London would not be able to stop the others from moving ahead if they really wanted a single currency nevertheless British negotiators would have more of a voice now that Britain was a member of the ERM. Given the govern-nment's position, outright opposition to other states' proposals would have been resented more. At least the hard ECU gave the British negotiators a locus in the debate and could be portrayed as a constructive, if different, approach to EMU, and anyway there were still significant obstacles to be overcome to achieve a negotiated Treaty solution.

To some extent John Major was caught on the horns of a dilemma. The hard ECU plan was designed and marketed as the means to exer-cise influence in the forthcoming IGC-EMU negotiations and one Cabinet minister felt the Prime Minister was unwilling to abandon it through 'pride of authorship'. To do so before the negotiations had even started would look 'whimsical and pusillanimous'. There was also some hope in government circles that when London's partners were confronted with the implications of a single currency they might settle for a more modest plan.

Aware of this, John Major's pressing need was to hold his party around the hard ECU position, while at the same time conscious that in the end-game a Treaty amendment establishing EMU would have to be conceded. Behind the cloak of the hard ECU plan and public oppo-sition to the principle of a two-speed Europe, he was therefore increas-ingly thinking in terms of securing an opt-out provision which left it to individual states to decide whether and when they should join a single currency. This was a somewhat weaker position than the one he had adopted six months earlier, when he had thought in terms of an opt in for those who wanted a single currency rather than an opt out for those countries who did not. To London the strategy was seen as the best means to allow the British government to take an active part in the negotiations and potentially shape the outcome, but permit it to post-pone a decision whether to participate in a single currency.

While there remained a deep ambivalence at the heart of John Major's policy, it was nevertheless the case that the search for alternatives in the run up to the IGC had produced some clear desiderata for the approaching negotiations. First, British policy-makers believed that Stage Two of the Delors Report should be as 'hard' as possible in the sense of securing convergence in prepara-tion for the new currency: thus Stage Two should contain elements that were worthy in themselves even if EMU did not come about. Second, policy-makers argued that there should be no bailing out of governments who ran excessive budget deficits, and that there should be an agreed set of steps that governments should take to reach monetary union. These were subsequently to become known as the convergence criteria.

Third, despite the conspicuous failure to garner German support for either the competing currency or hard ECU plan, there was a belief in both the Treasury and the FCO that the German government was the key to achieving British objectives. Germany was the leading economic power in the EC, and a single currency would be impossible if the Germans refused to sacrifice the Deutschmark. Moreover, while Bonn and the Bundesbank wanted to make the single currency as inflation proof as possible, they were also concerned to secure a cautious approach rather than participate in a rush towards monetary union. The immediate lesson of the pre-negotiation period was that London must harness German concerns and above all else avoid a timetable which set a clear deadline for the introduction of a single currency. Success of the Hurd-Patten strategy to develop a closer relationship with the Helmut Kohl and the Christian Democratic Union–Christian Social Union (CDU–CSU) – at least for government ministers – made it plausible for them to hope for German support.

In discussions between Treasury and FCO officials it was agreed that the major tactical move would be to try and separate the French from the Germans by playing on the differences between the two governments over the speed with which monetary union should be approached. In particular it was agreed to emphasize the importance of a 'long' rather than 'short' Stage Two and to advocate postponing the creation of a central bank until the end of Stage Two.[54] These evolutionary steps would, it was hoped, not only attract German support to the British cause but would also allow the British negotiating team to engage in the debate on the technical issues involved, without renouncing the British position of scepticism about the virtue of a single currency.

Although there was a high degree of support for these objectives across the Conservative Party, it must be noted that this support was something of an optical illusion. The fact was that the support stemmed largely from the ambiguity of the hard ECU plan. To the left wing, the plan represented a recognition of the need to move albeit slowly towards EMU, while to the right wing its original credentials as an alternative to EMU assuaged concern about the implications of EMU for national sovereignty.

Outside Westminster opinion was also very divided. One of the City's concerns was its importance as a financial centre in relation to

Frankfurt.[55] Some City figures feared that the government's nuanced position would diminish British influence if it did not accept the idea of a single currency. Others in the City opposed a single currency, but feared the consequences if it came about. The Confederation of British Industry had shifted its stance in the second part of 1989 from tacit to explicit approval of the principle of a single currency, but counselled caution.

THE TREATY NEGOTIATIONS

Given the preparations which had been undertaken on the subject of EMU, work on the issue moved swiftly ahead once the IGC opened in December 1990. The British negotiating team led by Sir Nigel Wicks worked to a tight brief, emphasizing the British position that only Parliament could decide if and when the UK would join a single currency, and that the final treaty should create no automatic obligation to participate. While British negotiators knew the hard ECU plan had little chance of being accepted, it was hoped that it might enable Britain to secure specific objectives in Stages Two and Three and there was evidence that the Spanish were interested in some aspects of the plan.[56]

Within weeks, however, the true weakness of the British position was apparent. France and Germany remained firmly united, and Britain's partners were evidently determined to forge ahead with the Treaty arrangements. Realization of this fact in February 1991 forced the British negotiating team to focus with increasing seriousness on the possibility of how Britain might stand aside from anything that might be agreed. At the official level and in the CCBG meetings, the team continued to make suggestions about Stages Two and Three in the hope of finding support on specific provisions, particularly on the role and functions of the EMI, and remained committed to the hard ECU policy. At the same time, however, British negotiators also began to promote the idea of a 'generalised option clause'. This was not an 'opt out' which implied a presumption that monetary union would take place, and Member States could only stand aside if they indicated a wish to do so. What the UK advocated was an 'opt in' clause which safeguarded Member States against any automatic commitment to join a single currency.

In April 1991, a finance ministers' meeting addressed the core issue of the transition from Stage Two to Stage Three. On this point,

Denmark, Germany and the Netherlands argued that convergence was necessary prior to any move to a single currency. A subsidiary question was whether a European Central Bank should be created at the start of Stage Two on 1 January 1994, as France and the Commission argued, or delayed further, as Germany and the Netherlands wished. It was finally agreed that a European Monetary Institute should be established at the beginning of 1994. This would act as the precursor of the ECB, thus satisfying the Rome Summit conclusions that institutional progress be made towards a single currency, but setting up neither a rival institution to the Bundesbank, nor eroding the independence of national banks during the second stage of monetary union – a position which was in line with British views on this issue.[57]

When the issue of who should participate in the single currency was discussed, British negotiators argued for a generalized option provision. Their position was weakened, however, by opposition from the Germans, who feared that a general provision would undermine the political commitment to achieve a single currency. It would also introduce the possibility of Germany standing aside from the creation of a single currency, something which other Member States were not willing to consider.[58]

At a meeting of Finance Ministers on 12 May, Jacques Delors proposed the idea of a unilateral opt out for Britain. This would allow Britain to sign the Treaty but permit a declaration stating that acceptance of Stage Three would require a positive vote at Westminster.[59] This was not an act of charity on the part of Delors, however, but rather aimed at defusing the 'British time-bomb'.[60] The informal proposal was primarily designed to neutralize the veto which John Major could wield if the outcome of the negotiations was unsatisfactory in terms of what the Conservative Party and Parliament could be persuaded to accept. A solution of the 'British problem' would also allow other Member States to concentrate without distractions on the key issue of how to manage the timing and transition from Stage Two to Three of EMU. It was thus a means to reconcile the British position with that of its partners. It would enable the UK to accept, as a last resort, a timetable leading to monetary union and in return the other governments would recognize that the British could not be forced to join a single currency.[61]

British reactions to the Delors proposal were mixed. The Chancellor, Norman Lamont, was considerably irritated by this very public and in his view premature attempt to further marginalize the

British in the negotiating process.[62] Concern was also expressed in parts of the Conservative Party, where the Bruges Group was deeply sceptical about allowing the others to move forward, fearing that pressure would mount for Britain to join a single currency. By contrast, the Cabinet was united in the view that the UK could in no way prevent two or more Member States from forming a monetary union, and that threatening to use the veto was an absurd over-estimation of the British government's negotiating strength.[63] By now it was clear that EMU was virtually unstoppable and at most, by refusing to sign a treaty, the British government would have forced EMU to be created by a separate agreement, but that would not have prevented a single currency being seen as an integral part of European integration by both the participants and outside onlookers. The leaking of a Bruges Group memo to the press showed the frustration of hard-line Eurosceptics with this position. This described John Major as 'a frightened compromiser' and threatened 'a serious split in the Tory party' if he continued on the path he had set out and refused to wield the British veto.[64]

In taking this line, the Group had an influential supporter in its President, Mrs Thatcher, who chose this moment to intervene publicly in the debate, first in speeches in the United States and then in Parliament. Speaking in the House of Commons for the first time following her resignation speech, she took issue with the idea of conceding the principle of EMU and a generalized option for those who did not wish to join a single currency. She argued that it was a mistake to think that exempting Britain from a single currency was the best deal to be struck, contending that the whole project should be vetoed.[65]

The European Reform Group, the largest Eurosceptic faction with 72 MPs, generally welcomed the Delors proposal. The Group saw in the proposal a means of realizing its long-cherished ambition of a two-speed Europe which would allow Britain 'to opt out of policies it did not like' such as the Common Agricultural Policy.[66]

It is true that the British negotiating team had up to now privately hoped for a generalized rather than a unilateral opt out. However, given its political isolation in the IGC-EMU negotiations, which had to some extent been hidden from the domestic audience, and some indication of Conservative Party support for a unilateral opt out, the government now recognized that a generalized option was not worth pursuing. Against this backdrop, the Chancellor's meeting with backbenchers provided the ideal means by which the government could bring its underlying position of conceding the principle of EMU, while securing an opt out of some kind, into the open. The meeting also had the merit of allowing the government to begin extricating itself from its official line of opposition to a two-speed Europe.

Notwithstanding the anxieties of the Bruges Group and Mrs Thatcher, the appeal of the new position so far as the government was concerned was the way in which it assuaged concerns on both wings of the Conservative Party. On the one hand, the government could argue to Eurosceptics that a Conservative government would not in practice want to participate in a single currency.[67] On the other hand, the government could argue to Europhiles that Britain could not be excluded from joining a single currency if the circumstances were right.[68] In this respect it is interesting if somewhat ironic to note that the opt out policy served many of the same domestic functions as the hard ECU policy had done.

Nevertheless, Major remained sensitive about his domestic position and, with German support, arranged that the Luxembourg European Council of 28–9 June should act as a stock-taking meeting only.[69] A great deal of diplomatic effort was also invested in clearing the hitherto informal Delors compromise with Kohl and Mitterrand, but especially with Lubbers who would chair the Maastricht summit. Although there was some discussion of convergence criteria, the European Council generally transferred the really difficult issues back down to the IGC-EMU and Finance Ministers.[70]

After a long summer break dominated by the crisis in Yugoslavia and a certain amount of delay on the part of the Netherlands Presidency, attention turned in earnest to the task of deciding the nature of the transition from Stage Two to Stage Three of EMU. In a series of meetings held in early September,[71] the proposals made in April for the creation of a European Monetary Institute in Stage Two were confirmed. It was further confirmed that a European Central Bank would be created in Stage Three when a single currency came into effect.

Regarding the mechanisms of transition from Stage Two to Stage Three, it was agreed that if a Member State made a commitment to Stage Three and met the convergence criteria it would automatically join a single currency. However, no single Member State would be able to exercise a veto over the process and no state would be forced to join a single currency. Thus if a Member State did not join in the first instance it could do so later if it met the convergence criteria. This compromise was clearly aimed at the British, but not exclusively so, since a number of other countries might not immediately meet the conditions for membership of a single currency.

The most important decisions, however, were those reached at the Apeldoorn ECOFIN meeting at the end of the month.[72] This meeting confirmed that 1 January 1994 should be the start date of the second stage, and decided that the Council of Finance Ministers would report within three years as to how many Member States had met the convergence criteria. It was further agreed that a minimum of six countries would be necessary for a single currency to go ahead. The decisions reached at Apeldoorn therefore signalled that EMU was on track to becoming a reality at Maastricht, and, stirred up by press reports, this realization caused an outcry from those on the Conservative backbenches still unreconciled to a British opt out.[73]

In reality, however, the British negotiating team was happy enough with the direction which the decisions were taking. The EMI which was proposed resembled the European Monetary Fund which Britain had envisaged, and the autonomy given to national banks throughout Stage Two would at least postpone the impact of the ECB and leave monetary policy as a national central bank responsibility until the introduction of a single currency. Indeed, the government sought to use these very facts to assuage backbench concerns by claiming that British ideas were winning support, and that the policy of engagement was producing dividends.[74]

But these claims were disingenuous, for the British were in fact becoming increasingly marginalized in the detailed negotiations. No effort, even of a token nature, was made to reconcile the substance of the hard ECU plan – which the British had still not officially abandoned – with the draft EMU clauses. Similarly, it was indicative that the Apeldoorn ECOFIN meeting should ignore Chancellor Lamont's demand that a minimum of eight countries must be ready to move to a single currency, deciding instead that only six would be necessary.[75] Likewise, some Bank officials had misgivings to the effect that even in their discussions in the CCBG and Committee of Alternates, the hard ECU plan had 'put too many eggs in one basket'.[76] Other officials were a little more sanguine, suggesting that there was by now little to lose and that from a technical perspective it provided intellectual coherence for British demands to have tough convergence criteria and a substantial Stage Two which became the British fall-back position.[77]

Most telling of all, however, was the fate of British efforts to secure a general opt out rather than the unilateral arrangement envisaged by the Delors compromise. Although the Dutch sought to make their October draft acceptable to the British by including a provision for a general opt out,[78] this was predictably enough rejected by the Germans and French. However, as a tactical device the negotiating team continued to argue for such a clause. In part this might allow the government to trade a general for a specific opt out, in the hope of securing other British objectives in return.[79] But it was also a position shaped by pressure from the government's domestic audience. Right-wing opinion was still a constraint, as the reaction to Apeldoorn and press delight at the inclusion of the general opt out in the Dutch draft underlined.[80] Negotiators therefore felt obliged to take a tough stance. Again, however, their efforts met with failure, with the formal rejection of the general opt out advocated by the British at both the ECOFIN meeting on the weekend of 30 November and a follow-up conclave meeting in Brussels the next day.[81]

That the British had, however, been working over the summer on the protocol for a unilateral opt out was a measure of their recognition of the true weakness of their position. This specific opt out, featuring an exemption for Britain from Stage Three of EMU if Westminster did not approve such a move and the right to join later if Westminster endorsed this, was now approved in principle by Finance Ministers, although the detail was left to be decided at the Maastricht European Council in December.[82] Even then it was emphasized by other negotiators that, despite abandoning its demand for a general opt out, Britain could not expect to gain concessions in other dossiers.[83]

The focus of attention now switched to the key issue of whether the convergence criteria were indicative or absolute. The chief protagonists were Germany, which favoured making the criteria inviolate,[84] and France and the Commission, which favoured a looser interpretation. The Dutch Presidency draft of 28 October 1991 had fudged the issue by suggesting tough convergence criteria, and specifying that a minimum of six countries should meet them before a single currency could come into effect – as agreed at Apeldoorn.[85]

The Dutch draft also left unresolved the problem of whether the EMI was simply to be a new guise for the Committee of Central Bank Governors, or whether it was an embryonic European Central Bank.[86] As in April, the major protagonists were again France and Germany, and the debate centred around three questions: the identity of the president of the EMI; what resources the institution should have; and what its powers would be, in particular whether it would have control over monetary policy.[87] The issue was eventually resolved with a Spanish/Danish compromise proposal that the president and vice president be appointed from the national central bank governors (as the Germans wished) and the managing director from outside (as the French wished).[88] In terms of the resources for the EMI, it was agreed that it would not have its own capital. Moreover, it would be left to governments to decide whether they wanted the EMI to manage their foreign currency reserves – a position strongly advocated by Germany – and the EMI was not given power over monetary policy.

Thus, by the time of the November parliamentary debate the British position in the negotiations was far more tightly constrained than 11 months earlier. Now the British were reduced to hoping that monetary responsibility remained a national responsibility during Stage Two, that economic policy remained as untouched as possible by a single currency, that clear and quantifiable convergence conditions were agreed, and that these criteria were met before a single currency emerged. As before, however, the bottom line remained that Parliament should decide whether Britain should at a later date join a single currency.

The government nevertheless had a fine line to tread. As early as the end of September one Eurosceptic MP, Tony Favell, had challenged the value of any British opt out and demanded a referendum on EMU. The government was sensitive to criticism from its own right wing that its position had shifted, from negotiating on the substance of the treaty to securing a suitable opt out, and was keen to build backbench support.[89] Even though they were not taken seriously in other national capitals, the government thus felt obliged to strike poses such as rejecting a declaration tabled by the Dutch in November concerning accelerated transition to Stage Three,[90] and Lamont's half-hearted attempt to resurrect the hard ECU in November 1991.[91] At the same time, however, the government was concerned to emphasize the dangers of staying aloof from EMU, and so court the pro-Europeans in its party and the City audience.[92]

Meanwhile, the government used its control of the parliamentary agenda to hold a set-piece debate on the British negotiating position. Ostensibly, the objective behind this was to secure parliamentary approval for a negotiating mandate. More importantly, the imposition of a three-line whip would silence backbench dissent and make it difficult for potential rebels to remove their support from any subsequent agreement.[93] It would also force the opposition parties to table substantive amendments that would show the Conservative Party as the most sceptical party on Europe. That said, it was also something of a high-risk strategy because the Prime Minister might find himself leaving hostages to fortune in the form of commitments which he could not subsequently deliver.[94]

The motion in the parliamentary debate held on the 20 November was thus carefully crafted to minimize divisions and maximize the Prime Minister's negotiating leverage. John Major's speech, moreover, argued that Britain might be interested in joining a single currency if convergence criteria were clear and quantifiable and a decision on who could join was based on genuine economic convergence.[95] And, though it was never a realistic prospect, he also restated the British position that a single currency could not be imposed on the UK by prior treaty commitment: a House of Commons decision would be essential, regardless of any European Council decision and whether the UK met the convergence criteria.[96] The outcome of the debate was a 101 majority in favour of the government's position, with only 6 rebels voting against the government and 9 abstaining. Dangerously, however, Mrs Thatcher now joined the small band of Eurosceptic MPs who doubted the value of a British opt out and used her House of Commons speech to call for a referendum.[97]

Domestically, this dual strategy appeared to be effective and, in the run up to Maastricht, Major secured widespread support both in the parliamentary party and in the press for the policy of preventing Britain from being frozen out of the negotiations, while keeping open the option of actually joining a single currency.[98] It should be noted that a key element of John Major's approach in selling the concession of the principle of EMU in conjunction with an opt out to his mixed audience of EMU enthusiasts and opponents was to argue that Britain was exercising real influence in the negotiations. He also treated the issue as an abstract exercise to try and construct EMU on an economic basis that would be as sound as possible, but without any commitment to participate. He thus sidestepped the thorny sovereignty issue completely.

This was in stark contrast to his predecessor, who viewed monetary union as fundamentally a political issue, dismissing the opt out as a 'trap', which would draw Britain into monetary union before long. Yet, so far as John Major was concerned, these continuing right-wing anxieties were not without their value as a negotiating weapon. Indeed, official reports and video of the Commons debate, including Mrs Thatcher's personal interventions, were sent to other

Heads of Government to remind them of the difficulties that EMU presented to London if a suitable British opt out were not forthcoming. This may also have been a misreading of other governments' likely reaction to evidence of a weak government failing to provide domestic leadership.[99]

In the last weeks before the European Council most of the remaining issues were clarified.[100] The unresolved issues were three-fold: the exact wording of the British opt out; the exact circumstances of the transition from Stage Two to Stage Three; and finally the location of the seat of the EMI/ECB.[101] Given the weakness of the British position during the pre-Maastricht phase of the IGC-EMU, the government had some grounds for satisfaction as the final stage of the IGC opened. Stage Two was less problematic than it had dared hope, with relatively little impact on national fiscal and monetary policies and genuine hurdles to be surmounted before countries could move to EMU. In this respect, the decision that governments did not have to make their central banks independent until the end of Stage Two rather than when it started in January 1994 was welcome as was the fact that countries were free to decide whether to give the EMI their foreign exchange reserves to manage. There was also relief that the creation of a Central Bank was deferred until Stage Three.[102] Finally, Britain had secured some symbolic victories, notably Norman Lamont's success in retaining the Queen's head on one side of the British ECU notes, with Scotland, and Northern Ireland able to keep their own designs too.[103]

Overall, however, these were decisions which owed little to British pressure. John Major and his negotiating team had played a difficult hand relatively well, but only in terms of managing the domestic audience. British negotiators were marginalized during the IGC-EMU negotiations in most issues that mattered, with the exception of securing the right to retain control of foreign reserves in Stage Two, which stood out as a British victory. Indeed, it was an irony of the British position that British participants, particularly Bank officials, only exercised influence if they put forward technical solutions to problems others had not thought of, thus speeding up the prospect of a single currency. Moreover, London had been unable to halt the tide of movement towards EMU and had even had to settle for a unilateral rather than a more general opt out clause. Ultimately, little effort was made to take British views into account 'when it was unwilling to buy a ticket for the ship', which reflected the underlying weakness of the British negotiating position.

THE MAASTRICHT EUROPEAN COUNCIL

Given the long months of detailed preparation and the inability of the British negotiating team to deflect its partners from their primary objective of EMU, the Maastricht European Council was in many key respects seen by the British negotiating team to be something of a rubber-stamping exercise, with one exception – the question of the timetable for starting EMU. The most significant debate in the European Council focussed on the transition from Stage Two to Stage Three and, in particular, whether the commitment to a single currency would be sufficient of itself to bring about EMU or whether a date should be specified for the guaranteed emergence of a single currency.

It was decided that if the European Council agreed by a qualified majority that a simple majority of willing Member States met the convergence criteria a single currency could come into effect in 1997. But at French insistence a treaty clause was also added specifying that a single currency would automatically be created in 1999 if a single currency was not created in 1997. Given German qualms about this clause, the arrangement has been attributed to a deal between President Mitterrand, Chancellor Kohl and Prime Minister Andreotti on the eve of the European Council.[104] One Bank official said that 'it was impossible to exaggerate the importance of a fall back deadline in giving impetus to the creation of a single currency' and another official 'that ultimately the weakness of the British position was that it was not consulted on this fundamental question'. The British, however, were in no position to become involved in discussions on the subject, having already made clear their intention to opt out of EMU.[105] In addition, the convergence criteria setting limits on budget deficits, public debt, long-term interest rates and requiring membership of the ERM were further diluted by the provision for their implementation to be interpreted flexibly. This was designed to reassure a number of Member States that feared exclusion through a strict interpretation of the criteria and was something which Britain had long opposed.

In the eyes of most governments, the detail of the British opt out was thus seen as something of a side issue. Indeed, the Chancellor, Norman Lamont, sought to present the opt out as a non-negotiable issue at the ECOFIN meeting of finance ministers on the second day of the European Council. His motives for so doing are unclear, given that the principle of an opt out had not only been accepted by all, but that the content of the protocol had been under discussion with the

Dutch Presidency since the autumn. Part of the answer might lie in reports that, as a tactical move, the Prime Minister had instructed that the IGC-EMU team should not disclose the details of the opt out until the last possible moment, to prevent other finance ministers from having time to 'pick holes in it'.[106] Hardly surprisingly, his fellow ministers were unsympathetic, and indeed insisted on discussing the draft opt out protocol on a line-by-line basis since it would form a formal part of the treaty.[107] Lamont's reaction was to withdraw the four members of the British delegation from the ECOFIN meeting, passing the issue to the Prime Minister for discussion by Heads of State and Government in the European Council.

It is possible that Lamont acted as he did because he wished to stake out his credentials as a tough negotiator in order to woo the Conservative right wing, and Lamont subsequently claimed the credit for negotiating the opt out and removal of a commitment to member-ship of the ERM contained in the main text.[108] But given his own lack of involvement in the day-to-day detail of the year-long negotiations, it is equally likely that Lamont either simply failed to appreciate the mood of the meeting and acted out of petulance or, as one official remarked, 'Lamont assumed absurdly that since it was Britain's opt out, the text could be of no concern to the others and had not both-ered to read his brief on the detail of the text and was simply unable to respond to the questions put to him.'[109] John Major was reportedly furious at Lamont's decision, and the issue was quickly resolved in a trilateral meeting between Major, Kohl and Lubbers, with the text of the protocol left just as the British had presented it.[110] But the point is that this could just as easily have been achieved by less confronta-tional means, since the eyes of all but the British and Danish who secured a similar opt out were focussed above all on the greater prize of Economic and Monetary Union.[111]

CONCLUSION

From the moment John Major became Prime Minister he had a diffi-cult hand to play on the question of EMU, though first as Chancellor and then as Foreign Secretary he had been involved directly in deci-sion-making. He inherited a situation in which Mrs Thatcher (though not Treasury and Bank officials) had failed to recognize the political momentum behind the EMU project. By November 1990, the key issue was how, rather than whether, a single currency might be created. British reluctance to embrace this goal and its attempts to muddy the waters with two schemes – the competing currencies and hard ECU plans – that were technically competent but politically naive had two consequences. First, refusal to commit to EMU inevitably marginalized the British in the negotiations and meant Britain was unable to influence the key issues in the debate. Second, persisting with the hard ECU plan, when others obviously were not going to agree, produced a certain amount of impatience from its partners. The IGC-EMU therefore began and ended with Britain on the defensive.

London's insistence on sticking to the hard ECU plan long after it served any useful purpose in the negotiations was not without rational foundation, however. The cloak of the hard ECU plan allowed Major to craft a strategy of constructive engagement that would, he hoped – somewhat forlornly, allow London to exercise influence in shaping a single currency, but would also allow a future government flexibility in deciding whether or when to join. Moreover, the hard ECU plan did give some important domestic dividends. It provided a screen which allowed a number of significant concessions to be disguised from right wingers. In particular, it obscured a departure from Mrs Thatcher's position of opposing any treaty amendment to include a commitment to EMU and the use of community institutions for the introduction of a single currency.

During the negotiations, the hard ECU plan thus held the Conservative Party together. Furthermore, the unilateral opt out protocol which ultimately superseded the hard ECU scheme served a similar purpose. Both the right and the left wing of the party could be persuaded that the opt out answered their concerns. The real problem was that the chosen means of holding the Conservative Party together came at the cost of reducing British influence in the negotiations.

British reluctance to participate in EMU, but grudging acceptance of it as a scheme for the EC, had by May 1991 prompted its partners to identify how to allow London to stand aside from a single currency without damaging the overall project. It is worth noting that there is little here to support the argument made in some quarters that the British extracted their opt out by dint of conceding recognition of the Croatian and Slovene Republics, a goal close to Chancellor Kohl's heart.[112] The point is that Britain was simply not in a position to bargain like this. Circumstances in 1991 meant the British Prime Minister could not come back with a treaty that committed the UK to a single currency in advance, since such a treaty had almost no chance of being ratified. Likewise, a British opt out appealed to its partners in its own right as a means of allowing them to concentrate on the detail of progression towards EMU without provoking a British veto, a point recognized as early as May 1991.

After this, London's remaining influence quickly deteriorated. Although certain of its objectives, such as the postponement of the creation of a European Central Bank, were achieved, the core issues were resolved between France and Germany, either bilaterally or through the assembly of coalitions on specific points. In all of this London played a role, but not the sort of role one might have expected from a large EC country with a major European currency. Ultimately, London was left to determine the terms and conditions of its own self-exclusion and negotiators concentrated on securing a UK opt out and the important right to reverse the initial position on it at a later date. This was an achievement of sorts, since it was by no means a foregone conclusion that the government would get an opt out which might allow Britain to join a single currency at a later date – though Denmark achieved a similar Treaty provision. The British Prime Minister also avoided a fundamental break between Britain and the EC and the emergence of a separate treaty to create a single currency.

However, while Major's handling of the EMU dossier was effective in terms of unifying the Conservative Party, even at the domestic level the policy was fraught with problems for the future. The outcome of the year-long negotiations was more like a stay of execution than a permanent reprieve from confronting the issues involved in EMU. It is true that Lamont's well-publicized Euroscepticism helped Major convince some backbenchers that 'nothing of substance had been conceded' and the Chancellor let it be known that as soon as the treaty was ratified Britain would exercise its opt out from a single currency.[113] However, the EMU negotiations contributed significantly to the growing ill feeling between John Major and his Chancellor, Norman Lamont, for whom the negotiations were something of a personal disaster.[114] But as hindsight reveals, Major also sowed the seeds of future discord by failing to engage the public or even his own party in a comprehensive debate about the costs and benefits of a single currency. The issues were instead reduced to theoretical arguments, and the government shied away from discussing the practical economic consequences of EMU. Just as importantly, it shied away from discussion of the practical political consequences of EMU, when opinion about these issues might still have been open to influence.

NOTES

1. There is an important distinction to be made between the key role Jacques Delors personally played in the negotiations and the limited role of the College of Commissioners. For Delors' personal involvement see Ross, *Jacques Delors*, op. cit., p. 80; Grant, *Delors: Inside the House that Jacques Built*, op. cit., p. 105.
2. Report to the Council and the Commission on the realization by Stages of Economic and Monetary Union in the Community, *EC Bulletin*, Supplement II–1970.
3. For the best account of this see Peter Ludlow, *The Making of the European Monetary System: a Case Study in the Politics of the European Community*, London, Butterworths Scientific, 1982.
4. Lawson, *The View from No. 11*, op. cit., p. 893.
5. Thatcher, *The Downing Street Years*, op. cit., p. 741.
6. Tommaso Padoa-Schioppa, et al., *Efficiency, Stability and Equity: a Strategy for the Evolution of the Economic System of the European Community*, Oxford, Oxford University Press, 1987.
7. Bernard Connolly, *The Rotten Heart of Europe*, London, Faber and Faber, 1995, p. 58.
8. Ross, *Jacques Delors*, op. cit., p. 80. See also Grant, *Delors*, op. cit., p. 117.
9. Thatcher, *The Downing Street Years*, op. cit., p. 741.
10. Ibid., p. 742.
11. Grant, *Delors: Inside the House that Jacques Built*, op. cit., p. 120.
12. Lawson, *The View from No. 11*, op. cit., p. 902.
13. Thatcher, *The Downing Street Years*, op. cit., pp. 740–1; Grant, *Delors: Inside the House that Jacques Built*, op. cit., p. 120.
14. Thatcher, *The Downing Street Years*, op. cit., p. 708. Dyson and Featherstone note that Mrs Thatcher had invited Pöhl to be a guest whilst she was on holiday in Switzerland and considered him 'one of us'. Kenneth Dyson and Kevin Featherstone, 'Britain and the Relaunch of EMU: Just Say No', paper presented to the panel Britain and Europe: Contemporary Aspects, Political Studies Association Conference, 10–12 April 1996, University of Glasgow, p. 8. In the event, Pöhl proved unhelpful, reportedly because he did not share Mrs Thatcher's 'nationalism and believed that sovereignty was limited in a modern economy'. Grant, *Delors: Inside the House that Jacques Built*, op. cit., p. 121.
15. The phrase is Lawson's, *The View from No. 11*, op. cit., p. 908.
16. There were others in the Bank of England from another school of thought who were more sceptical and considered the idea of a single currency as ill conceived and wished it would go away. Author's interview with Christopher Taylor.
17. Author's interview.
18. Committee for the Study of Economic and Monetary Union, *Report on Economic and Monetary Union in the European Community*, Luxembourg, 1989. For a discussion of the implications see Treasury and Civil Service Committee Fourth Report, 'The Delors Report', HC. 341, 1989.

19. Indeed the Delors Report (para. 43) warned against the adoption of deadlines – a pitfall into which the Werner Report had fallen. For a discussion of the Delors Report and its relationship to the final treaty articles see Alexander Italianer, *Mastering Maastricht: EMU Issues and How They Were Solved*, European Institute of Public Administration, Maastricht, 1993, pp. 51–113.
20. See the comments of Charles Powell quoted in Grant, *Delors: Inside the House that Jacques Built*, op. cit., p. 120.
21. Lawson, *The View from No. 11*, op. cit., p. 903.
22. Grant, *Delors: Inside the House that Jacques Built*, op. cit., p. 121.
23. For Alan Walters' view on the issue see *Sterling in Danger*, London, Fontana, 1990, p. 101.
24. For a discussion of this see Lawson, *The View from No. 11*, op. cit., pp. 419–20.
25. See, for example, the comments by Sir Terence Burns who blamed not joining the ERM on the increase in inflation bouncing back to double figures. *Economist*, 27 April 1991, p. 28.
26. Lawson argues it was FCO advice that British refusal to cooperate in Stage One of monetary union 'would be met with a decision to steam ahead with a two-speed Europe'. Connolly, *Rotten Heart of Europe*, op. cit., p. 68.
27. Helen Thompson, 'The UK and the Exchange Rate Mechanism, 1978–90', in Brian Brivati and Harriet Jones (eds), *From Reconstruction to Integration: Britain and Europe since 1945*, Leicester, Leicester University Press, 1993, pp. 227–40. For a discussion of Howe and Lawson's manoeuvring prior to the Madrid European Council see Howe, *Conflict of Loyalty*, op. cit., p. 580; Lawson, *The View from No. 11*, op. cit., p. 932.
28. Ibid., p. 939.
29. This position was set out by Lawson in a speech 'What sort of Financial Area?' at the RIIA, 25 January 1989. See Lawson, *The View from No. 11*, op. cit., p. 940.
30. Ibid., p. 942.
31. Ibid., p. 943.
32. Private information. For the plan see *An Evolutionary Approach to Economic and Monetary Union*, HM Treasury, November 1989.
33. See Paul Richardson, *The Next Stage in an Evolutionary Approach to Monetary Union*, London, British Invisibles Export Council, March 1990.
34. For an excellent discussion of the role of this Committee see Alasdair Blair, 'The UK and the Negotiation of the Maastricht Treaty 1990–1991', op. cit., pp. 225–7.
35. There was some feeling that the hard ECU was the lineal descendant of the competing currencies idea set out in *An Evolutionary Approach to EMU* (paras 22–4) and at least gave the impression of offering some consistency on this issue. Author's interview with Christopher Taylor.
36. For an excellent presentation of the merits of the hard ECU plan see Christopher Taylor, 'A Common Currency Route to EMU: the Hard ECU Revisited', National Institute of Economic and Social Science

Research, Discussion Paper no. 119, 1997.

37. Paul Richards was reportedly a little more cautious than Sir Michael Butler. Author's interview. See Butler's evidence to the House of Lords Select Committee on the European Communities, *Economic and Monetary Union and Political Union*, op. cit., pp. 26–37.

38. Thatcher, *The Downing Street Years*, op. cit., p. 725.

39. Ralph Atkins, 'Thatcher Balks at Prospect of Single Currency in Europe', *Financial Times*, 19 June 1990; John Major, *Beyond Stage One*, speech by the Chancellor, John Major, to the German Industry Forum, HM Treasury, 20 June 1990. For press coverage see Peter Norman, 'Major Presents Alternative Route to EMU', *Financial Times*, 21 June 1990. 'Economic and Monetary Union', *Economist*, June 1990, p. 64. See also House of Lords Select Committee on the European Communities, *Economic and Monetary Union and Political Union*, HL. 88 I (1989–90).

40. Margaret Thatcher, 'Dublin European Council', *Parl. Deb. HC*, 28 June 1990, cols 489–93.

41. Thatcher, *The Downing Street Years*, op. cit., p. 720.

42. Author's interviews with Bank of England and Treasury officials.

43. For an alternative view that the technical merits were more important than the tactical benefits see Taylor, 'A Common Currency Route to EMU', op. cit., p. 4. From the vantage point of 1997 this paper argues that, suitably modified, the hard ECU plan would have offered a better way to EMU.

44. Not least because the hard ECU by definition would be stronger than the Deutschmark. One Bank official suggests it was not self-evident when launched that the Germans would oppose the scheme, though this quickly became clear. Author's interview with Christopher Taylor. See also Peter Norman, 'Plan for Hard ECU Attacked by Pöhl', *Financial Times*, 3 July 1990.

45. Connolly, *Rotten Heart of Europe*, op. cit., p. 68.

46. Author's interviews with Bank of England and Treasury officials.

47. Philip Stephens, *Politics and the Pound*, London, Macmillan, 1996, p. 177. For Mrs Thatcher's insistence that the interest rate announcement take precedence over ERM entry in the press notice see ibid., p. 168.

48. Geoffrey Howe, *Parl. Deb. HC*, 13 November 1990, cols 461–5.

49. Thatcher, *The Downing Street Years*, op. cit., p. 725.

50. 'Economic and Monetary Union: Report by Mr Carli to the European Council', *Europe Documents*, 1657, 25 October 1990.

51. It was Nigel Lawson's view that this was exactly what Mrs Thatcher wanted, with diplomatic isolation in Europe the context for an election based on who should govern Britain – Brussels or Westminster.

52. 'Draft Statute of the European System of Central Banks and of the European Central Bank', *Europe Documents*, 1669/1676, 8 December 1990; 'Draft Treaty Amending the Treaty Establishing the European Economic Community with a View to Achieving Economic and Monetary Union', *Europe Documents*, 1675/1676, 20 December 1990.

53. One Bank official said that there was some reluctance on behalf of offi-

cials, who went to foreign capitals to sell the hard ECU, to report the extent of antagonism to the plan for fear of being seen as 'going native'. Author's interview.

54. 'The Spoilers', *Economist*, 9 March 1991, p. 48.
55. See Butler's evidence to the House of Commons Select Committee, November 1990, para. 139, p. 41.
56. Author's interviews with Treasury and FCO officials. The hard ECU plan was tabled immediately after the opening of the IGC-EMU in December 1990. 'Economic and Monetary Union – Beyond Stage 1: Possible Treaty Provisions and Statute for a European Monetary Fund', *Europe Documents*, 1683, 10 January 1991. For the objections raised to the hard ECU plan at the first personal representatives meeting, see *Agence Europe*, 10 January 1991.
57. *Agence Europe*, 12 June 1991.
58. David Buchan, 'Ministers Unworried by Idea of Two-Speed EMU', *Financial Times*, 13 May 1991.
59. Julie Wolf, 'Britain Offered Way Out of EC Currency', *Guardian*, 13 May 1991, p. 3. For a further discussion of this see *Agence Europe*, 13–14 May 1991.
60. Ross, *Jacques Delors*, op. cit., p. 154.
61. Author's interviews.
62. Author's interviews. See also Michael White, 'Tories Alarmed at Delors Deal', *Guardian*, 13 May 1991.
63. Author's interview with a Cabinet minister.
64. 'Mad, Mad Quite Mad', *Economist*, 15 June 1991, p. 38.
65. Margaret Thatcher, *Parl. Deb. HC*, vol. 139, 26 June 1991, col. 1011. For press coverage see 'She Makes Her Stand', *Economist*, 29 June 1991, p. 27.
66. 'But Can We Opt Out of the EC', *Economist*, 25 May 1991, p. 34. The ERG were very active with an organized campaign to harry the government in late night debates. For example Bill Cash's Early Day Motion gained 105 other MPs' signatures, congratulating the Prime Minster on resisting the latest IGC proposals.
67. For example the Foreign Secretary made clear in the House of Commons that the government would not be recommending acceptance of a single currency – at least not to the sitting Parliament. See Hurd, *Parl. Deb. HC*, 26 June 1991, col. 1012.
68. 'Major Lays Out Nation's Course in Europe', *The Times*, 15 June 1991; Robin Oakley, 'Major to Break with Thatcher Line Today', *The Times*, 14 June 1991.
69. John Major met Chancellor Kohl at Chequers on Sunday, 9 June. Nicholas Wood, 'Major Seeks to Avert Monetary Union Ambush', *The Times*, 6 June 1991; Ralph Atkins and David Marsh, 'Pact to Slow Down European Union', *Financial Times*, 10 June 1991.
70. *Bull. EC*, vol. 24, issue 6, 1991, p. 9.
71. The meetings took place on 3 and 11 September. See *Agence Europe*, 4 September 1991, and *Agence Europe*, 11 September 1991.
72. The Apeldoorn meeting took place on 20–2 September 1991. See *Agence Europe*, 4 and 25 September 1991.

73. Julie Wolf, Will Hutton and Michael White, 'EMU Moves Spark Fears of a Sell Out', *Guardian*, 23 September 1991; Colin Browne and David Usborne, 'Tories Warned Against Europe Split', *Independent*, 23 September 1991; Colin Browne, 'Tory MP Seeks Referendum on Monetary Union', *Independent*, 25 September 1991.

74. For example see John Major's Guildhall Speech, 11 November 1991, London, FCO Verbatim Service, VS031/91.

75. David Buchan, Rachel Johnson and Ivo Dawnay, 'UK Still Opposed to Imposition of a Single Currency', *Financial Times*, 23 September 1991; Peter Norman and David Buchan, 'Difficult Hand for Lamont to Play', *Financial Times*, 24 September 1991.

76. Author's interviews with Bank of England officials.

77. Author's interview with Christopher Taylor. One issue on which most officials agree the British 'won the argument' was preventing a super-visory role for the ECB.

78. 'Draft Treaty on Economic and Monetary Union', *Europe Documents*, 1740/1, 1 November 1991, art. 109G2.

79. Blair, 'The UK and the Negotiation of the Maastricht Treaty', op. cit., p. 254.

80. For press reports of the general opt out provision, see Boris Johnson and Barbara Smit, 'Britain Wins Right to Keep the Pound', *Daily Telegraph*, 29 October 1991; David Usborne, 'Delay on in Currency Fight', *Independent*, 29 October 1991; Christopher White and Larry Elliot, 'Compromise Allows Britain to Opt Out', *Guardian*, 29 October 1991.

81. *Agence Europe*, 2–3 December 1991.

82. 'Draft Treaty on Economic and Monetary Union', *Europe Documents*, 1740/41, 1 November 1991, art. 109F. The first draft produced by the Treasury omitted the UK's right to join later if it so decides and was corrected in later versions. Author's interview.

83. *Agence Europe*, 2–3 December 1991.

84. Quentin Peel, 'Bundesbank Deputy Calls for Tough Line on EMU', *Financial Times*, 19 September 1991.

85. *Agence Europe*, 28–9 October 1991.

86. 'EMU Knotty', *Economist*, 16 November 1991, pp. 146–51.

87. *Agence Europe*, 6 November 1991.

88. *Agence Europe*, 7 November 1991. 'Slow Man Out', *Economist*, 7 December 1991, p. 112.

89. Charles Goldsmith, 'Britain's Stance Won't Block Money Union, EC Maintains', *International Herald Tribune*, 30 October 1991.

90. *Europe Documents*, 1740/41, 1 November 1991; see also Colin Brown and David Usborne, 'Major Rebuffs EMU Declaration but Leaves the Door Open', *Independent*, 30 October 1991; Michael White and John Palmer, 'Cabinet Sop to EC-Sceptics', *Guardian*, 30 October 1991.

91. Kenneth Dyson, *Elusive Union: the Process of Economic and Monetary Union in Europe*, London, Longman, 1994, op. cit., p. 156.

92. See for instance John Major's statement to the House of Commons, *Parl. Deb. HC*, 20 November 1991, cols 269–81.

93. Author's interviews.

94. Hugo Young, 'Keeping Mum over Maastricht', *Guardian*, 29 October 1991.
95. John Major, *Parl. Deb. HC*, 20 November 1991, col. 274. See for example Geoffrey Howe's resignation speech in November 1990, which refuted the claim that a single currency might be imposed on the UK. Howe, *Parl. Deb. HC*, 13 November 1990, op. cit. Philip Stephens claims this was a deliberate attempt to change the terms of the debate within the Conservative Party. See Stephens, *Politics and the Pound*, op. cit., p. 200.
96. John Major, *Parl. Deb. HC*, 20 November 1991, col. 272.
97. *Parl. Deb. HC*, 20 November 1991, cols 293–8. Interestingly, Seldon claims that Major was sympathetic to the idea of a referendum, but did not want to be seen to be pushed around by Thatcher. Seldon, *Major*, op. cit., p. 244.
98. Editorial, 'A Sombre Prelude', *Daily Telegraph*, 3 December 1991.
99. 'Pre-Maastricht Tension', *Economist*, 7 December 1991, p. 38.
100. See for instance *Agence Europe*, 4 December 1991; *Agence Europe*, 6 December 1991.
101. 'Slow Man Out', *Economist*, 7 December 1991, p. 112.
102. Ibid.
103. The Governor of the Bank of England had remarked that he was surprised this was seen as so important since it was only in the 1960s that the monarch's image had been put on currency. 'Slow Man Out', *Economist*, 7 December 1991, p. 112.
104. Connolly, *Rotten Heart of Europe*, op. cit., p. 119.
105. On this see Hogg and Hill, *Too Close to Call*, op. cit., p. 149.
106. Ibid., p. 153; Seldon, *Major*, op. cit., p. 247.
107. Hogg and Hill, *Too Close to Call*, op. cit., p. 153.
108. Author's interview. For Lamont's claim see Stephens, *Politics and the Pound*, op. cit., p. 200.
109. Author's interview.
110. See *Treaty on European Union, Protocol on Certain Provisions Relating to the United Kingdom of Great Britain and Northern Ireland*, Luxembourg, Commission of the European Communities.
111. The British government offered to include the Danish in the British opt out text, but the Danish government preferred not to be associated with a country so unpopular at that moment – even though the Danish opt out text was perceived by the British negotiating team as being 'less meticulous'. Author's interview.
112. For the argument that an implicit deal was struck see David Buchan, *The Strange Superpower*, Aldershot, Dartmouth, 1993, p. 77. For the argument that it was an explicit deal see Seldon, *Major*, op. cit., p. 249.
113. Author's interview. See also Stephens, *Politics and the Pound*, op. cit., p. 200.
114. Seldon, *Major*, op. cit., p. 103.

3 Social Policy

The social policy negotiations were always going to be a tough part of the IGC-PU since there was a history of British opposition to further co-operation in this area. However, it was not clear at the outset that the whole IGC negotiations would, in fact, stand or fall because of it. For a start, even prior to British accession Community action in this area was slow and largely symbolic, while, following further enlargement of the EC, a number of poorer Member States were worried about a significant strengthening of employment legislation.[1]

The reason why social policy did in fact emerge as a key problem of the IGC negotiations was because of British domestic politics. John Major's refusal to make any concessions on this dossier stemmed from the evolving disagreements of his own party and government on the subject, and it was this refusal which was to bring the negotiations to the brink of collapse. Above all, the empirical evidence reveals that social policy developed in the course of 1991 into the symbolic issue on which the right of his own party were determined to make a stand. This was because of what they perceived as the corporatist overtones of social policy legislation, their deep suspicion of centrists and Christian Democrats in Westminster and abroad, and because a senior Cabinet minister was prepared to resist making concessions on this issue.

THE BACKGROUND

As with the idea of a single currency, the pre-Maastricht history of the social policy question was characterized by the increasing marginalization of Britain in the face of the growing enthusiasm of its partners to incorporate the issue into the integration project. Initially, it was the French who had led the way, with the Treaty of Rome containing concessions by others to French insistence on protecting its system of high social benefits. It was, however, underpinned by a consensus between the six founding Member States that social harmonization was essential to preventing unfair competition arising from some states having less generous employment legislation than others.

Tensions between those governments that wanted more social activism and those that did not, and between Member States with lower costs and less regulated employment systems and those with expensive continental systems, were reflected in the first package of formal treaty revisions effected through the SEA. The principal aim of the SEA was the construction of a Single European Market with particular emphasis on deregulation. It also made a commitment to build a social dimension as a pre-condition for labour mobility, in order to redress the unequal economic costs and benefits of the Single Market.[2]

With the progressive removal of barriers to a Single Market in the later 1980s, many governments with high national standards of social protection (in particular the Belgian, French and German governments) began to fear that low social costs and deregulated employment practices might act as a disincentive to inward investment.[3] The maximalist Member States, with Commission support, therefore sought to exploit the SEA's limited provisions for qualified majority voting (QMV) to overcome British opposition to the Community's social dimension.[4] These moves towards a more active social policy were vigorously resisted by the British government, principally because London feared that EC employment legislation would impose German wage costs and overheads on British industry, undermining British competitiveness and reducing levels of employment.[5] London took the view, therefore, that, rather than increase employment legislation, Community action should encourage Member States to compete in social as well as economic terms.[6] This ideological opposition, reflected in British approaches to national employment legislation, was inseparable from a 'hostility to any further weakening of national sovereignty' and a reluctance to transfer powers to the Commission.[7]

Finally, the Commission launched a declaratory 'Social Charter on the Fundamental Rights of Workers' in an attempt to break the deadlock – at best to get Mrs Thatcher to sign up to a social programme or, as a second best, demonstrate that the UK was in a minority of one.[8] This was a deliberately symbolic attempt to develop a social policy dimension to supplement the economic focus of the Treaty of Rome.[9] The Charter was followed by a Commission-drafted legislative programme outlining 47 proposals, 27 of which were binding directives to be implemented by January 1993.[10] Mrs Thatcher was again alone in rejecting the Charter at the Strasbourg European Council in December 1989, on two grounds, the absolute statement of rights which the government thought needed to be nuanced and qualified and opposition to the annexed legislative programme.

By 1990 there was, however, considerable external pressure from three sources on the British government to accept a more expansive social dimension to the Community. First, in December 1989, the 11 member governments agreed on a pro-active Social Action Programme.[11] Second, following the June 1989 European elections, the EP had a socialist majority and threatened to hold up agreement of Single Market directives if no action was taken by the Council of Ministers on a social dimension. Third, by the autumn of 1990, in preparation for the IGC-PU, a number of governments and the Commission had tabled a proposal that all social issues should be treated by majority voting and linked this proposal to further powers for the EP. The cumulative effect was that by the end of 1990 social policy was high on the EC's political agenda, with the British government both threatened and isolated in the debate.

THE DOMESTIC CONTEXT

The domestic British debate was primarily conducted within political circles, having a special relevance for the ruling Conservative Party and especially its right wing. Within this setting, responses to the mounting pressure for movement on the social issue were shaped by three factors. First, there was 'resentment' of the way in which the Commission used the provision for QMV on health and safety issues to secure its directives on working hours, maternity leave and protection of young children in the summer of 1990.[12] As one scholar has put it, 'nothing did more to turn Britain's Conservative Party against the Commission's plans for a social dimension than this cavalier approach to the legal base of its proposals'.[13] A major concern was if the Commission could go that far under Article 118A how much further might it go using majority voting.

A second concern was the perception that the Commission's proposals on social policy threatened the government's domestic agenda. Thatcherism was built on the premise that a decline in trade union power was the single and most important objective, and the undisputed success of 11 years of Conservative government. Any Commission proposals which were perceived as restoring the influence of trade unions, either in the work place or in the European policy-making process were accordingly considered unacceptable interference.[14]

A third concern was that proposed European legislation would undermine the government's attempts to generate employment through deregulation, greater flexibility in working time and limitation of the rights of part-time workers. However, there was also some concern that the government's industrial relations policy left Britain uniquely vulnerable to the partial imposition of any alternative method of industrial organization.[15] Given the ease with which workers could be dismissed, even modest changes imposed by the Community might actually result in massive restructuring.[16] Britain was also highly dependent on foreign direct investment (FDI), and this emerged as the centrepiece (arguably the only element) of the Conservative's industrial strategy in the 1990s.[17] This further heightened the government's fears that EC legislation would be damaging to the British economy and reduce the UK's attractiveness to multinational enterprises.[18]

At the same time, however, there is some truth in the argument that the social policy question meant different things to different wings of the Conservative Party.[19] To the political right and especially the Bruges Group, it was an issue that played up to all their own anxieties.[20] Not only did it confirm their perceptions of continental Europe as corporatist with a centralized political system, but it also fuelled their concern that the EC was dominated by Germany and its desire to impose *modell Deutschland* on the whole of Europe with French collusion.[21] Above all else, social policy was to them incontrovertible proof that the EC was bureaucratic and socialistic.[22] It was no surprise then that Mrs Thatcher's endorsement of John Major encouraged an expectation among the right wing that the new Prime Minister would be as resolute as his predecessor in opposing the Social Charter.[23] Indeed, it is fair to say that social policy became a 'litmus-test' issue that took on an almost mystical significance for Mrs Thatcher's personal supporters.[24]

To the left of the Conservative Party, the issue had a different resonance. The Heath/Patten view of Conservatism had much more in common with the Christian Democratic tradition of its continental conservative parties, and in particular the notion of social market and social partnership between industry and organized labour.[25] But although this tradition was advocated by an influential group of ministers associated with the Tory Reform Group,[26] back-bench support for this view of social policy was limited to a handful of MPs associated with the Catholic church, the European Movement and the old leadership of the Conservative Party.[27] There was thus a perceived distinction between a left-of-centre Cabinet and a right-of-centre parliamentary party.

As regards the position of the major domestic interest groups, this tended to reflect traditional cleavages.[28] The national employers' organization, the Confederation of British Industry (CBI), the influential Institute of Directors (IoD) and leading sectoral federations like the Engineering Employers Federation (EEF) held broadly the same views as government on the Community's social dimension and gave support to its position through publications, public statements and economic data.[29] However, behind a general preference for labour market deregulation, there were significant differences between these groups.[30] The CBI preferred to participate in European level dialogue and was explicitly closer to 'big business' than the IoD, which was composed of individual directors and chief executives and inclined to take a more neo-liberal line.[31]

The other key players in the domestic debate were of course the trade unions, and they shaped events in two ways. The unions' conversion to supporting European Community membership in 1988 had been a complex process which came about for a variety of reasons.[32] In the social policy issue, however, the Trades Union Congress (TUC) saw the means of reversing a decade of Conservative industrial relations legislation through Community level action. Accordingly, the more the trade unions championed the social dimension, the more the Conservative Party felt threatened by it.[33] The second way in which trade union involvement shaped the domestic debate was by the increase of TUC resources allocated to European lobbying. Particular attention was paid to developing a more active British role in the European Trades Union Congress (ETUC), and this culminated in the election of Norman Willis as the President of the ETUC in 1990.[34]

The views of the public on social policy issue were ambiguous. The issue of the Social Charter had been dramatically politicized by the Conservative Party with support from the right-wing press. This campaign was initially very effective, with Mrs Thatcher repeatedly linking opposition to it with general opposition to Brussels. But in the 1989 European elections, Labour was successful in turning the Social Charter against Mrs Thatcher by linking it to her unpopularity, while building support for the perceived benefits which specific measures would bring.[35]

In this way, the government's efforts to crystallize public opposition to the EC's social policy failed. Polling data indicated that while a majority of the public were against the Social Charter, the public was strongly supportive of the specific measures which the Charter contained, particularly a minimum wage and a maximum working week.[36] At the end of the day, however, the social policy issue was overshadowed, so far as the public were concerned, by 'domestic issues that appeared more directly relevant to daily life'.[37]

SOCIAL POLICY OBJECTIVES

Even before the negotiations opened the social policy issue was thus a highly political one for the British. Meeting to decide on desiderata for the talks, however, the view of the FCO was that social policy was not likely to prove the critical dossier on which the whole negotiations would hang.[38] Consulting closely with the Department of Employment, the negotiating team identified four objectives.[39] First, it wanted to ring fence existing Treaty commitments by detailing the specific competences to be handled at the EC level. Second, it wanted to strengthen the concept of subsidiarity to prevent 'unnecessary' EC-level legislation on the basis of the existing treaties. Closely linked with this was a desire to reform Article 118A to limit the use of QMV to genuine health and safety matters. Third, it opposed any extension of EC competence in the area of employee participation which might strengthen the position of the trade unions. Finally, it wanted to prevent any institutional changes concerning majority voting and any enhanced status for the European Social Partners in the policy-making process. It opposed the latter on the grounds of its corporatist overtones and in terms of its potential effect of enhancing the role of the trade unions in Britain.[40]

The achievement of these objectives was, however, complicated by the fact that the role of the Social Partners would in large measure be determined by a parallel set of negotiations being undertaken by the Social Partners themselves (comprised of the Union of Industrial and Employers Confederation of Europe [UNICE] and the European Trade Unions' Congress). If these negotiations were successful, the Luxembourg Presidency of the Council of Ministers, with support from the Christian Democrat and Socialist governments, had promised to incorporate the agreement into the final Treaty.[41] From the British side, only the CBI and the TUC were present in these negotiations with Norman Willis playing an important role as President of the ETUC. Unsurprisingly, the CBI negotiators came under considerable pressure from the Secretary of State for Employment to resist any agreement, thereby preventing any additional reference to the Social Partners in the final Treaty.[42]

THE TREATY NEGOTIATIONS

Although British objectives were thus essentially to stem the tide of encroachment of EC legislation into social policy questions, it was noticeable that a conscious effort was made, initially at least, to present a more conciliatory negotiating style. Hoping to break down assumptions built-up during Mrs Thatcher's period in office that the government was being unreasonable on this issue, the FCO encouraged Michael Howard to adopt a more positive tone in his dealings with the Commission during the first half of 1991.[43] This tone was in marked contrast to the accusations that the Employment Secretary had made only four months earlier that Commissioner Papandreou was bringing the EC into disrepute with proposals for directives on maximum working hours, employment rights for part-time workers and harmonized maternity benefits.[44] Above all, the FCO hoped that a change in style might lead to a scaling down of the more ambitious objectives among Britain's partners.

In substantive terms, however, the team made no proposals on social policy in the IGC-PU, waiting instead for its partners to take the initiative and then 'reserving' Britain's position.[45] At this stage, British tactics in so far as they existed were to encourage the so-called 'cohesion countries', particularly Portugal and Spain who might expect to suffer disproportionately from any strengthening of the Treaty's social provisions, to declare their own position rather than to 'free ride' on British opposition.[46]

Overall, in fact, little progress was made during the first three months of the negotiations, as international events preoccupied the negotiators, and, because the issue was difficult, the Presidency postponed addressing the issue. It was in the domestic debate that social policy increasingly adopted centre stage, emerging as a proxy issue in the struggle taking place over the direction of the Conservative Party.[47] The Party Chairman's endorsement of the social market economy in February 1991 was perceived by some on the right wing as the opening round of this struggle.[48] In the following month, Major made a speech in Bonn which set out an alternative vision to that of Mrs Thatcher's concerning Britain's role in Europe. Though never directly using the term social market, he strongly implied a commitment to social cohesion and partnership.[49] The experience of John Major's 'big idea', the Citizen's Charter, further undermined the Prime Minister's right-wing credentials with its emphasis on public service and standards, which carried with it the implied message that competition and privatization policies needed to be tempered by other considerations.

But it was the Bonn speech which caused consternation among the right wing of the party, not only because of its pro-German sentiments but also because they feared that the notion of the social market was an intellectual alternative to the neo-liberal ideas which had dominated the party in the 1980s. There was also considerable agitation on the backbenches,[50] although most activity came from the 'Friends of Bruges', which had run a slate in 1990 for all the posts on the Conservative Backbench European Affairs Committee. Bill Cash was particularly prominent on this platform, making repeated calls for the government to resist making any concessions, especially on social policy.[51] Nicholas Ridley too denounced voices in the Cabinet calling for a monolithic style of social market economy.

However, the influence of the Eurosceptics at this stage of the negotiations was diminished by the fact that there was no general merging of the various anti-Maastricht forces because of petty rivalries and deep-seated animosities between them.[52] Of particular importance was the schism between the European Reform Group and the smaller but more hard line 'Friends of Bruges' group.[53] Another problem for the Eurosceptic right was the lack of a significant leader around whom to group. Mrs Thatcher, for instance, preferred initially to keep her own counsel, at least in part because she felt under enormous constraint to ease her successor's job in winning the next election.[54] It was not until mid June that she broke her self-imposed silence, and even then focussed on EMU rather than social policy as the key issue.[55]

The development which finally made the Eurosceptic case on social policy impossible for the government to ignore was the spread of dissent among the ranks of the government itself. In September 1991, eight junior ministers and under-secretaries in the No Turning Back Group met the Chief Whip, Richard Ryder, and demanded a meeting with the Foreign Secretary in order to express their concerns about the conduct of the negotiations, though no concessions had been made or even hinted at by the negotiating team.[56] As dissent spread, Edward Leigh, a junior minister in the DTI, was eventually granted a private meeting with John Major.[57]

By the end of September, dissent had permeated to the highest level of government, with Michael Howard moving into open opposition. Howard had of course always been uneasy about the social policy question, refusing the Prime Minister's request earlier in the year to make a speech on the social market economy, on the grounds that this would undermine Thatcherite achievements and strengthen trade unions.[58] Now, in a private meeting with Major, Howard made it clear that, if any changes to the Treaty of Rome were accepted by the Cabinet, his own position in the Department of Employment would be 'untenable'.[59] Much to the annoyance of the FCO, Howard also directed his staff in the Department of Employment to make no effort to find compromises on the social policy dossier. The Secretary of State feared that the negotiating team's inclination would be to find a diplomatic solution and that it might ultimately press for a diplomatic surrender.[60] The result was that the FCO was left desperately trying to find solutions that might avoid a breakdown of the negotiations on social policy with little support from the minister or his department on the issue.[61]

The reasons behind Michael Howard's stance were various. He had been particularly concerned by the Presidency Conclusions attached to the Luxembourg summit where John Major had been 'bounced' into accepting 'renewed efforts to make progress on social policy'.[62] Above all, however, he was concerned that increased Community action in the social field would undermine his own legislative plans outlined in a Green Paper in June 1991. This Green Paper set out his plans for even greater labour market flexibility and trade union reform which had been stalled under his predecessors. It should be noted that Howard's personal ambitions were intimately linked to the success of these proposals. Specifically, they were seen by him and his supporters as a vehicle to promote his standing among the right wing of the party, and ultimately to become the undisputed champion of the right-wing faction in Cabinet.

Michael Howard's thinking may also have been shaped by the actions of Peter Lilley, his Thatcherite colleague in the DTI and rival for the right wing mantle. In taking a tough stance from his departmental bailiwick, Howard hoped to contrast his hard-line diplomacy inside the Cabinet with Lilley's semi-public anti-Maastricht rhetoric to Eurosceptic groups outside it.[63] This was a strategy which was to pay off, with the *Spectator* noting that Howard – and not, by implication, Lilley – had finally found a worthy agenda for the right wing of the party to rally around.[64] It should also be noted that Howard was further motivated by uncertainty concerning the Prime Minister's personal commitment to a Thatcherite agenda. In particular, he feared that the Prime Minister might buckle to pressure at Maastricht and sacrifice a firm line on social policy in the interests of an overall agreement.[65]

From September onwards the problem of Eurosceptic dissent was thus an increasing preoccupation for John Major. He was now forced to abandon his Party Chairman's attempt to chart a new intellectual path for the party, and to concentrate on the more immediate problem of holding the party together in the run up to the election.[66] Obviously this meant that his freedom to manoeuvre on the social policy dossier in the IGC-PU negotiations was more and more restricted. Exacerbating the problem, however, was the serious FCO miscalculation which now became apparent concerning the progress and the implications of an agreement by the Social Partners. Discussions between UNICE and ETUC unexpectedly reached agreement on 31 October 1991.[67] The FCO and Department of Employment were under the impression that the CBI would veto any potential agreement and was caught out unaware when it did not. Indeed the official response was that it was the result of a rogue CBI delegate who had simply made a rash agreement which was not significant.[68]

In reality of course it was neither rash nor insignificant. The CBI secretariat was unsure that John Major could or would hold out against his European partners in the face of their demands for extension of majority voting and addition of new competences.[69] The CBI negotiators therefore saw an agreement between UNICE and the ETUC as the least-worst available solution for British business; the Social Partners Agreement would almost certainly be inserted into the Treaty; and, at best, this might be acceptable to a number of maximalist countries as an alternative to changing the Treaty of Rome.[70] At worst, the business community would be able to influence EC legislation through a new role for the Social Partners in the legislative process. Either way, acceptance of the Agreement would allow large 'British' multinational companies to influence the agenda and shape any European-wide legislation.[71]

This decision was certainly contentious within the business community. In the CBI, the International Social Affairs Division (which negotiated the Social Partners Agreement) had always been more 'Europeanist' than the domestic branches.[72] Its analysis reflected the perspective of multinational companies and an instinct not to be marginalized in the formation of legislation. The Director General, Sir John Banham, on the other hand, represented the more nationally oriented companies, and opposed any agreement which would be perceived by smaller companies as a means by which multinationals could impose high European labour costs and employment practices on British companies.[73]

At the end of the day, however, it should be remembered that both the CBI and UNICE feared losing their privileged position in corporatist bargaining with the Commission. They were indeed under pressure from the Commission Social Affairs directorate either to reach agreement or face the prospect of the Commission opening up links with sectoral organizations who were pressing for more direct contact.[74] This provided an important incentive for UNICE (and the CBI as its most reluctant member) to come to some form of agreement.

The UNICE/ETUC agreement was immediately inserted into the second Dutch draft Treaty submitted on the 8 November 1991, radically decreasing the government's negotiating space.[75] On the domestic level, the credibility of a government committed to reducing the role of the trade unions could not but be damaged by press reports that British employers had broken ranks and agreed to the introduction of collective bargaining at the European level.[76]

Still more importantly, the Social Partners Agreement boxed the government into a corner in the negotiations themselves, since it now became a non-negotiable component of the social policy dossier. If the 11 governments endorsed the Agreement at Maastricht, it would allow the Social Partners to by-pass the Council of Ministers and the British veto by using an alternative legislative path to conclude EC-level collective agreements which could have the force of European law.[77] The effect of the Agreement was therefore to close down the scope for minor British compromises in trading an extension of competence for retention of unanimous voting procedures.[78] Increasingly, too, the Social Partners package became almost impossible to unpick, as the Socialist and Christian Democrat leaders came under domestic pressure from their own unions and industry to accept the Agreement.[79]

Against this backdrop of the increasing domestic volatility of the social policy issue and decreasing room to manoeuvre at the negotiating table, party managers swung into action in the immediate run up to the Maastricht European Council in an attempt to deliver backbench support for the government.[80] Party managers had in fact seen a successful negotiation as a means of boosting the image of the John Major,[81] and this motivation became stronger as the Conservative Party lagged further behind Labour in the opinion polls and all the economic indicators showed that there would be no significant upturn in the British economy before an election.[82]

Party managers particularly targeted the European Reform Group.[83] This grouping contained a high number of MPs in marginal

Conservative seats who thought they might lose their seats at the next election.[84] While members of the European Reform Group (ERG) were sceptical about greater ties with the EC, a large number had also been personal supporters of John Major in the leadership campaign. Indeed, a number of them, like Jonathan Aitken, hoped to be promoted into government posts if there was a fourth Conservative Party election victory.[85] These factors ensured that the majority were open to persuasion because their personal and political ambitions made them ultimately disposed to toe the government line.[86]

Where persuasion was used for the soft Eurosceptics, tougher tactics were employed against the irreconcilable.[87] The Whips orchestrated the ousting of the Bruges Group 'Friends' from the Conservative Backbench European Affairs Committee, replacing Bill Cash as the Committee Chairman by the loyalist candidate Sir Norman Fowler.[88] This was followed one week later by the replacement of the '92' group Eurosceptic Chairman of the Conservative Foreign Affairs Committee, Sir George Gardener, by Cyril Townsend.[89] Both Fowler and Townsend immediately used their access to the media to support the government's position in the run up to the negotiations at Maastricht.[90]

When the parliamentary debate finally took place on 20 November, Major presented a carefully worded motion intended to unite Tory dissidents behind him. Predictably, given the volatility of the issue, he was, however, equivocal as to what might actually activate a British veto. Although he did say that Britain would not sign a social chapter 'that undermined the ability of Britain to compete' he tempered this by pointing out that 'there would have to be give and take on all sides'.[91] The Opposition tried to highlight the difference between themselves and the government on social policy but this attack was blunted by sniping from Conservative backbenchers which led Neil Kinnock to lose his temper. The outcome of the debate on this issue was a 191 vote defeat for Labour's amendment to extend majority voting to social issues, suggesting that Major's strategy had paid off.[92] Perhaps just as importantly, though, the iron logic of the looming general election made all but the most irreconcilable anti-federalists vote with Mr Major.[93]

But while Major held the whip hand in managing the parliamentary party, he was still faced with the problem of holding his front bench together.[94] It was clear that Michael Howard was prepared to put the issue above his ministerial career and so provide the Eurosceptic backbenchers with the leadership of a Cabinet heavyweight to join the more junior No Turning Back ministers who numbered at least 14.[95] In other circumstances the resignation of a Cabinet minister and some junior members of the government might not have been critical. However, the situation was by no means normal. Major knew that back-bench support was extremely volatile since it was based on party discipline and the fear of an approaching election, rather than on a genuine debate about the issues, and his Chief Whip thought that 42 MPs might oppose any treaty agreed at the Maastricht European Council.[96] In these circumstances, the resignation of a senior minister who had assiduously cultivated the right wing of the party might provide the leadership for those disparate backbenchers who opposed the Prime Minister and his European policy, and might tear the party apart.[97]

Major therefore found himself on the horns of a dilemma. On the one hand, the majority in Cabinet approved a limited number of compromises on social policy and had granted him leeway to negotiate as he saw fit, mandating him to be tough on social policy but not to jeopardize the whole Treaty on this one issue. On the other hand, Major was sufficiently concerned about Michael Howard's position that he requested him to be ready during the summit for immediate consultation on the social policy dossier if this became necessary.[98]

On the eve of the Maastricht European Council, it was thus the domestic agenda which preoccupied John Major.[99] Failure at the Maastricht European Council was not considered by the leadership to be in the Conservative Party's electoral interest.[100] At the same time, acceptance of any social policy provisions would split the Cabinet and carry longer-lasting implications for the Conservative Party.[101] In this way, the issue of party unity had to be balanced with the need to reach some form of agreement.[102]

THE MAASTRICHT EUROPEAN COUNCIL

Although the preceding phase of the IGC-PU shaped the options available to John Major at the European Council, the agreements ultimately reached on the social policy dossier must clearly be understood in the context of the near chaos and hard bargaining which brought the negotiations to the brink of collapse at Maastricht itself.[103] In a careful handling of the summit agenda, Ruud Lubbers, President of the European Council, deliberately left the issue of social policy until last, in the hope that the British Prime Minister would not be prepared to veto the Treaty over one issue.[104] It was true that the Prime Minister's opening gambit was conciliatory, using the opening *tour de table* to out-line a number of British concessions, including some extension of EP powers and EC competence.[105] In this way, Major hoped that fellow Heads of Government would secure enough of their other proposals to be willing to reach agreement with the British on social policy.[106]

But by the time the discussion returned to the issue of social policy, it was clear that Britain was isolated.[107] To break the deadlock, Lubbers circulated a new text containing compromises that would allow more specific and limited powers for the Commission, would respect subsidiarity, and would maintain competitiveness. In partic-ular, the text restricted majority voting to health and safety, sex equality measures and employee information (but did not include consultation).[108] However, as a concession to the maximalist Member States it still contained the Social Partners Agreement.[109]

Acceptance of the Lubbers text would have represented a signifi-cant compromise on the part of the more maximalist Member States. It was therefore given very serious consideration by the Prime Minister and the British delegation. The CBI were not shown the text by the British negotiating team but, having received it from another national confederation, advised that, although it was imper-fect, they were prepared to accept it and would provide domestic support on Major's return to London.[110] The senior FCO official, Sir John Kerr, also suggested that Major should accept the Lubbers compromise text, but that he seek a watering down of some of the clauses in the hope that France, Italy and Belgium would not veto the whole Treaty for the sake of an imperfect social chapter.[111] However, the decisive factor in Major's judgement was the position of the Employment Secretary. Far from waiting patiently in London to be contacted if necessary, Howard was reported as being 'almost constantly on the telephone' demanding to know what was happening, and when eventually he was consulted on the Lubbers compromise he advised Major to give no ground. To do so would prompt Howard's resignation.[112]

Further complicating the picture, however, was the fact that other participants were also uneasy about the Lubbers compromise. Rather to the surprise of Lubbers and Major, Mitterrand, Andreotti and Martens declared that, for domestic reasons, they too could not accept the proposed text.[113] With failure looming ever larger, the debate turned instead towards a solution which would allow the 11 to accept the Treaty amendments in some form or other, whilst the British government could opt out of them.[114] Mitterrand and Delors proposed that the British should sign the social chapter and then opt out of it like EMU, or alternatively that Britain could opt out of specific social laws and then opt in again at a later stage, but Major refused to make any further concessions.

Finally, after six fruitless hours of talks, Mitterrand declared he was ready to fly back to Paris.[115] It was only at this point that, galvanized by the reality of a breakdown, the matter was settled, with a trilateral meeting between Kohl, Lubbers and Major proposing an 11-member 'opt in'. Formally, this would be outside the Treaty of Rome, but to satisfy the *communautaire* Member States for all practical purposes it was part of the treaty and would use the Rome Treaty procedures and institutions. In addition, the Agreement would form part of the *acquis communautaire* and would be justiciable by the ECJ. Major still had doubts about the arrangement because it created the two-speed Europe which both he and his Foreign Secretary had strived so hard to avoid, but caught between vetoing the Treaty or accepting this arrangement Major opted for the latter.[116]

CONCLUSION

The amendments to the social chapter were thus removed from the Treaty. Instead, a protocol attached to the Treaty noted that the 11 would make social policy according to the rules of the 'Agreement' and authorized them to use the EC institutions and procedures while doing so. The protocol modified normal voting procedures to take account of the absence of the British, and extended QMV to seven articles. It also provided a fast track for converting into law agreements reached by management and labour at the European level. It was an entirely political solution, with no participants sanguine about either its legality or practical viability. Indeed, many Heads of Government only acquiesced because they thought that John Major's days in Downing Street were numbered, and that an incoming Labour administration would immediately sign up to the Social Protocol.[117]

So far as the British were concerned, however, the outcome had considerable domestic benefits. The government seized the opportunity to talk up its opposition to the Social Protocol, which Douglas Hurd, for instance, denounced as corporatist.[118] Indeed, the Prime Minister made the opt out the centrepiece of his own statement to the House of Commons on his return from Maastricht, famously claiming to have won 'game, set and match'.[119]

So far as Conservative backbenchers were concerned, John Major could be presented as a leader whose tough negotiating skills had enabled Britain to pick and choose which parts of the European Union to sign up to – opting out of a single currency and enhanced social policy. At the same time it could be argued that Japanese and American investors would continue to invest in the UK rather than other EC countries.[120] The media concurred that the Social Protocol had no political or economic costs for Britain. In this they were assisted by timely support from the CBI and a number of companies, which, although in reality ambivalent about the outcome, nevertheless publicly welcomed it.[121] The issue of the Protocol also completely eclipsed compromises on other issues, in particular foreign and security policy and enhancement of the European Parliament powers.[122]

For all the ways the British government turned the outcome on the social policy dossier to its advantage, it is important not to lose sight of the fact that this outcome was neither intended nor particularly facilitated by the government. After all, the Conservative Party Chairman had made much of the social market, which implied some concessions on this issue, and which was only abandoned when it was clear that there was insufficient support for such moves. Even on the eve of the European Council, the Prime Minister thought that a deal was within reach without having to veto the Treaty, and the Protocol arrangement was in no way pre-bargained. Indeed, the evidence suggests that the British position was in large measure the product of miscalculation.

One aspect of the British complacency was the belief that the debate would move towards the lowest common denominator, and thus approach their position.[123] The most significant failure, however, was that of the FCO in underestimating the determination of a number of Socialist and Christian Democratic governments to make progress on social policy as a corollary to the Single Market.[124] There was also a misunderstanding of the extent to which the Social Partners' Agreement could be unravelled or disregarded by governments once European business and unions had endorsed it. It should here be noted that the government's failure to realize the implications of the Social Partners' Agreement undermines the argument of some scholars that the government's position was inspired by a desire to curry favour with the Conservative party's business supporters and financial backers.[125] Indeed, relations between the Department of Employment and the CBI were at an all-time low, and the CBI and British multinationals were sufficiently worried about the government's position to negotiate their own deal in the form of the Social Partners' Agreement.

The key factor in explaining the British position on, and indeed the outcome of, the social policy dossier was management of the party. It has been argued that the government's handling of the social policy negotiations was a sop to the far right of the Conservative Party and that it deliberately used these means to win over the majority of back-benchers to support the overall Treaty.[126] As we have seen, however, the sting was in fact largely taken out of Conservative back-bench dissent by the actions of the Whips' Office, manipulation of parliamentary procedures and the fear of the approaching election. Close examination of the negotiations rather shows that Major's principal need was to contain ministerial dissent which might provide the leadership for a wider split in the party, and it was this aspect of party management which did most to influence the negotiations.

Overall, then, the British government's position on the social policy dossier was characterized by short-termism and lack of forethought. The final outcome on this dossier, the British opt out from the Treaty's Social Protocol, was a last-minute expedient rather than the cleverly engineered product of British toughness, whatever the propaganda machine subsequently claimed. In the longer term, moreover, the fragility of the British victory was revealed in the ratification process, when the government's failure to build a consensus, the over-selling of the Social Protocol and the contradictory explanations given by the government for its behaviour became all too apparent.[127]

NOTES

1. Lange, 'The Politics of the Social Dimension', in Alberta Sbragia, *Euro Politics*, Washington DC, Brookings Institute, 1992, pp. 225–56, p. 245.
2. Juliet Lodge, 'Social Europe: Fostering a People's Europe', in Juliet Lodge (ed.), *The European Community and the Challenge of the Future*, London, Pinter, 1989, pp. 303–18, p. 303.
3. Alan Liepitz, 'L'Europe dernier recours pour une relance modiale', *Le Monde Diplomatique*, May 1989.
4. Philippa Watson, 'Social Policy after Maastricht', *Common Market Law Review*, vol. 30, 1993, pp. 481–513, p. 485.
5. David Lea, *The UK Government's View of EC Social Policy*, Speech to the Annual Conference of the Institute of Personnel Management, 1987: see also *Parl. Deb. HC*, 29 November 1989, cols 719–66.

6.   Paul Teague, '"Constitution or Regime", the Social Dimension to the 1992 Project', *British Journal of Industrial Relations*, vol. 27, no. 3, 1989, pp. 310–29, p. 326. Stephen J. Silvia, 'The Social Charter of the European Community: a Defeat for European Labor', *Industrial and Labor Relations Review*, vol. 44, July 1991, pp. 626–43.

7.   Tsoukalis, *The New European Economy*, op. cit., p. 164. See also Teague, '"Constitution or Regime"', op. cit., p. 311.

8.   See Commission of the European Communities, *Community Charter of Fundamental Basic Rights*, COM (89), Brussels, October 1989. For the role of the Belgian government in this see Alan Hansenne, 'Does Europe Want Flexibility through Deregulation', *Social and Labour Bulletin*, no. 4, pp. 1–8.

9.   R. Nielsen and E. Szyszczak, *The Social Dimension of the European Community*, Copenhagen, Handelshojskolens, Forlag, 1991, ch. 1.

10. See *Communication from the Commission concerning its Action Programme Relating to the Implementation of the Community Charter of Basic Social Rights for Workers*, COM (89) 568, Brussels, November 1989. For an optimistic assessment of the effect of the Charter see John T. Addison and W. Stanley Siebert, 'The Social Charter: Whatever Next?', *British Journal of Industrial Relations*, vol. 30, no. 4, December 1992, pp. 495–513. For a different view see Peter Lange, 'Politics of the Social Dimension', p. 229.

11. Robert Meyer, 'Key Year for Social Europe', *Industrial Relations Europe: 1992 Supplement*, newsletter, vol. 19, February 1991, p. 3S.

12. See for instance Thatcher, *The Downing Street Years*, op. cit., p. 743.

13. Charles Grant, *Delors: Inside the House that Jacques Built*, London, Nicholas Brealey, 1994, p. 86.

14. For a further discussion of this see Hugo Young, 'Sub Plot of the Social Charter', *Guardian*, 12 December 1991.

15. Christopher Lingle, 'The EC Social Charter, Social Democracy and Post-1992 Europe', *West European Politics*, vol. 14, No. 1, January 1991, pp. 129–38.

16. David Goodhart, 'Ground Rules for the Firing Squad', *Financial Times*, 13 February 1993. David Goodhart, 'A Government Dilemma over Labour Costs', *Financial Times*, 16 August 1993.

17. Robert Taylor, 'Low Wage Costs Fail to Draw Foreign Investment', *Financial Times*, 1 June 1993.

18. At Maastricht, DTI officials confessed that the UK was falling behind Germany for inward investment and that attracting inward investment and allowing part-time work and no statutory entitlement to holiday pay might help. Will Hutton, 'Major Puts Speed Limit on Fast Lane', *Guardian*, 11 December 1991.

19. Daniel Wincott, 'The Conservative Party and Europe', *Politics Review*, vol. 1, no. 4, 1992, pp. 12–16.

20. For example compare the language used by Ben Roberts, Julius Gould and Patrick Robertson, *The Bruges Group Looks at the Charter of Fundamental Rights*, Study Paper 1, London, Bruges Group, 25 October 1989.

21. For the argument that consensual corporatism was a modern version of

socialism see Robin Oakley, 'Party Sings the Same Song with New Melody', *The Times*, 12 October 1991.

22. The words Mrs Thatcher used in her Bruges speech. See Margaret Thatcher, *Britain and Europe: the Bruges Speech*, London, 1989; see also her comments that 'the social charter was a throwback to a Marxist period, a class struggle period', *Parl. Deb. HC*, 29 November 1989, col. 727.

23. Author's interview with Teressa Gorman MP.

24. Ibid.

25. This was spelt out by Chris Patten in his interview in *Marxism Today*, 'The Power to Change,' *Marxism Today*, February 1991, pp. 20–2. See also A. J. Davies, *We, the Nation: the Conservative Party and the Pursuit of Power*, London, Little Brown, 1995, p. 369.

26. 'Client' politicians in the Cabinet included David Hunt, Christopher Patten, William Waldegrave and John Gummer. For the difference between a left-of-centre Cabinet and right-of-centre parliamentary party see Peter Ridell, 'The Conservatives after 1992', *Political Quarterly*, vol. 63, no. 4, 1992, pp. 422–31. See also Neale Stevenson, 'The Right Way Forward: Building a Social Market Economy', *Tory Reform Group*, December 1990.

27. Tim Raison MP, 'Not Such a Bad Charter', *The Times*, 8 December 1989; see also *Parl. Deb. HC*, 29 November 1989. See also the comments by the Secretary General of UNICE that the Social Charter was 'a rather disappointing statement of the obvious'. *The European Community Social Charter*, Fourth Report, Employment Committee, House of Commons, Session 1990–91, House of Commons Paper 509, p. xii. The only neo-liberal to break the mould was Leon Brittan who echoed similar sentiments to those of Raison in Leon Brittan, *The Europe We Need*, London, Hamish Hamilton, 1994, p. 151.

28. Alan Butt Philip, 'British Pressure Groups and the European Community', in George, *Britain and the European Community*, op. cit., pp. 149–71.

29. For example see the memorandum submitted by the CBI to the Select Committee on the European Communities, House of Lords, session 1989–90, 3rd Report, House of Lords Paper 6, pp. 18–25. See also the text 'Europe of Opportunity for All', reproduced as an annex to the memorandum. See also 'EC Involvement Scheme Adds to Business Disquiet on 92', *Industrial Relations Europe*, vol. 18, December 1990, p. 1.

30. For example a British Institute of Management survey stated that 76% of managers were prepared to accept some form of legislation in the area of employee participation. Statistics quoted by the Labour Employment spokesperson, *Parl. Deb. HC*, 29 November 1989, col. 758.

31. Author's interview with a CBI official. See Howe, *Conflict of Loyalty*, op. cit., p. 456.

32. The most comprehensive account of the unions' position on this is Ben Rosamond, 'National Labour Organisations and European Integration: British Trade Unions and 1992', *Political Studies*, vol. XLI, September 1993, pp. 420–34.

33. John Cole, 'Unfinished Business', *New Statesman and Society*, 4 October 1991, p. 9.
34. Author's interview with David Lea, Deputy Secretary General of the TUC. For a wider discussion of this point see Robert Taylor, 'Mrs Thatcher's Impact on the TUC', *Contemporary Record*, vol. 2, no. 6, Summer 1989, pp. 23–6, p. 26.
35. During the 1989 Euro Elections the TUC even employed a public relations consultancy and placed advertisements in the press extolling the Social Chapter. See *Europe 1992*, London, TUC, August 1992, p. 3.
36. Gallup, 65% supported the Social Charter while 20% opposed it. Quoted in Anthony King, 'Fewer Back Thatcher's EEC Policy', *Daily Telegraph*, 9 December 1989.
37. Hugo Young, 'A Government Dispossessed', *Guardian*, 19 December 1991.
38. Author's interview with Sir John Kerr.
39. Author's interviews with Department of Employment and Cabinet Office officials.
40. Author's interviews with Department of Employment and Cabinet Office officials.
41. See Brian Bercusson, 'Maastricht: a Fundamental Change in European Labour Law', *Industrial Relations Journal*, vol. 23, no. 3, Autumn 1992, pp. 177–91.
42. Author's interview.
43. Author's interview with Timothy Collins, Special Advisor to Michael Howard.
44. *Independent*, 14 January 1991, quoted in Stephen George, *Contemporary Britain: an Annual Review 1992*, Aldershot, Dartmouth, 1993, pp. 68–75, p. 68.
45. This was one of the lessons drawn from the SEA negotiations when making proposals backfired on the British negotiators. See Thatcher, *The Downing Street Years*, op. cit., pp. 551–9.
46. In this respect the Dutch European Minister described the role of Garel-Jones as that of a 'spoiler', particularly with the Spanish Socialist government to which he had close links. Author's interview with Piet Dankert, European Minister, the Netherlands.
47. John Cole, 'Unfinished Business', *New Statesman and Society*, 4 October 1991, p. 9.
48. See Chris Patten's interview with David Marquand, 'The Power to Change', *Marxism Today*, February 1991, pp. 20–2; see also his interview with Sarah Baxter, 'Goodbye to All That', *New Statesman and Society*, 9 August 1991, pp. 12–13. For the hatred of Chris Patten by the right wing see Hogg and Hill, *Too Close to Call*, op. cit., p. 258.
49. John Major, 'The Evolution of Europe', *Conservative Party News*, 11 March 1991, pp. 11–13. 'Major to Underline Positive Approach to Europe', *Financial Times*, 11 March 1991; 'Major Signals Subtle Break with Past over Europe', *Financial Times*, 13 March 1991.
50. For the role of the social market in setting the post-Thatcherite agenda see Paul Heywood, 'British Politics in the 1990s: the Return of Consensus', *Talking Politics*, vol. 4, no. 2, Winter 1991–2, p. 74. See

also Will Hutton, 'A Rosier Shade of Grey', *Marxism Today*, April 1991, pp. 14–17.

51. Author's interview with Bill Cash MP. See Nicholas Ridley, 'Competition is the Key', *The Times*, 14 May 1991.

52. Thus Teresa Gorman's organization 'Conservatives for Small Businesses' and Michael Spicer's Eurosceptic dining club remained both distinct and exclusive as did Jonathan Aitken's Tory Philosophy Group. Author's interviews with Teresa Gorman MP and Bill Cash MP.

53. Robin Oakley, 'Delors Sets Euro Tongues Wagging Again in Europe', *The Times*, 16 May 1991.

54. Thatcher, *The Path to Power*, op. cit., p. 475.

55. On 15 June at Chicago and 18 June in New York. For press coverage see Andrew Grice, 'I'm Badly Disappointed in Major Says Thatcher', *Sunday Times*, 3 June 1991; and George Brock and Martin Fletcher, 'Thatcher Fires Broadside at Federal Europe', *The Times*, 18 June 1991.

56. The NTB ministers were Michael Forsyth in the Scottish Office, Eric Forth in the DE. In the DTI were Edward Leigh and John Redwood. Michael Portillo was at the Department of Environment. Neil Hamilton was an Assistant Whip.

57. Edward Leigh, 'The Judgement of Others', *Spectator*, 5 June 1993, pp. 16–19, p. 18.

58. Author's interview.

59. Author's interview with Timothy Collins and officials in the FCO, Cabinet Office and Department of Employment.

60. It was much to the chagrin of the junior minister, Timothy Eggar, that Howard had taken personal control over the formulation of the Department's position on the social policy issue. Author's interview with Department of Employment officials and Timothy Collins. See also Philip Stevens, 'Major Faces Renewed Warnings', *Financial Times*, 2 November 1991.

61. Author's interviews with FCO officials.

62. Watson, 'Social Policy after Maastricht', op. cit., p. 484.

63. Interview with Timothy Collins. For these proposals see *Industrial Relations in the 1990s*, London, HMSO, CM. 1602. Sarah Baxter, 'Howard's End', *New Statesman and Society*, 30 August 1991, p. 10.

64. Neil Malcolm, 'The Tories Throw Stones in a Glass House of Principles', *Spectator*, 10 August 1991, p. 6.

65. Author's interviews.

66. See John Cole, 'Unfinished Business', *New Statesman*, 4 October 1991, p. 9; 'Let Sleeping Dogmas Lie', *New Statesman*, 25 October 1991, pp. 8–9. See also Charles Leadbeater, 'Pragmatism Rules OK?', *Marxism Today*, November 1991, p. 18.

67. See the Social Partners Agreement for revised articles 118, 118A and 118B and a legislative role for the Social Partners, *European Dimensions of Collective Bargaining after Maastricht*, Brussels, European Trade Union Institute, 1992, pp. 63–8. See also 'Business Gives Some Ground on Euro-Deals – but with Riders', *Industrial Relations Europe*, November 1991, p. 1.

68. Even the Downing Street Policy Unit considered it this way. See Hogg and Hill, *Too Close to Call*, op. cit., p. 154.

69. One CBI official claimed that by the autumn relations between the CBI secretariat and the Department of Employment were 'at an all-time low and they were barely on speaking terms', though others suggest relations were 'warm and friendly' which is why the DE was surprised at the CBI's actions. This all took place in the context of a deterioration of relations between the CBI and the DTI over training and support for manufacturing. See Philip Bassett, 'Business Chiefs Fired Up for a Seaside Show Down', *The Times*, 1 November 1991.

70. Bercusson argues that the Dutch first draft, which included an extension of competences and majority voting, opened up the possibility of inserting an agreement of the Social Partners and was sufficient to induce UNICE to agree to a procedure for pre-emption of Community regulatory standards in a wide range of social policy areas. Brian Bercusson, 'Maastricht: a Fundamental Change in European Labour Law', op. cit., p. 185.

71. Author's interviews.

72. Wyn Grant and David Marsh, *The CBI*, London, Hodder and Stoughton, 1977, p. 151.

73. For the differences within the CBI compare Banham's article 'Social Charter Will Worsen Queues across Europe', *The Times*, 29 November 1991, with a letter from Deputy-Director General Richard Price, who negotiated the Social Partners Agreement, *Financial Times*, 29 November 1991.

74. Author's interview. See also Lange, 'Politics of the Social Dimension', op. cit., p. 251.

75. Hogg and Hill, *Too Close to Call*, op. cit., p. 154. For the Dutch Draft see *Agence Europe*, 6 November 1991.

76. Author's interview. These reports were 'placed' in the press by the TUC and through (un)fortunate timing coincided with the CBI's annual conference. See David Goodhart, 'Agreement Reached on Pay Bargaining', *Financial Times*, 5 November 1991.

77. The Agreement provides for two possible routes for implementation of texts agreed by the Social Partners, one in accordance with national practices specific to management and labour agreements, the other by a Council decision. It could be argued the first route does not exist in the UK, so the Council decision was the only option for Britain, and this would bring the UK back to the voting procedures as the key issue.

78. This had been the hope to which they had been clinging. Author's interview with Sir John Kerr.

79. Author's interviews.

80. For these efforts see Leader column, 'Quieting the Home Front', *The Times*, 6 November 1991.

81. Author's interview with Bill Cash MP. The election and the outcome of the IGC were formally linked in Major's Swansea speech in June. See for example John Williams, 'Major Says No Election This Year', *Evening Standard*, 14 June 1991.

82. Peter Ridell, 'Hung Up on Maastricht', *The Times*, 15 November 1991;

J. Catterall, 'John Major: His Rise and Record', *Politics Review*, vol. 3, no. 3, 1991, pp. 28–30, p. 30.

83. For the difference between the factions see Sarah Baxter, 'Dealing with Delors', *New Statesman*, 14 June 1991, p. 9.

84. As Chris Patten put it, these MPs had different 'bowel movements to colleagues with safe seats'. See comments by Chris Patten interviewed by Baxter, 'Goodbye to all that', *New Statesman*, 9 August 1991, p. 12.

85. Teresa Gorman argues it was the attraction of government office that won round one of the leaders of the ERG, Jonathan Aitken, after 18 years on the backbenches. See Gorman, *Bastards*, op. cit., p. 41.

86. Part though not all of the explanation may lie in the emergence of the career politician to whom election and reelection is everything. See Anthony King, 'The Rise of the Career Politician – and Its Consequences', *British Journal of Political Science*, vol. 11, 1981, pp. 249–85.

87. Author's interview with Bill Cash MP.

88. For the background to this see Gorman, *Bastards*, op. cit., pp. 29–35. See also leaders, 'Quelling the Home Front', *The Times*, 6 November 1991, and 'Whipping for Europe', *The Times*, 15 December 1991.

89. Robin Oakley, 'Torturous Struggle to Mend Party's Divisions', *The Times*, 13 November 1991; 'Oustings', *The Times*, 22 November 1991.

90. George Jones, 'Major's Men Move in on Euro-Sceptics', *Daily Telegraph*, 13 November 1991.

91. 'Not Quite Pulling Together', *Economist*, 23 November 1991, p. 35.

92. Robin Oakley, 'Major Secures Mandate for Maastricht', *The Times*, 22 November 1991.

93. Michael White, 'Tories and Labour Deride Calls for Referendum on EC', *Independent*, 18 November 1991. Philip Stevens remarked that having secured a majority in Parliament, those rebels who would not be reconciled were subsequently discounted. Philip Stevens, 'A Man Living with His Party's Past', *Financial Times*, 11 December 1991.

94. Peter Riddell, 'Agreement is Not in the Bag', *The Times*, 22 November 1991.

95. Author's interview with Timothy Collins. See also Seldon, *Major*, op. cit., p. 245; Seamus Milne, 'Victorian Jibe Stings Howard', *Financial Times*, 4 December 1991. To reinforce the point, two weeks before Maastricht the Department of Employment issued a paper spelling out Britain's opposition to EC social policy point by point. Sarah Baxter, 'The Game Is Up for Citizen John and His Charter', *New Statesman*, 13 December 1991.

96. Author's interviews.

97. Philip Stevens, 'Tories to Back Summit Deal by Isolating Rebels', *Financial Times*, 6 December 1991. FT writers, 'Backing for Hurd Stance', *Financial Times*, 29 November 1991.

98. Author's interview. Joe Rogaly, 'Duty Not Destiny', *Financial Times*, 6 December 1991.

99. 'Major Flies off on Tailwind of Conflicting Demands', *Guardian*, 9 December 1991; Alison Smith 'Major under Scrutiny from Critics at Home', *Financial Times*, 9 December 1991.

100. Robin Oakley, 'Tories Setting Less Store on an Agreement', *The Times*, 28 November 1991. The *Economist* remarked that one Cabinet minister said, 'the real F-word at Maastricht is failure'. 'Pre-Maastricht Tension', op. cit., p. 38.
101. John Cole, 'A Martian in Number Ten', *New Statesman*, 11 October 1991, p. 9; John Cole, 'Let Sleeping Dogmas Lie', *New Statesman*, 25 October 1991, p. 9.
102. Hogg and Hill, *Too Close to Call*, op. cit., p. 160. Leader, 'The Maastricht Calculus', *The Times*, 5 December 1991.
103. Officials and politicians have conflicting accounts of the order of events at the Maastricht European Council. For the social policy negotiations this section draws heavily on interviews with participants and the following sources: Grant, *Delors*, op. cit., pp. 201–2; Hogg and Hill, *Too Close to Call*, op. cit., pp. 150–6; Will Hutton, 'Street Fight over the Amended Wording', *Guardian*, 11 December 1991; Michael White, 'Eleventh Hour Attack Stole the Day', *Guardian*, 12 December 1991; Boris Johnson, 'Counting Down to a Crisis over the S-word', *Daily Telegraph*, 12 December 1991; Ronald van der Krol, David Buchan and Philip Stevens, 'Cool Hand Lubbers Scales His Summit', *Financial Times*, 14/15 December 1991.
104. Ronald van der Krol, David Buchan and Philip Stevens, 'Cool Hand Lubbers Scales His Summit', *Financial Times*, 14/15 December 1991.
105. For the contents of Major's speaking note at the opening day of the summit see John Palmer, 'Major Signals Concessions but Not over Social Policy', *Guardian*, 11 December 1991.
106. Author's interview with Sir John Kerr. See also Roy Pryce, 'The Treaty Negotiations', in Duff, et al., *Maastricht and Beyond*, op. cit., p. 50.
107. Philip Stevens, 'A Man Living with His Party's Past', *Financial Times*, 11 December 1991.
108. Will Hutton, 'Street Fight over the Amended Wording', *Guardian*, 11 December 1991.
109. Financial Times Writers, 'Single European Currency Due to Start in 1999', *Financial Times*, 10 December 1991; 'Britain This Week', *Economist*, 15 December 1991.
110. Author's interviews.
111. Grant, *Delors*, op. cit., p. 201; Daily Telegraph Writers, 'Counting Down to a Crisis over the S-word', *Daily Telegraph*, 11 December 1991.
112. Boris Johnson, 'Law on Jobs Becomes the Main Stumbling Block', *Daily Telegraph*, 12 December 1991. See also 'Howard Sets His Sights on the FO', *Sunday Times*, 1 January 1995. Michael Howard denies that he threatened to resign and argues it was right and proper that he be consulted and his opinion accepted as the best way forward.
113. Author's interview with Michael Welsh MEP. 'The Deal is Done', *Economist*, 15 December 1991, p. 55.
114. Andrew Grice, 'Master of Maastricht', *Sunday Times*, 15 December 1991.
115. At one point Garel-Jones told journalists that it looked as though the social chapter would not be removed and that Britain would have to settle for a vague social chapter. Philip Johnson, 'Major Strokes Put

Handbag in Shade', *Telegraph*, 12 December 1991.

116. Grice, 'Master of Maastricht', op. cit., p. 18.

117. Author's interview with Alain van Solinge and Georgio Maganza. See also Alan Barnard, 'A Social Policy for Europe: Politicians 1 Lawyers 0', *International Journal of Comparative Labour Law and Industrial Relations*, no. 8, 1992, pp. 15–31.

118. Douglas Hurd, *Parl. Deb. HC*, 19 December 1991, col. 480.

119. John Major, *Parl. Deb. HC*, 11 December 1991, col. 861.

120. Philip Stevens, 'Major Applies a Balm to Conservative Party Wounds', *Financial Times*, 12 December 1991.

121. Most of the companies that publicly supported the government, unsurprisingly, were also corporate supporters of the Conservative Party. See their letter in *The Times*, 13 December 1991.

122. Hugo Young, 'A Government Dispossessed', *Guardian*, 19 December 1991.

123. One British official was quoted as rather smugly remarking, 'things will move towards the lowest common denominator ... and that's us'. 'The Spoilers', *Economist*, 9 March 1991, p. 44.

124. One British official directly involved in the negotiations suggested that officials were aware of the commitment of the others to move ahead, but did not know how best to bridge the gap because British ministers were also very determined. Author's interview.

125. This is the argument put forward by both Lange, 'Maastricht and the Social Protocol', op. cit., p. 256, and Taylor, 'The European Community', op. cit., pp. 109–25.

126. Daniel Wincott, 'Much Ado about Nothing', in Brian Brivati and Harriet Jones (eds), *From Reconstruction to Integration: Britain and Europe since 1945*, Leicester, Leicester University Press, 1993, pp. 207–15, p. 215.

127. The post-Maastricht confusions are discussed by Wincott, ibid.

4 Foreign and Security Policy

The idea of adding a foreign and security policy dimension to the European Community was one of the explicit Franco-German aims in transforming the EC into a European Union. The reason why foreign policy became intimately linked to security policy in the IGC-PU, however, needs some comment. First, foreign and security policy raised the same sorts of issues concerning national sovereignty and autonomy. A foreign and a security policy role for the EC implied that Member States were surrendering their traditional nation-state functions, and that the integration project might eventually produce a superstate which was more than the mere sum of its parts.[1] Second, both foreign and security issues raised similar questions about the relationship between the EC and United Sates. If the Europeans had their own independent foreign and security policy, this would have inevitable repercussions for the American relationship and commitment to Europe and West European defence structures. Finally, though the British government may not have linked foreign and security policy, the issues were linked in the minds of its major partners France and Germany and indeed formed the centrepiece of the IGC-PU negotiations. Given the leading role Britain played in both these areas, the government's reluctance to consider any further supranational enhancement to foreign policy cooperation and outright opposition to a defence role, it was thought by the British negotiating team 'to be the issue that might break Maastricht', and it is to this issue which this chapter now turns.

THE BACKGROUND

No other set of policy issues under consideration in the IGC-PU brought with it such a lengthy history as that of foreign and security policy. The debate over whether to include a defence role within the European integration process dated from the inception of the project, although after early attempts to create a European Defence Community dramatically failed in 1954 defence issues were left to an expanded Western European Union (WEU).[2] This was an intergovernmental forum, subordinate to the wider grouping of states in the Atlantic Alliance and its military organization, NATO.

Despite the fact that the Treaty of Rome eschewed any mention of foreign and defence policy, tensions persisted between those Member States which wanted the EC to concentrate exclusively on trade and agricultural issues and those which wanted a foreign policy and defence dimension. The French government was the leading advocate of such a role, but for a variety of reasons its ongoing attempts on this front were resisted by its partners. France was eventually successful, but only in winning approval for an intergovernmental foreign policy dimension for the Community at the Hague Summit of December 1969, with defence questions left to other institutions.[3]

However, even on the issue of foreign policy, the Hague agreement on European Political Cooperation (EPC) did not represent a solution to the tensions surrounding the issue. The French, for instance, saw EPC principally as a means of increasing the influence of national foreign policies rather than as a means of deepening integration. Yet agreement to create EPC was reached only because it included sufficiently ambitious aims to satisfy the integrationists, while at the same time leaving procedures in the hands of national governments. The intergovernmental nature of this cooperation, and the limited European Commission involvement, differentiated this policy sector from others in the EC. The implications of a common foreign policy for both their own future as nation-states and the type of EC structure they wanted to create were thus sidestepped by Member States.[4]

Over the course of time, and driven by the enthusiasm of Bonn, EPC was made more effective through closer coordination of Community instruments in the areas of trade, aid and sanctions, but remained on an intergovernmental footing. These efforts culminated in the SEA, which for the first time provided a treaty base for EPC and made a commitment that Member States would pursue 'common actions' in the realm of foreign policy. However, there was nothing legally binding about this foreign policy cooperation and Member States were free to participate in it as much or as little as they pleased. By the late 1980s, 'procedure as a substitute for policy' thus increasingly characterized the area of EC foreign policy, and coordination was largely confined to economic questions.[5]

The inception of EPC did little to resolve differences over how to handle security and defence either.[6] Above all, 'Atlanticist' members of the EC were concerned that expanding the EC competence from

foreign policy coordination to include defence issues might undermine the American commitment to West European defence structures. Reflecting these concerns in the SEA negotiations, the British
government, with support from the Netherlands (and Ireland for
different reasons) continued to argue for a separation between
foreign and defence policy. In support of their case, they now introduced a distinction between defence and security issues, and successfully argued that EPC should be restricted to consideration of two
aspects only of security questions – the economic and political.[7]

For Britain the distinction between security and defence was thus
meant to set the limits to the expansion of EC competences. The EC
could on an intergovernmental basis consider broad issues relating to
the management of Western security, for example non-proliferation
and confidence building measures. Defence, however, defined as
those issues relating to military structures and operational command
of forces, would remain a matter for NATO and WEU. To many
governments, it has to be said that the distinction was wholly artificial
and not accepted as a fixed settlement of the issue of whether the EC
should acquire defence responsibilities.

However, in the short term, progress in Europeanizing defence
structures continued to take place outside the EC through the reactivation of WEU, since WEU did not raise the spectre of an alternative
military organization to NATO.[8] But it was not long before the issue
of further enhancing foreign policy and including a defence dimension in the EC came to the forefront of European debates again. This
was due to two key developments. The first of these was the collapse
of communism in the autumn of 1989, which encouraged Member
States which wished to move beyond pragmatic foreign and security
co-operation to put the case for a qualitatively new form of foreign
and defence integration within the EC.[9]

The second development was a major political initiative on the part
of President Mitterrand and Chancellor Kohl, who now explicitly
linked the objective of a European Political Union to the creation of
a common foreign and security policy.[10] Kohl's motives for this initiative were centred around his desire to give EMU a political dimension
and so secure domestic support, while Mitterrand wanted not only to
secure monetary union but also to bind a united Germany into an
even closer European institutional framework.[11]

So far as the British were concerned, this renewed agitation for a
deeper and qualitatively different integration was highly alarming.
There were two aspects to this. The first was that, greatly to the

surprise of the British, deepened integration attracted strong support from US Secretary of State James Baker.[12] This gave rise to considerable anxiety in London that an 'anti-British' element had won the ear of President Bush, with a number of opinion formers in the US openly talking up the idea of 'new' special relationships.[13] The second problem so far as the British were concerned was that the calls for deeper integration came against the backdrop of a failure to remodel NATO in the aftermath of the collapse of the Warsaw Pact. A 'window of opportunity' had thus apparently been created for the gestation of a distinct European defence identity outside the Alliance.[14] Equally worryingly, Bonn and Washington were increasingly taking the lead in setting the NATO agenda and brokering compromises, and it looked as though they were forging a new special relationship at the expense of London.[15]

Thus, by November 1990, when John Major became Prime Minister, there was growing external pressure on the British government to accept a strengthened foreign and defence dimension to the EC. At the same time, however, the British were fearful of an American withdrawal from the Alliance, since this might undermine one of the principal institutions through which Britain exercized its great-power status and activism on the international scene.[16] It would also unravel the long-standing British policy of using American leadership to counterbalance the economic and political weakness of Britain relative to Germany and France.[17] There was a feeling that in the 'New World Order', without special access to the US, 'Britain would be speedily reduced to the role of a suppliant cooling its heels in the ante-chamber of history'.[18]

THE DOMESTIC CONTEXT

Perhaps the most immediately striking factor shaping John Major's approach to foreign and defence policy issues at the IGC-PU was that these issues were in fact more contentious within the Conservative Party than between the two front benches. It was true that the Opposition was itself deeply divided over the issue of defence and Europe, and had only recently adopted both a pro-NATO and pro-EC stance. However, the Labour leadership was eager not to revisit all its recently concluded debates on the subject, even if it meant leaving the fundamentals of government policy unchallenged.[19]

In terms of the more important Conservative Party divisions, the split was essentially between an Atlanticist right wing and a more European oriented left wing. To the right, Anglo-Saxon solidarity was a higher concern than Britain's links with Europe, which were a matter for hard bargaining and practical politics.[20] Any step towards the Europeanization of foreign policy was a step away from Britain playing an independent role in international affairs.[21] To the smaller pro-European grouping, however, some Europeanization of foreign policy was both necessary and inevitable if Britain were to retain any influence in the world. The presence of Mrs Thatcher as leader, however, meant that this view received little airing in the party; Michael Heseltine, for instance, spoke out at the cost of his Cabinet job, and only then felt free to set out an alternative foreign policy agenda.[22] Nevertheless, the fact remained that hard questions of foreign policy were always likely to bump up against these competing Tory visions of the future of Britain, at its most stark a choice between an Anglo-Saxon or a European commitment.

Defence policy was intimately connected both to the foreign policy and European debates. It shared many of the features of foreign policy issues, being defined in terms of sovereignty, independence and symbolism. Moreover, the Conservative Party always perceived itself as the party of strong defence. But there were differences in emphasis here as well. To the Tory right, on the one hand, any Europeanization of defence was seen as a prelude to an EC common defence policy that would undermine Britain's capacity for independent action and which ultimately would not work.[23] To the left wing of the party, on the other hand and to most Conservative MEPs, a Europeanization of NATO, within certain limits, was seen as the most effective way to shore up the Atlantic Alliance and ensure a continuing American commitment to European defence.[24]

John Major was thus confronted by managing a party with different views which could have far-reaching consequences over the joint issues of defence and foreign policy. The problem was made all the more awkward by the fact that, unlike Thatcher, John Major himself had no particular interest in external affairs and no emotional commitment to the United States.[25] The Prime Minister's low profile on foreign and security policy thus attracted suspicion from the hitherto dominant right wing, who feared that he was more likely to be swayed by economic and political imperatives.[26] Nor was he helped by the lack of a pro-Major lobby in the Conservative press.[27]

Britain's steadily declining financial resources to pay for an active defence policy also had a heavy influence on Major's negotiating position. In the 11 years of Conservative government, Britain's conventional forces had suffered from the priority given to the procurement of the Trident nuclear system.[28] To a Conservative Party publicly committed to strong defence, this was very difficult to acknowledge, however, and left a yawning gap between the perception of the Conservatives as the party of strong defence and the reality of the MoD desperately struggling to keep up appearances.[29] The problem came to a head in the spring of 1990 when, following clashes between the Treasury and the MoD concerning the latter's budget, a second defence review in eight years was announced.[30] Ultimately, however, the outbreak of the Gulf War meant that the review was put on hold, leaving these issues substantially unresolved.

John Major's problems in dealing with foreign and security policy stand in significant contrast to the assumptions frequently made about the ability of the executive to dominate these areas. It was true that the number of participants in the debate was low, with the right-wing think tanks in particular in an intellectual vacuum following the fall of Mrs Thatcher.[31] But those who were involved tended to have very firm ideas of the outcome they wanted to see. The half-finished defence review, for instance, put en garde a well-entrenched network of domestic interests, including influential service associations and defence contractors.[32]

At the same time, public interest and involvement on the foreign and security issue remained inconsistent. On the one hand, survey data at the end of 1990 showed that 41 per cent of British people were 'very much in favour' of the development of a EC foreign policy while 38 per cent 'disapproved'. Concerning security and defence, surveys showed that 50 per cent of the British people supported the creation of a European common security and defence policy while at the same time 59 per cent wanted it to remain a national responsibility.[33] Although the imagery of the issues at stake was easy to grasp, complex institutional relationships between foreign ministries, and the fine detail of relationships between NATO, WEU and the EC, were of little concern to the general public. The implication so far as John Major was concerned was that presentation would be crucial in reconciling new initiatives with public perceptions – fed by 11 years of Conservative rule – that Britain was still a great, if not a world, power.

FOREIGN AND SECURITY POLICY OBJECTIVES

Foreign and defence policy was thus a difficult dossier in which two distinct elements coexisted and sometimes collided. On the one hand, the dossier was of great symbolic significance to the domestic audiences involved, and was also seen by the negotiating team as one of the most important issues under discussion in the IGC-PU.[34] On the other hand, the day-to-day handling of the dossier was confined to a narrow political elite. Indeed, in finalizing the British desiderata in advance of the IGC-PU, discussions were confined to the foreign and defence ministries, though in the run up to and early part of the negotiations Tom King, the Defence Secretary, was preoccupied by the British military response to the invasion of Kuwait, and thereafter King did not feel it necessary to intervene personally, given that the FCO was taking the lead in the negotiations and that his views were anyway similar to those of Hurd.[35]

The burden of policy-making therefore fell on the Security Policy Department of the FCO and the NATO/UK Policy Secretariat of the MoD with little need for direct involvement of the European Secretariat of the Cabinet Office.[36] This was a point of considerable importance, for these officials had a departmental interest in collective European action, and a very similar outlook on how the issue should be handled. Their shared interests were to do much to ease tensions as the negotiations increasingly took on a triple personality, taking place not only at the IGC-PU, but also in WEU and NATO.[37]

In terms of institutional objectives for foreign policy, the British delegation, and the Foreign Secretary personally, genuinely wanted to make progress in this area. The advantages of a united position expressed by 12 Member States, compared with exploitable differences or even contradictions, were overwhelmingly obvious and EPC was seen as having not been particularly effective. Of course 'progress' had to be in the right direction, and the FCO-inspired ideal was a common foreign policy conducted on the basis of the long-standing British preference for intergovernmental co-operation. This intergovernmental co-operation would be outside the Treaty of Rome, and so, as far as possible, under British leadership. There were two sub-components: one to avoid a policy-making role for the European Commission; and the other to prevent interference by the EP and ECJ. At the procedural level of foreign policy, London argued that Member States must be allowed to pursue a policy in whatever way they saw fit when vital national interests were at stake, and so opposed majority voting.[38] On the basis of these objectives the government proposed a modest strengthening of EPC.[39]

Concerning defence, the British feeling was that responsibility should continue to belong to the Atlantic Alliance with its central British role and proven efficacy. The key element of the British strategy was, however, to secure the restructuring of the Alliance before the question of expanded EC defence competence could be considered.[40] The hope was that Alliance members (and in particular the Americans) would in this way set the *de facto* limits to any European defence identity, forcing any new European responsibilities to be subordinate to NATO. There was also some hope among the negotiating team that, if London could 'hold the line' during the Maastricht negotiations, any future EC enlargement would increase the number of neutral Member States, and this would relieve any further pressure on London to concede a defence dimension to the integration process.

Given these preferences in the sphere of defence, London saw some scope for enhancing the role of European Member States in two areas: operations outside the geographical competence of the Atlantic Alliance; and a more equitable share of the defence burden with the United States within NATO.[41] In its desiderata for the IGC-PU, the government therefore proposed that WEU be given responsibility for military operations in partnership with the United States outside the NATO area.[42] In this way, a revitalized WEU would head off attempts to incorporate a defence organization into the EC directly. Focus on WEU had the added advantage that as a British creation it might also avoid a bitter dispute between the pro- and anti-European wings of the Conservative Party.[43]

THE TREATY NEGOTIATIONS

The general course of the Treaty negotiations on foreign policy, but particularly defence, was characterized by two key features. The first was the way in which the international environment affected the talks, with the outbreak of the Gulf War and the Soviet invasion of the Baltic States completely overshadowing early discussions and distracting negotiators from making any significant progress. An equally important feature of the international environment was the impact of the United States on the course of the negotiations.[44] The attitude of the US was especially significant in shaping British thinking, for while there was a widespread belief among its partners that London's objectives were 'a regurgitation of the American position',[45] the British themselves continued to be extremely concerned about confusing signals from the 'pro-EC' State Department and 'pro-NATO' Pentagon.[46] Indeed, on the question of defence, London's negotiating strategy was directed as much at Washington (in support of the Pentagon line) as it was at its European partners.[47]

The second key influence on the defence negotiations was the fact that three players – France, Germany and Britain – inevitably dominated the discussions. The German role had obvious geographic, economic and historical origins. That Britain and France were the only EC Member States with the necessary quantity and quality of military forces around which to create a European defence force also made these governments the major protagonists in the IGC-PU. Without British and French acquiescence, any new CFSP would be meaningless, and British negotiators were acutely aware of the additional leverage this gave them.[48]

The French position as the IGC-PU got under way was that the logic of European Union 'necessitated' inclusion of defence within the Union and not just a common defence policy. It should also be noted that Mitterrand's surprise declaration in June 1990 that all French forces would be withdrawn from Germany by 1994 added a new urgency to French arguments, since it made it vital for Paris to find a new European role for French forces that did not involve their reintegration in NATO.[49] In contrast, the German negotiators were caught between two competing visions, sharing not only part of the Atlanticism of London but also the pro-European sentiments of France.[50] Bonn, like London, hoped that the end of the Cold War and the collapse of the Warsaw Pact might provide an opportunity to draw the French back into NATO, if pro-NATO EC members took a conciliatory stand on developing a role for WEU.[51]

In the absence of a clear agenda and confusion surrounding what a CFSP might look like, the Luxembourg Presidency circulated a questionnaire and asked for specific Treaty amendments. Even this failed to kick-start negotiations, however, because of differences which now began to emerge between France and Germany over defence.[52] Increasingly, the defence ministry in Bonn began to think that the French preference for a declaratory policy rather than discussion of the detail of military integration reflected an unwillingness to consider any sort of military integration. For Bonn, it was this latter point which was the central purpose of any European defence identity.[53]

It was at this point that Commission President Delors intervened in an attempt to move the IGC-PU debate forwards. Delors provocatively unveiled ambitious proposals for a EU foreign and security policy in a speech at the International Institute for Strategic Studies in London, sure in the knowledge that it was bound to provoke a response.[54] The initiative backfired badly, however, with French and German negotiators rejecting the Commission initiatives and Washington – at British prompting – being moved to intervene directly in the negotiations, laying down three conditions for an 'acceptable' European defence identity.[55] These conditions stated: that no European caucus must be created inside NATO; that there must be no marginalization of non-EC European members of NATO (Iceland, Norway and Turkey); and that there could be no alternative European defence organization.[56]

Meanwhile, decisions on defence and security were being taken in NATO in the face of three pressures: the rapid withdrawal of national forces from Germany; nationally-based decisions to reduce defence expenditure; and constant British and American agitation to reach agreement on new tasks for NATO. Most importantly, at the end of May 1991, at the NATO Defence Policy Committee (DPC), the MoD and the Pentagon succeeded in their efforts to get an early decision on NATO force structure, in advance of the NATO Strategic Review to be announced in the autumn.[57] In addition, London secured the creation of a new Alliance Rapid Reaction Corps (ARRC) under permanent British Command.[58] In the absence of French participation in DPC meetings, German defence and foreign ministry officials had given Paris the impression that, as the largest contributor of conventional forces to NATO, Bonn would resist any such British *démarche*. After heavy lobbying, however, the German defence minister was convinced by his British counterpart that a major British command was the only means to guarantee a permanent British force in Germany, and in return the British supported the German request to command the air component of the ARRC.[59]

While developments in the sphere of defence were only taking place away from the IGC-PU discussion table, however, progress was now beginning to be made on the foreign policy aspect of the dossier. At the end of June, at the Luxembourg European Council, the institutional arrangements for a common foreign policy were formally unveiled, with a pillared structure for European Union. This clearly differentiated the way in which CFSP would be handled from other

EC business. The CFSP pillar was to follow intergovernmental rather than supranational procedures. It strictly limited the role of the European Commission to a shared rather than exclusive right to initiate proposals. Decision-making would take place in the Council of Ministers with the EP informed of decisions, but having no influence to change the decisions that had been made. Likewise, the European Court of Justice would be excluded from the CFSP pillar or policies agreed on the basis of CFSP treaty articles.[60] The distinction between supranational and intergovernmental procedures was broadly in line with British objectives, and London and Paris had formed a powerful coalition to secure this structure.[61]

London was worried by some aspects of the plan, particularly the proposal (and the majority view) for unanimity for the vote on the broad direction of a common foreign policy in the Council of Ministers and majority voting for the implementation of common policies (Article J.2).[62] This formula was considered unsustainable for three particular reasons: first, it would lead to perpetual argument over which category a given decision really belonged to; second, decisions on implementing a common foreign policy could be of major significance and could not therefore be relegated to a majority vote; and third, the pursuit of foreign policy aims required a genuine commitment and this could not be expected from a government voted down – in effect they would simply opt out or be a grudging and ineffective supporter.

In general, however, the government was by and large delighted by its success in the negotiations thus far. As the British had hoped, an intergovernmental approach had been adopted on the question of a European foreign policy and European defence remained firmly focussed on NATO.[63] Indeed, on the latter issue one official said, 'the important thing now is not to humiliate the French too far'.[64]

The government was greatly helped by the fact that domestic attention had failed to focus upon the CFSP dossier as might have been expected given its symbolic implications. This was despite the fact that the issue of a 'federal vocation', a phrase contained in the June draft European Union Treaty, sparked a furious row when the anti-European right, both inside and outside the Conservative Party, interpreted it as a plan for a European superstate with its own foreign policy.[65] In the House of Commons, Mrs Thatcher broke her silence and denounced this Luxembourg Treaty draft as the greatest abdication of national power and sovereignty, and talked of a 'conveyer belt to federalism' but decided to focus on the single currency rather than foreign and security policy.[66] Ironically, the truth was that the 'federal vocation' was seen by British negotiators as something of a 'straw man', easily knocked down at the end of the negotiations, and in the interim useful in diverting back-bench and media attention away from more difficult issues.[67]

The most significant development in diffusing the general back-bench concerns on the CFSP dossier was the failure on 30 September of the Dutch Presidency's attempt to replace the proposed intergovernmental structure of the treaty with a single 'federal' structure.[68] Somewhat disingenuously, the British government used this very public setback to argue that federalizing attempts had been decisively defeated, and that intergovernmentalism had won out.[69] The British negotiators saw this rebuttal as a 'godsend'[70] and, with considerable encouragement from the government's media managers, the British press seized on this 'victory' as a sign that Britain was winning the arguments. Though the commitment to a *vocation federale* remained in the Luxembourg draft, to which the negotiations reverted, the British negotiators remained confident that it would eventually be removed at the Maastricht European Council.[71]

At the same time, however, it should be noted that overturning the Dutch draft also meant a return to the Luxembourg formula of unanimity for deciding general principles of foreign policy and majority voting for the implementation of joint actions, a formula unacceptable to Britain, Ireland and Denmark.[72] Hurd argued that differences over how the EC should react to the dissolution of Yugoslavia illustrated the sobering difficulties of a common foreign policy. This could not be engineered by institutional tinkering but had to follow on from a genuine convergence of interests. The British government's resistance to majority voting was further stiffened by demands from Germany and Italy (unable to participate themselves) that European troops should be sent to Yugoslavia.[73]

Even the annual parliamentary debate on British defence, held in October, failed to ignite the spark of controversy concerning the CFSP dossier, with few MPs making the connection between the IGC-PU and NATO reviews.[74] Part of the explanation lies in the government's traditional domination of this sector: Parliament and the select committees have always been rather weak in scrutinizing foreign and defence issues. The government also managed to insulate the issues under consideration from domestic groups – including its own party – and opponents were seriously hampered by the lack of any alternative source of information.

Notwithstanding this, the symbolism of the dossier meant that the government was careful to reassure its own backbenchers that what was under negotiation in the IGC-PU and NATO was not a reorientation of Britain's defence posture, but a pragmatic adjustment to changed circumstances. In particular, the Alliance Rapid Reaction Corps was assiduously presented as tangible evidence of great-power status in the aftermath of German unification.[75] Likewise, the strengthening of WEU was portrayed as an adjustment to NATO arrangements and an alternative to EC defence.

Meanwhile, the Labour Party front bench continued to feel itself vulnerable on defence, not wishing to be seen as undermining NATO or suggesting concessions which might imply that they were ready to sacrifice British sovereignty.[76] The issue of foreign and defence policy was therefore subordinated to the questions of public services and the economy – both issues on which party unity was more likely.[77] Against this backdrop, the bulk of the October debate was not therefore concerned with international status, institutional options, or even the balance between the three services, but dominated by parochial pleas from backbenchers that the army was bearing the brunt of the defence cuts and that particular regiments be reprieved.[78] Indeed, five short references to the negotiations in the IGC-PU in 11 hours of debate were a reflection of how successfully the implications of the defence review were divorced from the defence discussions in the IGC-PU.[79]

Having overcome the potentially difficult hurdle of a parliamentary debate on the restructuring of British armed forces, government negotiators now felt more able to make some concessions in the IGC-PU without unpalatable domestic ramifications.[80] There was also a feeling that NATO had sufficiently Europeanized itself to head-off any alternative in the EC, as the ARRC would be the principal focus of national resources for any out of area capability. This was particularly important given that any independent European defence force would involve an additional level of defence expenditure beyond that which most West European states would be willing to pay.[81] There was also some genuine convergence between the major protagonists about the need for the Europeans to do more for their own defence, though the French preferred to use the language of a 'European defence identity' and the British that of a 'European pillar' of NATO.[82]

Prompted by its new-found readiness to make concessions, London therefore agreed a joint defence initiative with Rome in October.[83]

The choice of partner was an important part of the initiative. By demonstrating that it could reach a consensus with one of the most federal-minded Member States, London hoped to set the parameters of an eventual deal. The involvement of two large countries would also act as a counter to the Franco-German axis which, though hitherto ineffective, was still feared.[84] In terms of the substance of the initiative, London was now prepared to accept calls for the Union to have a gradual role in the formulation of a *defence policy*, but not yet matters relating to a *common defence*. The European Union could formulate strategy and policy, but not create an independent command structure or an integrated military command. WEU was not to come under the direct control of the European Union, and was only required to take into account the decisions of the European Council along with the Alliance. In operational terms, London proposed a European Reaction Force involving 'double-hatted' NATO troops.

As Douglas Hurd admitted, the shift to a common defence policy 'was a fairly substantial move' from the initial position.[85] But the absence of opposition to this initiative from any part of the Conservative Party underscored how successfully the government had diffused domestic concerns on the defence dossier. Indeed, the major effort of ministers was now focussed on reassuring Washington that British concessions on defence would not threaten the long-term viability of NATO.[86]

The Anglo-Italian initiative soon attracted a Franco-German response. Made on 11 October, this argued that the Union should have a common defence policy now, and a common defence in the long run.[87] The Council of Ministers was to oversee relations between the Union and WEU which was 'an integral part of the process of European Union'.[88] The difference was significant: the Anglo-Italian proposal recognized the primacy of NATO, linking WEU indirectly to the Union; the Franco-German initiative in contrast emphasized the primacy of WEU as the defence arm of the Union, indirectly linked to NATO. To reinforce the point Roland Dumas insisted that relations between WEU and the European Union were 'of a different nature' to those between WEU and NATO.[89] Most contentious was the proposal to invite other members of WEU to join the existing Franco-German Brigade to create a Euro Corps which would form an embryonic European Army to be placed at the disposal of the European Union.

The problem was, however, that Bonn and Paris had consulted none of the other governments which supported a European defence identity, and this alienated other maximalist Member States.[90] Paris and Bonn were also attacked for issuing a separate invitation to sympathetic governments to a meeting in Paris, and 'effectively usurping the Presidency from the Dutch to force through their own views on defence'.[91] The Franco-German proposal paid little attention to detail, particularly the command structure or operational role of the Corps.[92] One German official candidly stated that 'the simple fact is that we have to have a way of allowing the French to save face. A Europeanisation of NATO cannot be the answer for Paris; these proposals offer a solution'.[93] But Belgium, Spain and Luxembourg – in principle all sympathetic to a Euro Corps – were sceptical of a European military unit in which Germans could not operate out of area and French forces were not prepared to operate inside it.[94] Thus the Franco-German initiative failed to win support, greatly to the relief of Britain.

It was, however, the NATO Rome summit on 7–8 November 1991 which was the key event in the immediate run up to the Maastricht Council, and more specifically in the preparation of the British package for the final phase of the negotiations. In substantive terms it marked agreement between France on the one hand and the United States on the other, in the form of a compromise to the effect that France was not going to rejoin NATO, and that, in return for American recognition of a complementary role for European multi-national structures, France would recognize the primacy of NATO as the essential forum for discussions on defence.[95] In domestic British terms, there were two key outcomes from the turbulent debate at the Rome summit. First, the Prime Minister held the debate up as 'proof' that, in the face of tough questioning from the American President, all European members of the Alliance recognized the centrality of NATO and the need for American forces in Europe.[96] Second, the summit provided political cover for London's key concession concerning a defence policy role for the European Union which, after intense British lobbying, the Americans now accepted.[97]

Nevertheless, as the Maastricht European Council loomed ever larger, the Foreign Secretary felt it necessary to launch a diplomatic offensive aimed at two audiences: that in national capitals and that in his own party. Hurd was particularly worried that his negotiating counterparts had not yet realized that, in contrast to what had happened under Mrs Thatcher, British intransigence on foreign and security policy would not be followed by substantial last-minute compromises.[98] For the benefit of his overseas audience, Hurd argued that London 'was prepared to compromise on everything except the fundamentals' and that, if London's partners were prepared to scale down their demands, it was ready to sign a treaty which would mark a significant move from the SEA.[99] To the domestic audience he took a more bellicose line, attacking the Commission's interference in 'the nooks and crannies of daily life', in the hope that talking tough would persuade potential rebels that London had fought as hard as possible and that if agreement could be reached it would be the best possible outcome for Britain.[100]

There were also selective government leakings to the press to the effect that Britain had already made concessions on a European defence policy and that, although Britain could accept joint actions in foreign policy, London was not willing to compromise on majority voting in foreign policy.[101] In the debate held in the House of Commons on 20 November, moreover, the motion re-echoed these themes and proposed that co-operation in foreign policy should safeguard the country's national interests. Tellingly, the debate passed without any detailed consideration of the issues, with both Mrs Thatcher and Neil Kinnock supportive of the government's position.[102]

The main difficulty faced by the government in the weeks immediately preceding Maastricht was in fact to come not from home but from abroad. Here, in private meetings with British officials, the Greek government made it clear that if WEU were to be a separate defence arm of the European Union as Britain advocated, and if it were denied WEU membership, it would veto the whole Treaty. The question of WEU enlargement, something to which Britain had long been opposed, therefore resurfaced to cast a shadow over the government's success in achieving many of its goals prior to the opening of the Maastricht Council.[103]

Aside from this, however, there remained four key points to be settled at Maastricht. First, there was the question of the exact wording of the defence clause: should it include the framing of a defence policy and not defence? Second, there was the question of whether WEU should be directly subordinate to the European Council, or whether, as the British argued, it should have issues sub-contracted through general guidelines. Third, there was the question of the purpose of the 1996 Treaty review of the defence clauses: should the next IGC automatically incorporate WEU into the EU as its defence identity, or should it be a stock-take of existing procedures? Fourth, there was the question of whether there should be a separate WEU declaration, implying independence for WEU, or whether it should be attached to the Treaty, suggesting subordination. The negotiating team recognized that having already secured its principal objectives, some concessions on these issues would be necessary to reach agreement.

THE MAASTRICHT EUROPEAN COUNCIL

In stark contrast to the traditional high politics assumption that issues of foreign policy and defence are non-negotiable, what was most striking about the debates at Maastricht on CFSP was that so much of it confirmed agreements which had already been reached. This was in stark contrast to the drama surrounding the social policy and EMU debates.[104] A key reason for this was that the negotiations were by now concerned with abstract questions about negotiators' preferences for one set of phrases rather than another. Indeed, at the end of October one minister frankly remarked that it was much easier to envisage acceptable compromises on foreign policy and defence, through a combination of 'fudged' Treaty language and deferred decisions, than in the areas of competence and institutional change.[105] The second-order profile of these issues was underlined by the fact that the defence clauses were negotiated in the margins of the Summit by the foreign ministers and WEU council, and then rubber stamped by the Heads of State and Government in the European Council.[106]

From the British point of view, the most important confirmatory elements were approval of the pillared structure of the Treaty and the removal of the federal vocation of the Union by the Dutch Presidency. The general objectives of a common foreign policy were approved, as were the institutional changes to incorporate the EPC secretariat in the Council of Ministers secretariat. At the request of the British Foreign Minister, the (rotating) presidency of the European Council, and not the Commission, represented the Union in all matters relating to CFSP. The Member States would share the right of policy initiative with the Commission. As for the constraint on independent action when a common policy had been agreed, an obligation to uphold the Union's position was agreed, but, when matters of vital national interest were at stake, a Member State could free itself from this commitment. In the UN Security Council, both Britain and France had to consult their partners about their positions, but were not obliged to uphold the Union's position (Article J.5[4]).[107]

There was again heated debate concerning majority voting for implementing joint actions in foreign policy, which by now was the most crucial point in the whole CFSP text. Douglas Hurd, with support from Denmark, Ireland and Portugal, continued to resist this. In searching for a compromise solution, diplomats drafted Article J.3(2), which permitted majority voting only when all Member States agreed so to do. In effect this agreed the principle of majority voting, but in practical terms rendered the formula unworkable.[108] The attached declaration which required members to avoid preventing unanimous decisions did not have a compulsory character.[109] Despite a year-long debate on what issues should automatically be considered for joint action, differences remained and London was successful in limiting the list to four areas in which majority voting might be considered.

On defence, the debate was contentious in so far as the majority of Member States still pressed for a commitment to the framing of defence policy. The eventual formula agreed was that the Treaty 'shall include all questions related to security of the Union, including the eventual framing of a common defence policy, which might in time lead to a common defence'. The Union was formally permitted to address defence policy in the short to medium term, but acquiring a defence role remained an issue for the longer term, with an open review of these arrangements in 1996.[110] This represented a concession from the British delegation, which had been opposed to any defence competence, although the concession was sufficiently nuanced to be imperceptible to all but the diplomats and governments closely involved in the debate.

Concerning WEU, in line with the Prime Minister's statement to the House of Commons in November, the British stubbornly resisted the formal subordination of WEU to the European Union, with some support from Ireland and Denmark. Here the agreement was that WEU would be the defence arm of the European Union *and* a contribution to the European pillar of NATO. This compromise formula permitted the European Union to request WEU 'which is an integral part of the development of the Union, to elaborate and implement decisions and actions of the Union, which have defence implications'.[111] But WEU retained autonomy and an identity independent of the European Council. The Treaty also endorsed closer co-operation between WEU/EU staffs and harmonization of the rotation and timing of the presidencies.

At British and Dutch request, a separate declaration created a small WEU operational planning cell of military personnel, and provided that the civilian secretariat would move from London to Brussels to be closer to the European institutions and NATO. In practical terms, WEU was given no military forces under its direct command and would remain dependent on NATO for surveillance, intelligence gathering and long-range transport support.[112] The price for London of this compromise on defence in the IGC-PU, however, was the enlargement of WEU, to which it had long been opposed. Thus the declaration extended an invitation to Denmark, Greece and Ireland, and the three non-EC European members of NATO, to accede or become observers to WEU. This was particularly galling given that the British had been opponents of Greek accession to WEU for some time. On balance, however, it was judged wisest not to call the Greek bluff over their threatened veto of the overall Treaty if accession to WEU was denied them.

CONCLUSION

The CFSP discussions at the IGC-PU touched on questions at the heart of the ambiguous identity of the European Community, and reopened wounds which had existed since the Community's inception. From the British perspective, the first imperative was to manage the actions and demands of its partners so as to achieve its own desiderata. As to how far it succeeded in this, the NATO Secretary General suggested that it was 'a points win to Britain'.[113] The creation of an intergovernmental pillar to deal with foreign and security policy issues and the greater coherence of West European foreign and defence efforts were all developments in the mainstream of British thinking and could be traced back to long-standing British preferences on foreign and security policy. Yet in defence discussions the government itself considered that it had made considerable concessions and, further, had accepted integrationist encroachments on British sovereignty. Unsatisfied with simply dealing with security issues, London had conceded that the European Union would have a defence policy competence which might even eventually include defence, a position to which they had been long opposed. On foreign policy, too, the government had over a 12-month period moved a considerable distance away from its starting point of accepting incremental adjustment to EPC towards acceptance of an ambitious rhetorical commitment to create a common foreign and security policy as a key component of the European Union, which included the possibility of majority voting.

But what was noticeable was the way in which the government successfully concealed these compromises from the public at large and from backbenchers in particular. The principal means by which it did this was to link a major restructuring of Britain's defence forces to the reshaping of NATO, rather than to a European defence identity. The reactivation of WEU was thus seen as an Atlanticist, NATO-friendly development which in principle and reality would reinforce rather than undermine NATO. It thus diffused domestic opposition to a major reduction of British armed forces whilst avoiding the appearance of any major reorientation of British defence policy away from NATO and towards Europe.

Moreover, few backbenchers were fully aware of the details of the CFSP clauses, and the government did all that it could to withhold detailed information and the draft treaty texts from them. Backbenchers were also unintentionally reassured by Delors' claim that ambitious objectives for CFSP were not matched by the procedural requirements to achieve them.[114] The government was aided along the way by the NATO Rome Summit, the failure of the Dutch 'federalist' draft and the removal of the federal vocation, all of which were presented to backbenchers as proof that the government's views on the dossier were prevailing.[115]

It would be wrong, however, to conclude from this that domestic concerns over the CFSP dossier were akin to the dog which failed to bark in the night. The point was that the government was acutely sensitive to the implications of back-bench dissent and the danger of being perceived to have sacrificed NATO and the British veto on foreign policy – especially if this was linked to the inevitable defence cuts following the end of the Cold War. The government's actions were therefore substantially shaped by the need to pre-empt, distract and reassure the domestic audience. Thus, there was a central tension in the government's handling of the CFSP dossier since, although on the face of it, defence and foreign policy was dominated by the executive the government was tightly constrained by the need it perceived to manage domestic pressures on the issue. Since this tension was exacerbated by the external pressures of international events and the actions of Britain's negotiating partners, it was ultimately perhaps surprising that the government managed to make both as many, and as few, concessions as it did.

NOTES

1.   See Nicole Gnesotto, 'Défense européenne: pourquoi pas les Douze?', *Politique Étrangère*, vol. 55, no. 4, 1990, pp. 881–3.
2.   See Edward Fursdon, *The European Defence Community: a History*, London, Macmillan, 1980.
3.   See William Wallace, 'European Defence Co-operation: the Reopening Debate', *Survival*, November–December 1984, vol. XXVI, no. 6, pp. 251–61, p. 252.
4.   Philippe de Schoutheete, 'The Creation of the Common Foreign and Security Policy: the Reform Debate during the IGC on Political Union', in Elfrieda Regelsberger, Philippe de Schoutheete and Wolfgang Wessels (eds), *Foreign Policy of the European Union: From EPC to CFSP and Beyond*, Boulder, Col./London, Lynne Rienner, 1997.
5.   William Wallace, 'Political Cooperation: Procedure as a Substitute for Policy', Wallace, et al., *Policy Making in the EC*, Chichester, John Wiley, 2nd ed., 1983, pp. 227–48.
6.   Geoffrey Edwards and Simon Nuttall, 'Common Foreign and Security Policy', in Duff, et al., *Maastricht and Beyond*, op. cit., pp. 84–103, p. 86.
7.   Panos Tsakaloyannis, 'The EC from Civilian Power to Military Intervention', in Juliet Lodge (ed.), *The European Community and the Challenge of the Future*, London, Pinter, 1989, pp. 241–55, pp. 247–8. Philippe de Schoutheete, *La Coopération Politique Européenne*, Brussels, Labor, 2nd ed., 1986.
8.   For the general implications of the reactivation see Panos Tsakaloyannis (ed.), *The Reactivation of WEU and Its Institutional Implications*, Maastricht, EIPA, 1985. For the links to the EC see Philippe de Schoutheete, 'Sub-systems of the European Community', in William Wallace, *Dynamics of European Integration*, London, RIIA/Pinter, 1990, pp. 106–20, p. 118.
9.   See Karel de Gucht and Stephan Keukeleire, 'The European Security Architecture: the Role of the European Community in Shaping a New European Geopolitical Landscape', *Studia Diplomatica*, vol. XLIV, no. 6, 1991, pp. 29–90.
10.   The Franco-German letter is reproduced in *Agence Europe*, 5238, 20 April 1990.
11.   See Louis W. Pauly, 'The Politics of European Monetary Union: National Strategies, International Implications', *International Journal*, vol. 47, 1991–2, pp. 93–111; Wayne Sandholtz, 'Choosing Union: Monetary Politics and Maastricht', *International Organisation*, vol. 47, no. 1, Winter 1993, pp. 1–40.
12.   For initial support for this idea see the speech by James A. Baker, *A New Europe, a New Atlanticism, Architecture for a New Era*, US Mission to the EC, Public Affairs Office, 12 December 1989.
13.   See President Bush's Berlin speech in May 1989; see also Peter Tarnoff, 'America's New Special Relationships', *Foreign Affairs*, vol. 69, no. 3, 1990, pp. 67–80.
14.   Author's interview with Nicholas Williams, Defence Policy Planning Section, NATO.

15. Author's interviews with NATO officials, Brussels, and MoD London.
16. Trevor Taylor, *Reshaping European Defence*, London, Royal Institute of International Affairs, 1994, p. 78.
17. Robert Keohane and Joseph Nye, 'Introduction', in Robert Keohane, Stanley Hoffmann and Joseph Nye (eds), *After the Cold War*, Boston, Mass., Harvard University Press, 1994, pp. 1–19, esp. 3–4.
18. Christopher Coker, 'The Special Relationship in the 1990s', *International Affairs*, vol. 68, no. 3, July 1992, pp. 407–22.
19. As to why this consensus came about see Anthony Forster, 'The United Kingdom', in Charles Anstis and Alexander Moens (eds), *Disconcerted Europe: the Search for a New Security Architecture*, Boulder, Colorado, Westview, 1993, pp. 135–58, p. 138. For a detailed discussion of this issue see Dan Keohane, 'The Approach of British Political Parties to a Defence Role for the European Community', *Government and Opposition*, vol. 27, no. 3, Summer 1992, pp. 299–310.
20. Conveniently overlooking the Suez fiasco, many on the right pointed to a long history of European indecisiveness, of weak countries often led by coalition governments unwilling to match foreign policy declarations to a commitment to deploy military force. The lack of support in the Falklands War and the Belgian government's refusal to sell munitions to the British in the Gulf War were only the most recent examples. Tim Congdon asserted in the *Spectator* that the world remained dominated by English-speaking nations and that 'Europe was by comparison something of a sideshow', quoted in 'Time to Choose', *Economist*, 26 September 1992, p. 36.
21. See Christopher Coker, 'The Special Relationship in the 1990s', op. cit., p. 416.
22. See Michael Heseltine's comments in *The Challenge of Europe: Can Britain Win?*, op. cit.
23. The clearest statement of this was made by Bill Cash in the defence debate in October 1991. *Parl. Deb. HC*, 14 October 199, col. 92. For the sovereignty argument see Norman Tebbit, *Parl. Deb. HC*, 21 November 1991, col. 482.
24. See *Defence and Security in the New Europe*, London, European Democratic Group, 1991.
25. Junor, *Major Enigma*, op. cit.
26. Author's interviews with Bill Cash and Teresa Gorman.
27. 'Against the Current', *Economist*, 8 June 1991, pp. 31–2.
28. Keith Hartley, 'The Defence Budget', *Defence Implications of Recent Events*, House of Commons Paper 320, Session 1989–90, London, HMSO, 1990, pp. 125–8, p. 125.
29. See David Greenwood, 'Expenditure and Management', in Peter Byrd (ed.), *British Defence Policy: Thatcher and Beyond*, London, Philip Allan, 1991, pp. 36–66, p. 58. See also *Defence Implications of Recent Events*, Tenth Report of the House of Commons Defence Committee, London, HMSO, 1990.
30. See Colin Brown, 'Treasury Demands 1 Billion Defence Cuts', *Independent*, 10 May 1990. See the 1990 Defence White Paper, *Statement on the Defence Estimates 1990*, Cmd 1022–1, London,

HMSO, April 1990.

31. Author's interview with Graham Mather, Director of the European Policy Forum. See also 'Any Ideas?', *Economist*, 7 November 1992, p. 30.

32. For an analysis see editorial, 'A Battle Shirked', *The Times*, 26 July 1990. See also 'Counting the Ploughshares', *Economist*, 2 June 1990, p. 31. For the importance of defence companies see Keith Hartley, Farooq Hussain, Ron Smith, 'The UK Defence Industrial Base', *Political Quarterly*, vol. 58, no. 1, January–March 1987, pp. 62–72, p. 63.

33. Public opinion in the European Community, Directorate General of Information, *Eurobarometer*, no. 34, 11 December 1990.

34. Author's interview Sir John Kerr.

35. Author's interviews with MoD and FCO officials.

36. Author's interviews with Cabinet Office, MoD and FCO officials.

37. For an analysis of the connection between the EC and NATO debates, see Anend Menon, Anthony Forster and William Wallace, 'A Common European Defence?', *Survival*, vol. 3, no. 34, Autumn 1992, pp. 98–118. The key players at official level in London were Sir John Goulden and Michael Ryder in the FCO and, in the MoD, Crispin Hain-Cole, Paul Flaherty and David Chuter and, in Brussels, Sir Michael Alexander and Catherine Roe.

38. The clearest public statement of this was made by Douglas Hurd quoted in David Usborne, 'Dutch Seek British Flexibility', *Independent*, 18 October 1991.

39. See the UK's non-paper of September 1990 contained in Presidency document 9233/90, Annex 2.

40. Author's interview with MoD and Foreign and Commonwealth Office officials and Sir John Kerr.

41. See the UK's non-paper *Draft Treaty Provisions on CFSP*, 26 February 1991 (unpublished).

42. The Alliance summit in July 1990 had declined the British initiative to give NATO this out-of-area mandate. See the British government submission to the IGC-PU, 'Defence and Security in Europe', dated 15 December 1990, unpublished. These points were reiterated by Douglas Hurd in the Churchill Memorial Lecture, Luxembourg, 19 February 1991.

43. See Michael Carver, *Tightrope Walking: British Defence Policy since 1945*, London, Hutchinson, 1992, p. 166.

44. Trevor Salmon, 'The Growing Pains of European Adolescence: Groping for a European Pillar', *Journal of European Integration*, vol. XVI, nos 2–3, Winter 1993, pp. 209–23.

45. Comments made by Pascal Lamy, Delors' Chef de Cabinet, quoted in Ross, *Jacques Delors*, op. cit., p. 96.

46. Calls from the State Department for a stronger West European role within the Alliance were matched by Pentagon warnings about a European caucus in NATO, and even the fear that Irish neutrality might through the European Council influence WEU and NATO. See Anthony Hartley, *America and Britain: Is the Relationship Still Special?*, London, Centre for Policy Studies, no. 137, 1994, p. 25.

47. Author's interview, Sir John Kerr and MoD officials.

48. Lawrence Freedman, 'Defence Policy', in Kavanagh and Seldon, *Major Effect*, pp. 269–82, p. 278.
49. For a discussion of the French perspective see Anand Menon, 'From Independence to Cooperation: France, NATO and European Security', *International Affairs*, no. 71, 1995, pp. 19–34.
50. Gnesotto, 'Défense européenne: pourquoi pas les Douze?', op. cit., pp. 881–3.
51. Author's interview Hans Mauch, responsible for WEU relations, Auswärtiges Amt, Bonn.
52. Author's interview Auswärtiges Amt officials. See also Philippe Lemaitre, 'Francais et Allemands – pourtant à l'origine du projet d'union politique?', *Le Monde*, 25 June 1991.
53. Author's interview with defence ministry officials, Bonn. For French preference for rhetoric over practical detail see the comments by Roland Dumas that all talk of details and procedures 'were secondary to the great question of principle'. Quoted in David Buchan, 'US Envoy Denies Nato's Holding Up EC Progress on Common Security', *Financial Times*, 2 May 1991.
54. See Ross, *Jacques Delors*, op. cit., p. 96. For the speech see Jacques Delors, 'European Integration and Security', *Survival*, March–April 1991, vol. XXXII, no. 2, pp. 99–109.
55. The so called 'Bartholomew Telegram' is discussed in *International Herald Tribune*, 14 March 1991. For continuing concern see Peter Ridell, 'America's Uneasy at New Europe', *Financial Times*, 28 June 1991.
56. See David Usborne, 'US Warns EC Not to Disrupt Role of NATO', *Independent*, 6 March 1991; Sarah Lambert, 'Washington's Alarm at EC Defence Plan', *Independent*, 9 March 1991.
57. Author's interviews NATO Headquarters, Brussels. For the DPC Press Communiqué see M-DPC-1 (91) 38, NATO Press Service, esp. para. 9.
58. Author's interviews, Auswärtiges Amt Bonn. See Michael Evans 'British Troops to Spearhead New NATO Force', *The Times*, 25 May 1991, and Joseph Fitchett, 'The New NATO: a Mobile Force for Post-Cold War Era', *International Herald Tribune*, 27 May 1991.
59. Author's interviews.
60. But Article 228A of the EC pillar on trade sanctions is justiciable.
61. For the Luxembourg draft see *Europe Documents*, 1722/3, 5 July 1991. Schoutheete argues that the implications of the Luxembourg draft treaty were more far reaching than was realized at the time. Schoutheete, 'Creation of the CFSP', p. 13; for the Commission's view see Ross, *Delors*, op. cit., pp. 146–8.
62. This was an idea initially put forward by the Commission in March 1991. See *Europe Documents*, 1697/98, 7 March 1991. For the full text see *Europe Documents*, 1722/23, 5 July 1991.
63. David Buchan, 'Horse Trading Before High Noon', *Financial Times*, 28 June 1991.
64. Ibid.
65. Initially Major had said that any commitment to a federal vocation depended on how the term was defined. In response to back-bench pressure, Major's position hardened *after* the Luxembourg Summit.

Compare the comments of Major in the House of Commons, Question Time, 27 June 1991, with his statement, 30 June 1991, on his return from the Luxembourg European Council; see *Keesing's Contemporary Archive*, June 1991, 38295.

66.   'She Makes Her Stand', *Economist*, 29 June 1991, p. 27.

67.   Author's interview with Sir John Kerr.

68.   Author's interviews with Sir George Gardiner and Bill Cash.

69.   In fact this was far from true, since the defeat of the Dutch draft was brought about by nine Member States that agreed in principle with the draft, but felt that too little time was left to re-examine many of the issues which a new structure raised. Only Britain, France and Denmark opposed the Dutch draft treaty in principle. See Robert Wester, 'The Netherlands and European Political Union', in Laursen and van Hoonacker, *The IGC-PU*, op. cit., p. 172. Ross, *Delors*, op. cit., p. 171.

70.   Hogg and Hill, *Too Close to Call*, op. cit., p. 140.

71.   George Brock, 'Dutch Challenged over Draft Treaty', *Daily Telegraph*, 28 September 1991, p. 9; Robin Oakley and Philip Webster, 'Hurd Seeks to Calm Tory Fears on Federal Europe', *The Times*, 9 October 1991.

72.   The Dutch had proposed unanimity for joint actions, except where Member States decided unanimously to do otherwise (Article B.2). See *Europe Documents*, 1733/4, 3 October 1991.

73.   Menon, et al., 'A Common European Defence', op. cit., p. 109.

74.   See *Statement on the Defence Expenditures: Britain's Defence for the 1990s*, presented to Parliament by the Secretary of State for Defence, cmnd 1559–I, London, HMSO, 1991, p. 39. For the paucity of the defence debate see John Wilkinson, *Parl. Deb. HC*, 15 October 1991, col. 205.

75.   Louise Richardson, 'British State Strategies', in Robert Keohane, Stanley Hoffman and Joseph Nye (eds), *After the Cold War*, Boston, Mass., Harvard University Press, 1994, pp. 148–69, p. 160.

76.   Private information. See articles by John Reid and Menzies Campbell both in the *Independent*, 17 August 1991; see also Carver, *Tightrope Walking*, op. cit., p. 172.

77.   See the comments of one shadow minister quoted in Ivo Dawnay, 'Labour Becalmed in Euro Fog', *Financial Times*, 4 December 1991.

78.   These fears were compounded by criticisms by Prince Charles. Even the Queen was reported to have made her dismay clear to senior Tories. See 'Royal Family and Generals Unite to Fight Defence Cuts', *Sunday Times*, 13 October 1991.

79.   The references were made by Martin O'Neill, *Parl. Deb. HC*, 14 October 1991, col. 69; Julian Amery, ibid., col. 78; Bill Cash, ibid., col. 92; John Wilkinson, *Parl. Deb. HC*, 15 October 1991, col. 204; John Cartwright, ibid., col. 215. Only Cartwright and Cash directly referred to the IGC-PU in the debates.

80.   Author's interviews at the Foreign and Commonwealth Office and MoD. Senior ministers did, however, remain concerned about Mrs Thatcher's position on these issues.

81.   A Royal United Services Institute sponsored study suggested that a European defence force would require 1.5% of GDP on top of current

expenditure levels sustained for ten years. Quoted in 'The Defence of Europe', *Economist*, 25 February 1995, p. 25.

82. Author's interview, Sir John Kerr.
83. The Anglo-Italian Declaration is reproduced in *Europe Documents*, 1735, 5 October 1991. For the genesis of the Anglo-Italian Declaration see *Europe Documents*, 1735, 5 October 1991. The Italian foreign minister claimed Hurd offered support for this initiative in return for Italian support in defeating the Dutch draft treaty though some sort of initiative had been under discussion since Easter of 1991. See Gianni de Michelis, *La Stampa*, 16 October 1991.
84. There was also a close personal relationship between Douglas Hurd and the Italian Foreign Minister, Gianni de Michelis. For the latter's views of the significance of the Anglo-Italian Declaration see *Europe Documents*, 5589, 15 October 1991.
85. Douglas Hurd quoted in Philip Stevens and Robert Mauthner, 'Hurd Treads a Slow but Confident Path to Summit', *Financial Times*, 5 December 1991.
86. Author's interviews with Foreign and Commonwealth Office officials and Sir John Kerr.
87. The Franco-German Initiative is reproduced in *Atlantic Documents*, 1738, 18 October 1991.
88. *Atlantic Documents*, 1738, 18 October 1991.
89. Roland Dumas, Speech to WEU Council of Ministers, 29th October 1991, *Ambassadé de France*, London, Service de Presse.
90. Author's interview, Rene de Maesschalck, NATO/WEU Policy Planning Section, Belgian Ministry of Defence.
91. David Usborne, 'Near Hysteria at Castle de Haar', *Independent*, 8 October 1991. For the wider discussions of the initiative see *Financial Times*, 29 October 1991.
92. The Franco-German initiative was prepared in the Auswärtiges Amt and was unveiled by Kohl with a great deal of irritation from his own pro-NATO defence ministry. Author's interviews in the Auswärtiges Amt, Bonn.
93. Quoted in David Usborne, 'Bonn and Paris Derail Britain's Defence Plans', *Independent*, 7 October 1991. The French immediately announced that one of three armoured divisions in Germany would remain, to form part of the new Euro Corps. Quentin Peel, 'An Odd Couple Still in Tune', *Financial Times*, 14 November 1991.
94. Author's interview, René de Maesschalck. For the British reaction see 'Service Chiefs Launch Assault on Euro-Army', *Sunday Telegraph*, 3 November 1991.
95. Author's interviews, NATO Headquarters, Brussels. For the communiqués see 'The Alliance's Strategic Concept', in *Transformation of the Alliance*, NATO Office of Information and Press, 1991, pp. 50–1, para. 52.
96. See John Major's Lord Mayor's Banquet speech, quoted in Philip Stevens, 'UK May Make Concessions on EC Integration', *Financial Times*, 12 November 1991.
97. Author's interviews with MoD officials.

98. In June Mitterrand had said that a solution would be found in the last five minutes of the Maastricht European Council, implying that Britain would cave in if enough pressure were applied.
99. Douglas Hurd, *The European Community in a Wider Europe*, Speech to the Atlantic Council in the Hague, 5 November 1991, Verbatim Service, VS026/91, p. 2.
100. See for example Philip Stevens, 'Hurd Seeks EC Deal in His Own Image', *Financial Times*, 6 November 1991; Douglas Hurd, 'Our Message for Maastricht: Progress Without Shackles', *Financial Times*, 12 November 1991.
101. George Jones, 'Major Aims at Compromise on Political Union Treaty', *Daily Telegraph*, 8 November 1991; Michael Binyon, 'UK Ministers Hint at Bottom Line', *Daily Telegraph*, 13 November 1991; 'An Omen for Maastricht', *The Times*, 13 November 1991; Peter Ridell, 'Hung up on Maastricht', *The Times*, 15 November 1991.
102. For Mrs Thatcher's comments, see *Parl. Deb. HC*, 20 November 1991, col. 293. For Mr Kinnock's speech, see *Parl. Deb. HC*, 20 November 1991, col. 290. The sole reference to the shift which had occurred on CFSP since the start of the IGC-PU was made by George Robertson MP, Labour spokesman on European Affairs, at 1.30 am on 18 December in an almost deserted Chamber: see *Parl. Deb. HC*, 18 December 1991, col. 413.
103. 'Greece's Price is Place in WEU', *Independent*, 9 December 1991; *Financial Times*, 29 November 1991. For the range of Greek motivations see Arthur den Hartog, 'Greece and European Political Union', in Laursen and van Hoonacker (eds), *Intergovernmental Conference on Political Union*, pp. 79–97, p. 94.
104. See for instance Schoutheete, 'The Creation of CFSP', op. cit., p. 21.
105. Quoted in *Financial Times*, 26 October 1991.
106. Author's interview, Richard Tibbles, WEU Secretariat.
107. The article says that permanent members of the Security Council will ensure the defence of the position and interests of the Union.
108. Author's interview with David Williamson, Secretary General of the European Commission. The solution was modelled on Article 130S (environment as introduced by the SEA), where provision for QMV had never actually been used.
109. See Florika Fink-Hoojer, 'The Common Foreign and Security Policy of the European Union', *European Journal of International Law*, vol. 5, no. 2, 1994, pp. 173–98, p. 180.
110. *The Treaty on European Union*, Art. B Title One, *Treaty on European Union*, Brussels, European Communities, 1992.
111. Article J.4(2), ibid.
112. See the comments by Secretary General Manfred Wörner to the European Peoples' Party Colloquium on Security and Defence, 2 July 1991.
113. Hella Pick, 'Points Win to Britain Says NATO', *Guardian*, 12 December 1991, p. 2. Christopher Hill described it as a 'partial victory'. Christopher Hill, 'Foreign Policy', in Peter Catterall (ed.), *Contemporary Britain: an Annual Review 1992*, Aldershot, Dartmouth,

1993, pp. 132–44.

114. Delors' speech to the European Parliament is reproduced in *Bulletin to the European Communities*, supplement 1/92, Luxembourg, 1992. See also Ross, *Delors*, op. cit., p. 189. Lord Bruce later remarked, 'the text is itself is replete with generalities, ambiguities and inferences open to a wide variety of interpretation, which studiously avoids precise definition'. 'Reading Between the Maastricht Lines', *The Times*, 1 May 1992.

115. See Tristan Garel-Jones, *Parl. Deb. HC*, 18 December 1991, col. 301.

5 Institutional Reform: the European Parliament

A wide range of institutional and legal questions were debated in the IGC-PU. Among the most important were proposals for developing the role of the European Court of Justice, strengthening the role of the court of auditors and the establishment of a committee of the regions. There was also much discussion of the institutional arrangements necessary to make common policies effective in the key Justice and Home Affairs areas of frontier controls, internal security, and asylum and immigration policies. These debates were linked by two key factors. The first of these was the question of the pillared structure of the proposed EU and whether it should have one institutional mix of responsibilities, competences and decision-making procedures which would be used for all issues which it handled. The alternative to this was a different mix of Commission, EP and ECJ involvement, depending on the policy sector in question. The second factor which linked the institutional debates of 1990 to 1991 was concern over the legitimacy and democratic credentials of existing institutions. This meant that the institutional debates were closely bound up with discussions at the IGC-PU of how to strengthen the legitimacy of decision-making, discussions in which the role of the European Parliament played a pivotal part.

So far as Britain was concerned, furthermore, the debates concerning the role and competences of the EC's supranational institutions raised two particular questions. These were the symbolic issue of the sovereignty of Parliament, and the role of Westminster in the British political system. Indeed, as has been described in Chapter 1, these were two of the questions which had for a long time stood at the centre of British ambivalence about Europe. While all the institutional debates touched on these questions, however, it was the issue of the European Parliament which highlighted them most clearly. It is thus principally with the European Parliament, and the concomitant questions of the relationship of the Commission and the European Council with it, that this chapter is concerned.

The paradox of this particular issue is why, despite the symbolic importance of the issue of enhancing the powers of another parliamentary institution, the British government ended by making a wide range of concessions on EP powers. Some scholars have argued that British behaviour can be traced to the influence of Chancellor Kohl and Bonn's linkage of strengthening of the EP to the issue of Economic and Monetary Union, and certainly Kohl was at the forefront of arguing the case for strengthening the EP.[1] However, close examination of this issue reveals that, while external pressure on the British government did lead to some convergence between Britain and its partners, the exact nature of the concessions offered by the British government was ultimately shaped by some important domestic considerations.

THE BACKGROUND

The origins of the European Parliament lay in the Treaty of Rome, which had provided for a Common Assembly (from 1966 formally termed the European Parliament though the term was not included in the SEA) with limited power to approve an annual report and power of censure over the Commission. The Assembly also had power to approve parts of the budget of the Communities, and the right to be consulted on legislative proposals on some issues. Overall, it was clear that the crucial relationship was that between the Council and the Commission, since the Assembly was perceived as little more than democratic window-dressing with few real powers.[2]

Thus the EP was 'born hungry and frustrated' and, in the absence of any final constitutional settlement, it continued to lobby Member States for greater powers and a federal structure.[3] By 1975, incremental enhancements had given the EP some important budgetary powers, namely the power to have the final word (within pre-determined limits) on the level of non-obligatory expenditure, the right to reject the budget as a whole and the power to call the Commission to account on their management of expenditure. Importantly, too, a 'conciliation procedure' was introduced which made the EP a direct interlocutor with the Council on legislative measures with substantial budgetary implications. In other legislative areas, the Parliament built on its limited right of consultation, although its role remained advisory only.

With the boost to its legitimacy of the first direct European elections in 1979, however, Members of the European Parliament felt empowered to demand greater influence, notably in the areas of monetary and foreign policy co-operation. This demand was premised on a more democratic decision-making process in which the Parliament hoped to play a leading role.[4] But it was to be the 1987 Single European Act which was the major breakthrough in terms of the scope of the EP's legislative role.

The SEA, for example, gave the EP the right to reject the Council's text, with the Council then needing unanimity to override the veto. It also introduced a two-reading procedure for legislation which allowed the EP the right to propose amendments to the Council's text (instead of just the Commission's proposal), with the possibility that the Commission could reject them, with the Council left with the final decision.

During the period from 1987 to the end of 1990, the EP proved itself capable of reorganizing its internal procedures to accommodate its new powers and used the provision of specific time-limited stages to the legislative process to great practical effect.[5] In addition, by asserting its claim as the legitimate representative of the European electorate, it also threatened to hold up any EC enlargement which was not accompanied by a strengthening of the EP.[6]

Following the agreement to convene the IGC-PU of 1990 to 1991, the EP was the first to put forward proposals.[7] These fell into four categories. The first concerned its legislative functions, which it argued should be shared with the Council through a co-decision procedure. In effect, the Council and EP would act as the co-legislator, with nothing reaching the statute book unless the majority of 518 Members of the European Parliament approved it. The second proposal was the right to initiate legislation when the Commission failed to act. Third, MEPs demanded the right to elect the President of the Commission and the College of Commissioners, by aligning the mandate of the Commission with that of the EP. Finally, the EP argued for powers of assent for Treaty amendments in effect giving it a veto over any new treaty. These formed the core of the EP's proposals for the IGC-PU and were elaborated in further submissions.[8] At their heart, the proposals implied a federal structure, with the Council and EP to serve as the two chambers of a joint legislature.

The Commission's submission to the IGC was by contrast based on the general premise of maintaining the existing balance of power between the three main Community institutions.[9] It opposed giving the EP co-decision powers and a right of initiative, particularly the latter, since it would undermine the primary role of the Commission as filter in the legislative process. It also opposed EP approval of individual Commissioners, which it feared would undermine the collegiate nature of the Commission.[10] In general, MEPs felt a certain amount of resentment that the Commission 'had its snout in the negotiating trough' and could not be relied upon to look after the Parliament's interest.[11]

However, neither the EP nor the Commission was directly involved in the negotiations, and both had to rely on sympathetic proxy governments to argue their case. In this regard, the German, Italian and Belgium governments were the most active in supporting the EP's demands. A number of the EP's ideas were specifically reiterated in the Belgian Memorandum published in March 1990.[12] In April, these received further support from Kohl and Mitterrand, who reaffirmed that priority should be given to strengthening the Union's political legitimacy.[13]

Overall then, by November 1990 when John Major became Prime Minister, the conventional wisdom among a majority of Member States was that the way to provide a stronger democratic legitimacy to EC decision-making was to reinforce the powers of the European Parliament, the most important of which were legislative powers and investiture of the Commission.[14] Alongside Britain, there was a small group of states that opposed this, including Portugal, Denmark and Ireland. However, this group had indicated to British negotiators that they would eventually accept a strengthening of the EP at the closure of the negotiations. The position of France was more significant and more unpredictable. The French government, historically the closest to the overall British position of scepticism, was an increasingly uncertain partner on the question. To British officials it was not clear how far a French (socialist) government was willing to subordinate the issue of enhancing the EP to its more important goal of securing Monetary Union.[15] Since Chancellor Kohl had linked the EP's fortunes to those of the EMU talks, the battle over the Parliament threatened to be divisive.[16]

THE DOMESTIC CONTEXT

The sovereignty of the Westminster Parliament is a central concern of British political elites. As Anne Deighton notes, Westminster has 'acquired an extraordinarily potent image as the font of democratic authority, accountability and law'.[17] Both major political parties see this parliamentary sovereignty as a key component of national sovereignty, despite or perhaps because of the erosion of the influence of

Westminster in shaping European legislation. There is also a bipartisan belief that the legitimacy of the EC comes from governments acting in the Council of Ministers, and not through the directly elected MEPs in the European Parliament.

It is true that the Labour Party had become more pro-European in the 1980s, but it should also be remembered that it took very little to look pro-European in comparison with the implacably hostile policy of Mrs Thatcher.[18] Moreover, Labour's pro-European stance was largely a product of the leadership's position, *renovateurs* within the party and success in the 1989 European elections, rather than a widespread shift in the position of the parliamentary party or the constituencies.[19] The Labour Parliamentary Party was particularly uneasy about the concept of 'Political Union' and in one survey nearly half the Westminster MPs were opposed to giving more powers to the EP.[20] In practical terms, the Labour leadership was therefore only cautiously supportive of increasing the powers of the EP, and reluctant to move beyond a vague rhetorical commitment to solve the democratic deficit. It was not because they had no ideas that the Labour front bench made no proposals – these were amply supplied by an active British Labour Group secretariat in Brussels – but rather because any proposals might raise the spectre of internal divisions for little electoral advantage.[21]

Of the two main parties, however, it had always been the Conservative Party which identified itself most consciously and vociferously with the notion of parliamentary sovereignty, viewing Britain's role as a great power as part and parcel of that sovereignty. It was true that as developments inside the EC increasingly cast doubt on this claim, some Conservative leaders, notably Sir Geoffrey Howe, modified their argument, contending that what was really happening was a 'pooling of sovereignty' which still preserved Britain's influence.[22] Overall, however, the position was that practical moves towards closer integration went ahead, yet government ministers continued to repeat their customary mantras about the importance of parliamentary sovereignty.

The ultimate proof of successive governments' reluctance – and inability – to come to terms with the dichotomy between European integration and parliamentary sovereignty was Mrs Thatcher's negotiation of the SEA, which extended the powers of the EP through the co-operation and assent procedure. So far as the Prime Minister was concerned at the time, these were insignificant concessions surrendered in exchange for the more significant goal of establishing the single market.[23] It was only subsequently that Thatcher's misgivings were aired, when in her Bruges speech in September 1988 she raised the spectre of diminished Westminster sovereignty *vis-à-vis* the EP and warned against any further transfer of powers to Strasbourg.

Thatcher's view found widespread support on the right wing of the Conservative Party, especially in the No Turning Back Group which was even more explicit in arguing that the sacrifice of sovereignty embodied in the SEA was only made in order to overcome opposition to the creation of the internal market. Having secured this goal, a line could now be drawn against any further diminution of the sovereignty of Westminster.[24] But the left wing of the party was not predisposed to enhance the powers of the EP either. Michael Heseltine's suggestion for an upper house composed of national parliamentarians who would share the parliamentary function[25] was ill-received by the EP, which considered the proposal no substitute for increasing the primary powers of Strasbourg.[26]

The only element inside the Conservative Party pressing for greater powers for the EP was the Euro MPs. They argued in pragmatic terms that holding the Commission to account and permitting the EP to initiate legislative proposals would effectively constrain the European Commission.[27] However, the influence of the Conservative MEPs within the party 'was almost non-existent'.[28] MEPs had no significant profile in domestic politics[29] and were treated with suspicion and as professional rivals by most Westminster colleagues.[30] Moreover, as Mrs Thatcher turned against the European Community, a growing gap emerged between the Prime Minister and Conservative MEPs, whose influence was further reduced by the loss of a quarter of their members in the 1989 European elections.[31]

As far as public opinion was concerned, the evidence was that there was no particular interest in the European Parliament, or the democratic deficit, with turnout at European elections the lowest in the Community.[32] Eurobarometer data collected in October 1990 showed that 42 per cent of those sampled wanted a more important role for the EP compared with 30 per cent against it, and 39 per cent of no fixed view.[33] This neutral data therefore underlined that the issue of EP enhancement was most immediately of concern to the political elite.

By the opening of the IGC-PU in December 1990, the forces of domestic opposition to increased EP powers were thus already massed. Enhancing the powers of the EP was seen by both parliamentarians and the government as a threat to British sovereignty and a challenge to Westminster, and ministers were acutely aware that backbenchers 'had a juicy bone in their mind's eye' when they thought of EP ambitions.[34] Moreover, although opposition was articulated largely within the political elite, there was every chance that it would spill over into public opinion in view of the issues of national sovereignty and identity with which it was bound up.

OBJECTIVES FOR THE EUROPEAN PARLIAMENT

There was, therefore, bipartisan agreement at Westminster that EP enhancement had gone far enough with the SEA.[35] This was in keeping with the general feeling amongst policy-makers that control of the integration process should ultimately rest with Member States themselves using intergovernmental procedures, rather than with the EP, perceived as by far the most integrationist of the supranational institutions. In addition to the constitutional and political implications of strengthening the EP, there was also an unquantifiable feeling that the EP could normally be guaranteed to oppose the British governments on specific issues, for example always wanting to spend more and consistently resisting reform of the Common Agricultural Policy.

Yet in formulating its negotiating objectives, the government had to balance its own objections against the clear desire of a majority of its partners to act over the EP. There were two additional reasons for not coming to the negotiating table empty handed. The first was a feeling that London, 'the home of the mother of parliaments', should be seen to be making a positive contribution to the debate on parliamentary democracy. The second was the more practical consideration that the EP might have to be offered something to avoid a head-on confrontation over the ratification process.[36]

The substance of the British proposals, however, reflected very clearly the government's desire to respect the concerns of MPs. Hurd was prepared to countenance some changes to the EP's non-legislative roles based on the Westminster model.[37] The British therefore proposed to increase EP scrutiny powers, making it the watchdog of the Community's finances. In Britain, the Audit Department backed by Parliament's Public Accounts Committee is an extremely important element of financial control. The expenditure programmes and policies of the Commission were thought by the government to 'cry out' for similar control and, although the Audit Court had long existed, the Commission treated it with contempt. The British government therefore hoped to improve matters by harnessing the Audit Court's findings more closely with the EP, which the Commission might find more difficult to ignore.

The government also proposed a greater role for national parliaments, taking as its template the work of the House of Commons Select Committee on the European Communities.[38] This would secure a number of goals. First, it would reduce the influence of the Commission, a popular move among the government's own supporters, since Commission power was a perennial fear of the right wing of the Conservative Party.[39] Second, it offered the tactical advantage that London would appear open to persuasion on at least some of the issues on the agenda. Third, it might exploit the tension between the EP and the Commission and deflate the EP's more ambitious demands by directing its institutional militancy towards reining in the powers of the Commission rather than the Council.[40]

The proposals were also in part a tactical response to the demands from London's partners to enhance the role of the European Parliament.[41] This then was not a genuine attempt to strengthen the EP, because the government did not want the EP to adopt wholesale the Westminster parliamentary model of executive scrutiny and accountability. Nor was there a strong commitment to these ideas, and London was certainly not willing to pay a price to secure these goals. At root, the British proposals were based on the hope that they would shift their partners' focus of attention away from granting the EP new legislative functions, a move which was perceived as provocative to Westminster MPs.[42]

It should be noted that most officials directly involved in the negotiations, notably Sir John Kerr, expressed considerable doubts concerning these proposals on two counts. First, they doubted whether the proposals would be accepted by other governments in place of greater legislative powers.[43] In particular, officials argued that, whilst the EP would not refuse new powers of scrutiny and accountability, its primary interest was not in controlling the EC executive, but rather in inserting itself more directly in the legislative and decision-making process. Over the longer term, this implied a diminution of both the powers of the Commission and the Council of Ministers, and it should therefore be this ambition which the government should address. Second, the negotiating team did not have a clear line from ministers on what they might be willing to accept, beyond the limited proposals the British had put forward.

The negotiators were therefore concerned this might weaken their ability to indicate particular sticking-points for the government. However, these arguments fell on deaf ears at ministerial level, and the British position as the IGC-PU opened therefore remained vague, based on increased powers of scrutiny and accountability for the EP and opposition to any form of co-decision, investiture or extension of the assent procedure.

THE TREATY NEGOTIATIONS

The situation as the IGC-PU commenced was that a majority of Member States (Belgium, Germany, Greece, Italy, the Netherlands, Spain and to some extent France) had in principle accepted the EP's request for co-decision powers with the Council, whilst Britain and Denmark were against, and Portugal and Ireland were not persuaded.[44] However, as the negotiations got underway, different alliances appeared on specific issues. Thus, on the central issue of a legislative role for the EP, Germany supported a right of initiative for the EP, and a form of co-decision which strengthened the role of the EP in the legislative process.[45] In contrast, Belgium, the Netherlands and Italy, while generally considered 'pro-Parliament', did not support a right of initiative or any proposal that undermined the powers of the Commission.[46]

A second feature of the debate was that the united front of the EP and the Commission quickly broke down, leading to acrimonious relations between the Commission President and the European Parliament.[47] This forced the Commission to fight on two fronts, while it continued to argue for increased EP power and its own continued role as initiator of proposals and filter of EP amendments.[48] Ultimately, however, the Commission proposals tabled in March 1991 were perceived by Member States as a transparent 'and wholly absurd' attempt to increase its own power.[49]

In this situation, the British supported proposals to establish an EP Committee of Enquiry, the right of petition, and the creation of a community ombudsman which were the only detailed reforms which were widely acceptable.[50] The issue of enhancing the role of national parliaments in the EC decision-making process attracted less support, since national parliamentary traditions varied across the EC, and it was difficult to agree a particular model on which to base Treaty clauses.[51] Nevertheless, the British negotiating strategy was an early tactical success, since it bolstered the credibility of the UK's bargaining position without increasing the legislative power of the EP.

However, when the Luxembourg Presidency produced a first treaty draft, pulling together its ideas on 12 April, and then published a formal draft treaty on 17 June, it was clear that the British had not succeeded in heading-off proposals for legislative powers.[52] The draft also included an article on co-decision to which the government, alongside Denmark, had from the outset been implacably opposed.[53] On the issue of Commission investiture, the draft proposed consultation between the Council and the EP on the nomination of the President, with the whole College of Commissioners submitted to the EP for approval (so-called assent procedure).[54] On the remaining issues, the draft was either silent or maintained the *status quo*. On the subject of other legislative functions, no mention was made of an EP right of initiative, or the assent procedure. On the issue of extending the Commission term to coincide with the EP's mandate it proposed that the four-year term of office of the Commission was retained.

There were some elements of the draft that appealed to the British government since the number of occasions on which the co-decision procedure came into operation would be relatively few.[55] In contrast, the draft would undoubtedly enhance the power of the EP in the legislative process, not least by giving it power of scrutiny over delegated (implementing) legislation, which had hitherto been decided by governments and the Commission through the comitology process.[56] There was also the implication from British ministers that opposition to co-decision was, in the end, something on which 'it would not be impossible to compromise'.[57]

By June, moreover, the production of a second draft treaty by the Luxembourg Presidency, coupled with the scheduling of the first full Westminster parliamentary debate on the negotiations on 26 June, had triggered active domestic dissent on the European question. As already noted, in the second week of June, the Bruges Group called for an orchestrated campaign to force the Prime Minister to take a tougher line in the IGC.[58] In an interview with the *Evening Standard*, Nicholas Ridley publicly raised doubts over the Prime Minister's failure to give a lead, and, in an echo of Enoch Powell's stance in 1974, claimed that European policy was more important than party unity.[59]

Douglas Hurd led moves to isolate potential rebels, and the Prime Minister also weighed in with two speeches emphasizing the damaging electoral impact of party divisions and emphasizing that there would be no general election until the IGCs were concluded.[60] Yet, critically, although Europe now became a live issue in the domestic debate, the right wing of the Conservative Party failed to focus on the issue of the EP.[61] In some respects there was an accidental aspect to this. The rapid replacement of the first Luxembourg draft treaty by the second wrong footed opponents of any compromise on the EP. Moreover, the House of Lords Select Committee, one of the most important sources of information for MPs, found its own enquiry on the first draft was overtaken by this turn of events.[62]

At the same time, the government was careful to try to manage the situation to its advantage. Not only did the Foreign Secretary specifically ask that no draft treaty be deposited in the House of Commons Library,[63] but the government also studiously avoided providing an interpretation of these technically complex drafts in memorandum form.[64] Instead, the Prime Minister gave general assurances that a willingness to participate in the negotiations was not incompatible with a robust defence of British interests.[65] With little evidence to the contrary, MPs had little choice but to accept the government's arguments that nothing had been decided and that Britain was not isolated on the issue of the EP.[66]

In the parliamentary debate held two days before the Luxembourg Council (both took place at the end of June) attention therefore focussed on the recently aired possibility of a British opt out from Stage Three of a single currency and the federal vocation contained in the Treaty.[67] One explanation for this was that the sheer number of issues at the top of the political agenda crowded out the issue of the EP. In particular, however, the issue of the federal goal became the one most clearly identified as a threat to national sovereignty.

On the question of why this happened, Eurosceptics had good reason to avoid the issue of the EP, because an anomaly lies at the heart of the Eurosceptic claim that the EC was undemocratic: to democratize the EC would lead to greater accountability and legitimacy for EC actions and thereby strengthen it in relation to national parliaments.[68] There was also some feeling amongst pro-Europeans in the party that Eurosceptics had spent so long deriding the EP and MEPs that they would look ridiculous if they now claimed it was an issue which engaged British sovereignty in the same way as a single currency.[69] This helps shed light on why the commitment to a federal goal (alongside EMU) was taken up as the main challenge to British sovereignty, rather than enhancing the powers of the EP, even though some of the Eurosceptics realized the removal of the term 'federa' from the second Luxembourg draft was little guarantee of anything.[70]

If Mrs Thatcher had chosen to point her guns at the issue of the European Parliament it is possible that the dossier might have played differently.[71] But without a significant senior figure in the party to speak out on the issue, and with little information in supply, the EP figured little in the 26 June debate. The Labour Party chose to avoid the issue,[72] and it was in fact only mentioned by a lone right-wing Conservative back bench MP, Jonathan Aitken. Aitken raised two fundamental issues, the single currency and the question of co-decision. He argued that co-decision was 'unworkable in practice and wrong in principle', constituting a 'litmus test' of whether Britain should veto the political union Treaty.[73] Though a lone voice, it should be noted, however, that Aitken was Joint Chairman of the influential European Reform Group and headed a faction whose support would be crucial for the ratification of any agreement reached at Maastricht.[74] The EP issue was therefore never fully diffused and, as with the foreign and security policy, the events of June left the Prime Minister wary of its potential to mobilize opposition.[75]

This awkward domestic situation, in which the issue of the EP was not directly addressed but concepts closely affecting it, such as national sovereignty, were well to the fore, led to a dual negotiating strategy emerging. First, the government sought to postpone decisions that had awkward domestic ramifications. Major, for instance, devoted considerable effort to convincing fellow Heads of Government, particularly Mitterrand and Kohl, that the Luxembourg Summit be used as a stocktaking exercize rather than an occasion to endorse specific clauses in the Luxembourg draft treaty.[76] In this he was successful, and the summit communiqué was deliberately vague on the question of co-decision.[77]

The second element of government strategy was the deliberate 'talking' up of opposition to the draft treaty to provide a smoke screen which would 'throw potential rebels off the scent'. Thus in the press conference after the Luxembourg Council, John Major specifically referred to British opposition to the proposals for the EP, echoing his Foreign Secretary's position that legislative power for the EP 'was not at all attractive'.[78] This strategy of a tough posture on the EP, and the postponement of potentially difficult problems, largely paid off, and the government emerged from this period looking tough on the question of enhancement of EP powers in the eyes of both fellow negotiators and its own backbenchers.[79] Meanwhile, the government had avoided disclosing its negotiating hand fully.[80]

With the parliamentary recess of the summer of 1991 providing an opportunity to review the negotiations,[81] it became increasingly apparent that the issue of enhanced powers for the EP was less important from the British perspective than had initially been anticipated. Up to this point, ministerial meetings to discuss the issue of the EP had been repeatedly cancelled or the agenda overtaken by more pressing matters, notably foreign and security policy, social policy and the single currency, where the negotiations were furthest away from British objectives. Meetings scheduled to discuss the EP, in particular co-decision procedure, new competence chapters and majority voting, were squeezed off the agenda or the time devoted to them so limited that the British government's position remained unclear until the Prime Minister was directly engaged in the discussions.

Despite the fact that the German negotiators continued to argue that the Luxembourg draft did not go far enough and continued to press for 'full co-decision', that is to say positive approval by both EP and Council, as a condition of adopting legislation, there was now no clear majority for this view.[82] What was also apparent was that, although the British strategy of proposing non-legislative functions in the hope of preventing legislative proposals had been unsuccessful, the majority of governments was not in fact considering a true sharing of legislative functions between the EP and the Council. What they envisaged was rather the power for the EP to block some legislation in a very limited range of areas, something which was less out of tune with British wishes, and there was some indication at official level that the French government considered it in the same way.[83] A number of meetings with Chancellor Kohl had also underlined to Major the extent to which Kohl was publicly committed to enhancing the EP's powers. Though there is no evidence in the public domain to support or refute the argument that concessions were explicitly traded, it was nevertheless the case that Major was aware of the goodwill which would be generated in Bonn by British movement on the EP and of the leeway he now had to make some concessions.[84]

The scene was therefore set for the British to consider concessions on the EP issue, but what provided the immediate trigger was the fact that the Prime Minister himself was out of sympathy with the argument that any enhancement of the EP would automatically erode the powers of Westminster.[85] On the issue of co-decision, his feeling was that, although the term was an emotive and misleading one, what it really gave the EP was a power of veto over Council of Ministers' actions. It did not imply shared power with the Council of Ministers to adopt draft legislation. Thus Major did not see it as a fundamental sticking-point, since it did not diminish Westminster powers in areas where majority voting already existed and, so long as the nomenclature was changed, he was willing to concede this point.[86]

Major also saw some scope for compromise on the issue of investiture of the Commission by the EP and the extension of the mandate of the Commission from four to five years (which was on the agenda but not in the Luxembourg draft). From the Prime Minister's perspective, these were relatively cost-free political steps, since they did not undermine the capacity of the Heads of Government to agree a candidate for the presidency of the Commission, where unanimity had to prevail. Moreover, the EP could already censure the Commission as a whole and demand its resignation, although these were powers which the EP had never had the nerve to use. What was particularly appealing to Major about these compromises was, therefore, that they could be marketed as mere modifications of existing practice agreed under his predecessor.

In short, the nature of the concessions the British government was willing to make was shaped by the Prime Minster's view that it would be easier to sell the deepening of a concession made by his predecessor than to make new concessions.[87] Where British influence had already been lost Major was relaxed about further concessions – but, where Mrs Thatcher had stood firm, he too felt unable to make concessions. However, there were two further reasons why the concessions could be sold to nervous backbenchers. First, they could be depicted as a move that restored democratic control where it was most lacking, in majority voting decisions where individual national governments could be outvoted.[88] Second, play could be made of the way in which the powers of the (democratically elected) EP had been turned against the (unelected) Commission.[89]

In formulating these compromises, John Major was flying in the face of his negotiating team's advice. Their view was that while the political ramifications were rightly held to be low, the institutional implications of aligning the Commission and EP mandates were fraught with danger.[90] Here, the team's analysis coincided with that of a number of leading MEPs who argued that, following the five-yearly European elections, the first act of the new EP would be to determine the character of the Commission and hold confirmation hearings of the remaining Commissioners. This was in line with its aspirations to follow the American Congressional model, using its powers to deadly effect.[91] The FCO further argued that the compromises envisaged would ultimately pave the way for the EP to elect the Commission from among its own membership.[92]

While the government did in fact hold back from offering its concessions straightaway at the negotiating table, this was not because FCO reservations ultimately prevailed. Rather, it was that Major remained cautious about allowing the issue of the EP to become politicized, perhaps undermining his ability to deliver ratification of the Treaty. Second, he did not want to offer hostages to fortune by making premature concessions which might hinder the government's ability to sustain back-bench support prior to the Maastricht European Council. Third, British negotiators wanted to play up their opposition to issues they were now willing to concede in order to extract maximum kudos when the compromises were finally made.[93]

The first British concessions were therefore agreed at the Noordwijk Foreign Ministers meeting on 12 November. Britain now accepted the co-decision procedure in substance, but succeeded in getting the provocative term co-decision itself removed from the second draft. It was instead referred to in the Treaty draft in the less inflammatory form of Article 189B, or in British parlance the 'Negative Assent Procedure'. With French, Danish and Irish support, London was also successful in limiting the EP's power to a blocking veto at the third reading of a bill when the Council of Ministers and European Parliament disagreed.[94] Nevertheless, it was an indication of the government's continuing caution that it was left to the junior FCO minister, Tristan Garel-Jones, and not the Foreign Secretary himself – who left the room for the duration of this aspect of the negotiations – to agree to the notion of co-decision, lest the news cause an outcry among Conservative backbenchers.[95]

However, since the co-decision procedure was now so limited, a majority of Member States pressed for a much wider application than the Luxembourgers had proposed in their second draft. At Noordwijk, the French position on this changed, with the minister Elisabeth Guigou now supportive of co-decision for a far wider number of issues, thus removing an important British ally. Thus some 15 areas for co-decision were agreed in principle at the Noordwijk conclave, a much wider number than the British had expected. In addition, delegates to Noordwijk left unresolved the issue of extension of the assent procedure, that is to say the areas in which parliamentary approval for (but not amendments to) rules was possible. Given the financial implications, the British were particularly opposed to applying assent for the definition of and ceiling on Own Resources (Article 201) and treaty amendment. British negotiators argued that since both issues involved national parliaments there was no democratic deficit. However, these issues were left for a decision by the Heads of Government at Maastricht, along with the areas to be decided by co-decision.

As Major had hoped, the compromises made at Noordwijk occasioned little domestic controversy, leaving some officials with the impression that, if government had moved earlier on the principle of co-decision, perhaps the negotiators could have argued more effectively on the coverage. The Eurosceptics found it difficult to argue against a blocking power for the EP when the Council made decisions by majority voting, since to do so would lay them open to the charge of being anti-democratic.[96] Indeed, even Nicholas Ridley favoured giving the EP this power of veto, arguing that it would diminish the powers of the Commission, while the *Spectator*, no friend of the European Parliament, also welcomed the prospect of 'greater control of the Assembly [*sic*] on the Commission'.[97] At the same time, Eurosceptics were distracted from the EP question by euphoria over the collapse of the 'federalist' Dutch draft of 30 September.[98]

By a fortunate coincidence, back-bench MPs were also voting on the composition of the Tory Backbench European Affairs Committee on the same day as the Noordwijk meeting. Events in Holland were therefore overshadowed by the successful challenge to Bill Cash by Sir Norman Fowler. Thus, the most likely opponents of the government 'had sand kicked in their faces' at a crucial moment in the negotiations. This was not without some timely assistance from the Dutch, who were made aware of the elections and went out of their way in their dealings with the British press to play down the significance of the British concessions.[99]

Any remaining Eurosceptic unease was also assuaged by the tougher rhetoric coming from both the Foreign Secretary and the Prime Minister. Far from being a mere negotiating tactic, this appeared to many Eurosceptic backbenchers to be a genuine move towards the sceptic position as the negotiations drew to a close.[100] At the same time, care was taken to assure the remainder of interested Conservative backbenchers that the compromises reached were a pragmatic codification of existing powers, giving the EP the appearance but not the reality of a greater legislative role.[101]

Using the parliamentary debate of 20 November to reaffirm the government's position on the EP dossier, John Major repeated

London's belief that the EP should not have the right to initiate legislation or power of co-decision as an equal partner of the Council of Ministers, 'but on both issues the risk had long since disappeared'.[102] Tellingly, however, little further discussion of the EP took place during the debate, and this was testament to the overwhelming success of the government's management of its own backbenchers, along with Labour's unwillingness to contest the government's position.[103] Of the government's opponents, only Bill Cash spoke out, noting that the House had been given no opportunity to debate the issue of the European Parliament, with Jonathan Aitken, previously the most outspoken on this issue, noticeably silent.[104]

Thus with the backing of the European Reform Group and support from the 'silent majority' of the Party, the Prime Minister won an overwhelming majority in support of his position.[105] As Major left for the Maastricht European Council, he was therefore less concerned by the issue of the EP and its potential for division within his party and was prepared to make a number of concessions. With little discussion beyond that in Whitehall and with his FCO ministers, he had not only won Cabinet backing for concessions on Commission investiture and the synchronization of EP and Commission mandates but had also secured the Cabinet's remit to use his own judgement concerning the application of the co-decision and assent procedures. Indeed, the EP dossier was one of the few areas in which Major felt he had room for manoeuvre at the European Council. Notwithstanding his personal preferences, he was therefore mentally prepared to make still further concessions if it proved essential to the overall deal, though he remained determined not to allow the application of assent to the Own Resources article and Treaty amendment.[106]

THE MAASTRICHT EUROPEAN COUNCIL

The Prime Minister's first move at the European Council was to announce a wide range of British 'concessions' on enhancing the EP. In the legislative area he formally endorsed the co-decision procedure and left open the areas to which it should be applied. He confirmed acceptance of the Dutch proposals for investiture of the Commission President and College of Commissioners and even indicated that he could accept the extension of the mandate of the Commission to align it with that of the EP.[107] In addition, he accepted the principle of extending the assent procedure but, as with co-decision, left open the areas to which it should be applied. The conciliatory position was greeted with both surprise and delight, and generated considerable goodwill among the pro-Parliament supporters – especially Chancellor Kohl.[108]

After fierce arguments for a wider application of co-decision procedure, the Prime Minister ended by agreeing to its application in 15 areas, a number in excess of that proposed in the Luxembourg draft which he had claimed was unacceptable.[109] It was true that co-decision would not apply to all areas covered by majority voting and excluded transport, social policy, agriculture, development, environment legislation, individual research programmes, development and regional and social funds. Nevertheless, it was a wider set of areas than that covered by the co-operation procedure and meant that co-decision was now applicable to one-quarter of all EC legislation. To defuse further tension on this issue and to placate Chancellor Kohl, Major also accepted a specific undertaking that the possibility of extending the co-decision procedure would be reviewed in 1996.[110]

On the question of assent, Major approved the application of the procedure to a further four issues (citizenship, structural funds, cohesion funds and international agreements with significant budgetary implications or which modified decisions taken under co-decision).[111] The EP also gained an extension of consultation (simple majority required) for nine new issues and a weak and non-binding right of consultation on CFSP and JHA issues.[112] Although this chapter has focussed on the issue of the EP, it should be noted that this effective exclusion of the EP from CFSP, JHA and, indeed, EMU is an important reminder of the way in which debates on the EC's institutional arrangements were linked. Discussion of the powers of the various EC institutions not only raised similar practical questions of procedure and the division of responsibilities between Member States and the institutions. They also touched on the same concepts of legitimacy and sovereignty.

On the issue of JHA, for instance, there was fierce argument over a number of issues which critically affected the balance of power between states and EC central institutions. Bonn was insistent that asylum and immigration policies be included as EC common polices, and was also at the forefront of those pressing for a European Police (EUROPOL) organization with intelligence gathering powers and the potential for an operational capability.[113] The British and Danes were against this, but eventually acceded in order to secure the greater goal of an intergovernmental arrangement for the remainder of the JHA pillar. Again at German insistence, a clause was also included to ensure compliance with the European Court of Human Rights and the 1951 Convention on the Status of Refugees.[114]

At the Maastricht European Council, though long accepted, it was formally agreed that the JHA pillar should come under the authority of the European Council. In addition, Britain and Denmark reluctantly conceded eight areas of common interest.[115] In these areas the Council might adopt common positions, and promote cooperation and joint actions by unanimity. Although in other areas of immigration policy unanimity was preserved, the Treaty moved certain aspects of visa policy into Community competence in Article 100C, which specified the use of QMV from January 1996. More general provision was also made for the possibility of majority voting on other issues through the *passerelle* procedure.[116]

The JHA question also involved discussion of another key EC institution, the ECJ. Here Britain was rather more successful in securing its objectives. Throughout the IGC-PU, Court of Justice powers to rule on disputes were proposed by Belgium, Germany and the Netherlands, and equally doggedly opposed by Britain and Denmark. Agreement was eventually reached around the London/Copenhagen position to make implementation of conventions a national concern, but with the possibility of ECJ intervention subject to a consensus. Britain also won agreement for its proposal that in the EC pillar, the ECJ should be able to fine Member States which failed to comply with its judgements or to implement legislation.

Other debates touched more explicitly on the question of the legitimacy of EC institutions and indeed of the EC itself. The Germans, for instance, proposed the establishment of a consultative committee of the regions, an idea which gained support from Belgium, but met with resistance from Britain, because it could see no point in such an institution, and France and Spain for different reasons. However, both this proposal and the scheme whereby regional ministers could represent Member States in the Council were eventually accepted. From a British point of view it posed few problems simply because it did not matter to the government who came to the Council, provided they could commit their national government. The IGC negotiations also saw calls for the creation of a concept of European citizenship by the Spanish government.[117] This would enhance the status of Union citizens when in other Member States, giving them the right to vote and stand in municipal and European elections.

While this proposal was widely accepted, specific issues such as voting arrangements in the Council caused difficulties. There were also particular problems in Luxembourg where 28 per cent of the population were other nationals, and in Denmark where foreign nationals were not permitted to buy holiday homes. At Noordwijk, the Luxembourgers secured a general derogation from measures granting EC nationals the right to vote and stand in municipal and European elections, while the Danes gained a protocol making legal their prohibition on the sale of second homes to non-Danish citizens. This solution resolved the citizenship issue and the concept was therefore included in the final Treaty draft.

CONCLUSION

The emotive issue of the democratic deficit, and its role in launching the second IGC, gave the debates on the EC's institutional arrangements a particular edge. The EP dossier occupied a vital position in these debates, since the majority of Britain's partners regarded the EP as the chief forum in which to remedy the democratic deficit. Faced with this, and given also the history of British antagonism to the EP, the dossier thus threatened to be extremely difficult for the government to manage.

While it was true that the British all along overstated their hostility to enhanced EP powers as a negotiating tactic, the government was, however, ultimately prepared to make important concessions on the issue. The key reason for this was its success in controlling opponents of EP enhancement in the domestic arena, above all those within the Conservative Party itself. One explanation for this was the relatively insulated nature of the IGC-PU, which permitted the British government to conceal the course of the negotiations from informed opinion. In addition, however, the government was able to keep a very tight rein on the supply of information about the EP dossier, and was greatly assisted by the extremely technical nature of the Treaty amendments under discussion.

When the proposals were eventually published and opposition to the draft clauses gathered momentum, the government managed to play a clever tactical hand, talking up its opposition to the draft clauses while at the same time taking effective action to bolster back-bench support. Luck was also on its side, however, for the government was fortunate that the sheer number of items on the IGC agenda obscured the issue of the EP. The pillared structure of the EU also helped the government to assuage the concerns of backbenchers that the most sensitive issues affecting British sovereignty – JHA and CFSP – should be handled using an intergovernmental process which gave the appearance of safeguarding the British veto. The government therefore secured passive support from the majority of its backbenchers to negotiate on enhancing the EP as it saw fit, so long as the changes proposed did not significantly affect either the executive's powers in the Council of Ministers or Westminster's powers.

With all governments facing external pressure to reach a compromise solution, and with his domestic audience under close control, Major became increasingly prepared to make concessions on the EP. This position was underpinned by two considerations. First, Major believed – FCO doubts notwithstanding – that the legislative proposals under discussion were not as significant as initially feared. The second consideration was that pro-Strasbourg Member States would not veto the overall Treaty if only the British could accept some limited strengthening of the EP. What is equally important to note, however, is the type of concessions the British government was prepared to make. Major would only countenance concessions which were extensions of those made by his predecessor, and which could be presented as codifying pre-existing practices. He therefore reordered his negotiating priorities on this basis.

Thus while external pressure on the British ensured some convergence between Britain and its partners as the Maastricht European Council approached, and while the government was ostensibly successful in controlling domestic concerns on the EP, domestic political considerations continued to loom large in the government's calculations. Compromises were offered and ultimately accepted, but the nature of those compromises reflected clearly the government's preoccupation with domestic and, above all, party political concerns. The end result, nevertheless, was a significant shift away from the government's initial negotiating position. It also represented a volte face in the government's thinking on the principle of subsidiary, that is to say, its belief that the EC/EU should only do what could not be done at the national level.

NOTES

1. David Andrews, 'The Global Origins of the Maastricht Treaty on EMU: Closing the Window of Opportunity', in A. Cafruny and G. Rosenthal, *The State of the European Community: the Maastricht Debates and Beyond*, London, Longman, 1993, pp. 107–42.
2. See William Wallace and Julie Smith, 'Democracy or Technocracy? European Integration and the Problem of Popular Consent', *West European Politics*, July 1995, vol. 8, no. 3, pp. 137–57.
3. Martin Westlake, *The New European Parliament*, London, Pinter, 1994, p. 28.
4. See the 'Draft Treaty Establishing the European Union', *Official Journal*, no. C.77, 19 March 1984.
5. Richard Corbett, 'Testing the New Procedures: the EP's First Experiences with its New Single Act Powers', *Journal of Common Market Studies*, vol. XXVII, no. 4, June 1989.
6. Though the two issues were not formally linked the SEA required EP assent for enlargement. See Juliet Lodge, 'The European Parliament – from "Assembly" to Co-legislator: the Changing Institutional Dynamics', in Lodge (ed.), *The European Community and the Challenge of the Future*, London, Pinter, 1989, pp. 58–82.
7. See 'Resolution on the IGC in the Context of the Parliament's Strategy on European Union', *Official Journal*, no. C.96, 17 April 1990.
8. For the full range of proposals see the EP resolution adopted on 22 November 1990, *Official Journal*, no. C324, 24 December 1990.
9. See *Agence Europe*, 24 October 1990.
10. 'Commission Opinion of 21 October 1990 on the Proposal for Amendment of the Treaty Establishing the EEC with a View to Political Union', *Bulletin of the European Communities*, supplement 2/91, Luxembourg, pp. 75–82.
11. Author's interview, Michael Welsh. See also Martin Westlake, *The Parliament and the Commission: Partners and Rivals in the European Policy-making Process*, London, Butterworths, 1994.
12. The Belgian Memorandum is reproduced in *Agence Europe*, 29 March 1991.
13. The text of the Kohl-Mitterrand letter is reproduced in *Agence Europe*, 20 April 1990.
14. For the academic conventional wisdom see Shirley Williams, 'Sovereignty and Accountability in the European Community', in Robert O. Keohane and Stanley Hoffmann (eds), *The New European Community: Decision-making and Institutional Change*, Boulder, Col., Westview, 1991, pp. 155–76; Otto Schmuck and Wolfgang Wessels (eds), *Das Europäische Parlament im dynamischen Integration prozess*, Bonn, Europa Union Verlag, 1989.
15. Interestingly French officials remained much more reticent on this than the main protagonists until a late stage. Author's interview with Sir John Kerr and Cabinet Office officials.
16. 'The Road from Strasbourg', *Economist*, 13 April 1991, p. 19.
17. Anne Deighton, 'Une maladie imaginaire: England's Europäische

Dilemma', in Beatrice Beutler (ed.), *Reflexions über Europa*, Munich, Akteul, 1992, pp. 52–63, p. 56.

18. Ivo Dawnay, 'Labour Consummates Marriage to Europe', *Financial Times*, 23 October 1990.

19. For the concern that Euro elections one day might work against an incumbent Labour government mid-term see Denis McShane, 'Europe's Next Challenge to Britain', *Political Quarterly*, vol. 66, no. 1, January–March 1995, pp. 23–35, p. 30.

20. See Hugo Young, 'Guardian Survey' that 32 of 66 MPs questioned were opposed to giving more powers to the EP. *Guardian*, 21 November 1990. See John Piennar, 'Kaufman Admits Flaws in EC Policy', *Independent*, 7 July 1991.

21. See *Opportunity Britain: Labour's Better Way for the 1990s*, London, Labour Party Publications, 1991.

22. Geoffrey Howe, 'Sovereignty and Interdependence: Britain's Place in the World', *International Affairs*, vol. 66, no. 4, 1990, pp. 675–96.

23. In government, Mrs Thatcher continued to refer to the European Parliament in dismissive terms as an 'Assembly'. See *The Downing Street Years*, op. cit., p. 60 & p. 558.

24. See *Choice and Responsibility*, No Turning Back Group, London, Conservative Political Centre, September 1990, pp. 9–10.

25. Michael Heseltine, *The Democratic Deficit: the Balance in Europe for Britain to Redress*, Centre for Policy Studies Paper no. 10, 1989, London, pp. 22–8, esp. 25. For a more detailed exposition see also Heseltine, *The Challenge of Europe*, op. cit., pp. 24–37.

26. Author's interview with Richard Corbett.

27. Bill Newton Dunn, *A Conservative Agenda for the European Community*, Wandsworth, London, 1990, p. 10. Sir Christopher Prout, *Federalism, Integration, Sovereignty, Union and All That*, Wandsworth, Conservatives in Europe, 1990, p. 12.

28. Author's interview with Sir Christopher Prout.

29. For example a Gallup poll found that 85% of the electorate could not name their MEP. Reported in *The Times*, 4 December 1989.

30. See Stafford T. Thomas, 'Assessing MEP Influence on British EC Policy', *Government and Opposition*, vol. 27, no. 1, 1993, pp. 3–18, pp. 13–15.

31. See, for example, the near-unanimous open letter which attacked Thatcher's vision of the future of Europe and remarked on the breakdown in communication between Number 10 and Tory MEPs. *The Times*, 17 November 1989, p. 2a.

32. In 1989 this was 36.2%. See Neil Nugent, *The Government and Politics of the European Community*, London, Macmillan, 2nd ed., 1991, p. 133.

33. See *Euro Barometer*, no. 34, December 1990.

34. Douglas Hurd, evidence to the Select Committee on the European Communities, *Economic and Monetary Union and Political Union*, House of Lords Paper 88–II, 27th Report, session 1989–90, p. 211.

35. Douglas Hurd, evidence to the Select Committee on the European Communities, *Economic and Monetary Union and Political Union*, House of Lords Paper 88–II, 27th Report, session 1989–90. See also

Martin Eaton, Legal Counsellor, Foreign Office, evidence to the Select Committee on the European Communities, *Political Union: Law-Making Powers and Procedures*, session 1990–91, 17th report, 1991, House of Lords Paper 80, p. 13.

36. Author's interviews with FCO officials.

37. Douglas Hurd, evidence to the Select Committee on the European Communities, *Economic and Monetary Union and Political Union*, House of Lords Paper 88–II, 27th Report, session 1989–90.

38. See the House of Commons Select Committee on Procedure, *The Scrutiny of European Legislation*, session 1988/9, House of Commons Paper 368–I and II. In January 1991 the House of Commons debated the need to establish two new committees for the scrutiny of EC legislation. See *Parl. Deb. HC*, 22 January 1991.

39. Introduction to the Select Committee on the European Communities, *Law-Making Powers and Procedures*, session 1990–91, 17th report, 1991, House of Lords Paper, p. 17.

40. For the clearest exposition see Douglas Hurd's statement to the House of Commons, 26 June 1991, *Parl. Deb. HC*, col. 1016.

41. Author's interview with Sir John Kerr.

42. Author's interview with Alain van Solinge, General Secretariat of the European Commission.

43. Author's interviews.

44. Denmark like Britain was also strongly attached to the notion of sovereignty, while those with few representatives in the EP (Portugal and Ireland) were concerned that the Parliament had yet to take root in European political life. David Buchan, 'MEPs Seek to Lay Down Law on Legislative Powers', *Financial Times*, 13 August 1991.

45. See *Agence Europe*, 16 February 1991.

46. For the fluidity of national positions in this dossier see *The Times* editorial, 'Corridor Diplomacy', 1 July 1991.

47. See, for example, Delors' speech to the EP debate on Political Union, 17 April 1991, and reports of the stormy press conference which followed the Intra-Institutional meeting of 15 May 1991.

48. This is one explanation of why the Commission badly overplayed its hand in the negotiations, looking after its own interest in the IGC rather than searching for common ground. See David Buchan, *Financial Times*, 8 April 1991; Helen Wallace, 'Britain out on a Limb', op. cit., p. 277. For the Commission perspective on this see Ross, *Jacques Delors*, op. cit., pp. 100 and 209.

49. Author's interview with a Cabinet Office official. See also Ross, *Jacques Delors*, op. cit., p. 100.

50. These were contained in the British proposal Conf UP 1762/91, 8 March 1991.

51. See Karl-Heinz Neunreither, 'The Democratic Deficit of the European Union', *Government and Opposition*, vol. 29, no. 3, Summer 1994, pp. 299–314, p. 307.

52. For the texts see 'Non-Paper Draft Treaty Articles with a View to Achieving Political Union', *Europe Documents*, 1709/10, 3 May 1991; and *Europe Documents*, 1722/3, 5 July 1991. For the British position see

the discussion documents attached to the 4th and 8th Permanent Representatives meetings, SEC (91) 261 and SEC (91) 491.

53.   See Article 189A, *Europe Documents*, 1722/3, 5 July 1991.

54.   Jacques Poos, the Luxembourg Foreign Minister, argued that in reality this was a double investiture since in practical terms the chances were slim of appointing the commission president without Strasbourg's approval. *Agence Europe*, 12 June 1991.

55.   Development aid and framework programme for research and development (passed every four years); regional and social funds (passed every five years); environmental programmes (spread over several years); and indicative plans for trans-European infrastructure (schemes that do not yet exist). For a discussion of this see *Agence Europe*, 10 July 1991.

56.   See the evidence of Sir Christopher Prout MEP to the Select Committee on the European Communities, *Law-Making Powers and Procedures*, session 1990–91, 17th report, 1991, House of Lords Paper 80, p. 22.

57.   Author's interview with a Cabinet Office official.

58.   Charles Reiss, 'Split Threat to "Scared" Major', *Evening Standard*, 11 June 1995.

59.   Charles Reiss, 'Ridley Stokes Furore', *Evening Standard*, 12 June 1991. George Brock, 'Major Adopts Macawberist Policy to Dodge European Pitfalls', *The Times*, 18 June 1991.

60.   Douglas Hurd made a strong condemnation of Euro rebels to the Foreign Press Association. See Charles Reiss, 'Hurd Scorns Euro Rebels', *Evening Standard*, 13 June 1991. Major made two speeches to party activists, on 14 June to the Welsh Conservative Party and on 27 June to the Conservative Womens' Conference. See John Williams, 'John Major Says No Election This Year', *Evening Standard*, 14 June 1991.

61.   Boris Johnson, 'Blue Print Unveiled for Federal Europe', *Daily Telegraph*, 21 June 1991.

62.   All the oral evidence to the House of Lords select committee was made prior to the publication of the second Luxembourg draft treaty which meant the final report was based on outdated information. See the Introduction to *Political Union Law-Making Powers and Procedures*, Select Committee on the European Communities, session 1990–91, 17th Report, House of Lords Paper 80, p. 6.

63.   For the difficulty of MPs getting hold of Treaty texts and the discovery that the government had asked for drafts not be made available see Christopher Moncton, 'Signing on the Dotty Line', *Spectator*, 12 October 1991, p. 12.

64.   In part this might be explained by the fact that the government did not know how many of the procedures would work, but there was also a tactical dimension to this. Author's interview.

65.   George Jones and Philip Johnston, 'Tories Rally to Major's Euro Stance', *Daily Telegraph*, 13 June 1991.

66.   Author's interviews with Bill Cash and Sir George Gardiner.

67.   Boris Johnson, 'Row Over EC Deal on Single Currency', *Daily*

Telegraph, 11 June 1991.
68. Colin Pilkington, *Britain in the European Union*, Manchester, Manchester University Press, 1995, p. 116.
69. Author's interview with a Cabinet minister. For this argument see Colin Pilkington, *Britain in the European Union*, 1995, p. 116.
70. Noel Malcolm, 'Lies Damned Lies and Federasts', *Spectator*, 22 June 1991, pp. 8–9. George Brock, 'Draft Treaty Puts Federal Rule at Top of EC Agenda', *The Times*, 22 June 1991. K. Middlemas, *Orchestrating Europe: the Informal Politics of the European Union*, London, Fontana, 1995, p. 193.
71. Author's interviews with Bill Cash MP and Teresa Gorman MP.
72. For an analysis of why Labour adopted this position see editorial, 'Parliament and Europe', *Evening Standard*, 27 June 1991, which argued it was to prevent Labour splits; and John Hibbs, 'Labour Split over Policy on Europe', *Daily Telegraph*, 27 June 1991.
73. Jonathan Aitken, *Parl. Deb. HC*, 26 June 1991, col. 1054.
74. Robin Oakley, 'Delors Sets Tongues Wagging Again in Europe', *The Times*, 16 May 1991.
75. For example the *Independent on Sunday* noted that 33% of Conservative MPs would vote against the government if it conceded real legislative powers to the European Parliament. Reported in Robin Oakley, 'Major Launches Summit Strategy with Dunkirk Meeting', *The Times*, 24 June 1991.
76. For the background to this see George Jones, 'Major Postpones the Showdown', *Daily Telegraph*, 25 June 1991.
77. For the extent of this watering down on the issue of EP powers see the pre- and post-summit versions of the communiqué, reproduced in *Agence Europe*, 5 July 1991.
78. *Agence Europe*, 30 June 1991.
79. Author's interviews with Philippe de Schoutheete, Piet Dankert and Bill Cash MP.
80. George Brock, 'Major Adopts Macawberist Policy to Dodge European Pitfalls', *The Times*, 18 June 1991.
81. Author's interview with Sir John Kerr.
82. See for instance Quentin Peel, 'German SPD Threatens to Block EC Treaty', *Financial Times*, 15 November 1991. For the argument that Kohl was never as fully committed to the EP as his public rhetoric, see Fabian Richter, 'British and German Attitudes to the European Parliament', undergraduate dissertation, University of Oxford, Trinity Term 1995.
83. One official noted the self-deception of ministers on this point since they were warned that in reality the EP could and would use this veto power in order to get measures amended in their direction. Author's interview. See Michael Binyon, 'EC Ranks Split over New Role for Parliament', *Financial Times*, 28 June 1991.
84. See Wayne Sandholtz, 'Monetary Bargains: the Treaty of EMU', in Rosenthal and Cafruny, *State of the European Community*, pp. 125–42.
85. Author's interviews with Sir John Kerr and Cabinet Office official. The point is also made in Hugo Young, 'The Prime Minister', *The Major*

Effect, op. cit., pp. 18–28, p. 23.

86. Michael Jay made the same point that this was not a real loss of power for national parliaments to the House of Lords Select Committee, see *Political Union Law-Making Powers and Procedures*, Select Committee on the European Communities, session 1990–91, 17th Report, House of Lords Paper 80, pp. 49–50.

87. For the antecedents to this thinking see John Major's speech to Welsh Conservatives, when he pointedly noted that it had been Mrs Thatcher who had conceded majority voting and co-operation powers to the EP.

88. See Boris Johnson, 'Euro Court Wins Right to Fine Governments', *Daily Telegraph*, 13 November 1991.

89. The *Evening Standard* was the first to advocate this line of reasoning; see 27 June 1991.

90. Author's interview with Sir John Kerr.

91. George Tsebelis, 'The Power of the European Parliament as a Conditional Agenda Setter', *American Political Science Review*, vol. 88, 1994, pp. 128–42.

92. Author's interview with Sir John Kerr. For a further discussion of this see Richard Corbett, 'The Intergovernmental Conference on Political Union', *Journal of Common Market Studies*, vol. XXX, no. 3, September 1992, pp. 271–98.

93. Sir John Kerr was reported to have put his concerns on the record, lest there be any misunderstanding about the quality of advice given to the Prime Minister which might 'rebound on the FCO at a later date'.

94. The Commission's right to vet Parliament's proposals was also maintained. See Richard Corbett, 'The Intergovernmental Conference', op. cit., p. 292.

95. Author's interviews with FCO and Cabinet Office officials.

96. Author's interview with Bill Cash MP.

97. Editorial, 'No, No, No', *Spectator*, 2 November 1991.

98. Author's interview with Bill Cash MP.

99. David Buchan, 'UK Signals Flexibility on EC Law Making Powers', *Financial Times*, 13 November 1991.

100. See Simon Heffer, 'Mr Major Prepares to Don His Tweeds for England', *Spectator*, 9 November 1991. Boris Johnson, 'Tougher Line by Britain on EC Power', *Daily Telegraph*, 5 November 1991.

101. Author's interview with Sir George Gardiner MP.

102. Author's interview. John Major, *Parl. Deb. HC*, 20 November 1991, col. 278.

103. Kinnock mentioned the EP only once during a 36-minute speech: see Neil Kinnock, *Parl. Deb. HC*, 20 November 1991, col. 289.

104. Bill Cash, *Parl. Deb. HC*, 20 November 1991, cols 319–20. For the silence of Jonathan Aitken see Gorman, *Bastards*, op. cit., p. 41.

105. Robin Oakley, 'Major Secures Mandate for Maastricht', *The Times*, 22 November 1991.

106. Author's interview with Sir John Kerr.

107. This was contrary to the expectations of the EP and had initially been opposed by Britain, France, Greece, Ireland and Portugal. See Sophie van Hoonacker, 'The European Parliament', in Laursen and

Hoonacker, *Intergovernmental Conference on Political Union*, p. 222. Richard Corbett notes this is 'perhaps one of the clearest examples of Parliament's involvement in the IGC producing a clear result'. Corbett, 'The Intergovernmental Conference', op. cit., p. 293.

108. Author's interview with Philippe de Schoutheete.
109. Author's interview with Sir John Kerr. See also Richard Corbett, 'The Intergovernmental Conference', op. cit., p. 291.
110. Article 189B (8).
111. The SEA had already applied assent to Association Agreements.
112. Citizenship; transport; harmonization of legislation; entry and residence of third country nationals; industry; cohesion; research programmes; and environment. See *Report of the Result of the IGC*, EP Committee of Institutional Affairs, 155.444/fin./Party 111.
113. The best narrative account of these negotiations is Monica den Boer, 'The Quest for European Policing: Rhetoric and Justification in a Disorderly Debate', in Malcolm Anderson and Monica den Boer (eds), *Policing across National Boundaries*, London, Pinter, 1994, pp. 174–196, p. 175.
114. Lutz G. Stavenhagen, 'Durchbruch zur politischen Union – vor dem Maastrichter-Gipfel', *Integration*, vol. 14, no. 4, 1991, pp. 143–50.
115. Asylum policy, rules governing the crossing of external borders of Member States; immigration policy and policy regarding nationals of third countries; combatting drug addiction and fraud; judicial cooperation in civil matters and criminal matters; customs cooperation and police cooperation.
116. For British opposition to QMV in these areas see the evidence of Garel-Jones to the Foreign Affairs Committee, *European Council Maastricht*, col. 69, p. 16.
117. See the revised Spanish text concerning European Citizenship, dated 21 February 1991, reproduced in Laursen and van Hoonacker, *Intergovernmental Conference on Political Union*, op. cit., pp. 325–32.

6 Explaining British Policy in the IGCs

It is impossible to consider the overall balance-sheet of British success and failure in the negotiation of the Maastricht Treaty without reference to the British Prime Minister's own claim that he had won at Maastricht 'game, set and match'.[1] There is a case for arguing that this picture of British success was true so far as Major's own role went, for, by most accounts, he gave the most impressive performance at the Maastricht European Council, both in terms of setting out his case and the tenacity with which he held to his position.[2] However, when one examines the outcome against the three guiding principles of British policy – a preference for intergovernmentalism, opposition to a two-speed Europe and acceptance of the principal of subsidiarity – the outcome of the negotiations was not an absolute success. Indeed, in terms of the chapter and verse of the Treaty itself, it is more accurate to say that the Treaty as finally agreed represented a mixture of 'wins' and 'losses' for all concerned. It was a measure of the success of the Dutch Presidency in drafting the TEU that no one Member State 'lost' to a degree that it was prepared to veto the Treaty, and that all could claim to a greater or lesser degree that they had won the arguments.

The British government most clearly lost on the issue of EMU and enhanced powers for the EP. On EMU, it failed to halt the momentum of its partners towards a single currency, and was left to negotiate the terms of its own self-exclusion. On the EP, the Treaty clauses extended co-decision to major sectors of British policy which included internal market legislation, incentive measures in education, and research and development. Unanimity was now only required in the Council of Ministers for research and development framework programmes, environmental action programmes, guidelines for trans-European networks, public health, culture and consumer protection.[3] This tilted the balance of power away from the Commission towards the European Parliament in general action programmes, meaning that the EP had clearly gained substantial new influence in these areas. Together with its additional powers in the areas of assent and investiture of the Commission – all gained contrary to the British government's initial wish – the EP had been significantly strengthened, so that, in less than five years after the signing of the Single European Act, the government had acquiesced in yet another major change in the EP's powers and conceded on a number of key principles which might be used against them in the future.

Matched against the government's stated position at the outset of the negotiations, London 'won' most clearly in social policy. Here it secured the removal of the social policy provisions and a restatement of the position on social policy defined by the SEA. Yet this success came only at the price of a British opt out from the Social Chapter and the abandonment of Britain's hitherto adamant opposition to the idea of a two-speed Europe. The departure from this long-standing principle was further underlined by the second British opt out, that on EMU. It was the EMU debates which highlighted most clearly the dangers of resorting to opt outs, for on this dossier the British negotiating team was almost totally unable to exercise influence on the course of the negotiations, commensurate with her political and economic importance.

The British achievements in the Maastricht Treaty thus reflect a complex mix of partial successes and partial failures. It is also a similar story with the institutional question of Treaty structure. Here Britain succeeded in getting the federal goal removed, and two intergovernmental pillars were created to handle Justice and Home Affairs on the one hand and foreign and security policy on the other. These intergovernmental pillars excluded the ECJ (except on visa policy), downgraded the importance of the EP and Commission, and excluded automatic recourse to the EC; budget and decisions based on cooperation in these pillars did not have the effect of EC law.

Nevertheless, the government had to concede majority voting on visa policy in the JHA pillar, and, at least in principle, majority voting could also take place on foreign policy issues. As regards CFSP, moreover, although the government 'won' in the battle to prevent the EC immediately taking on defence responsibilities, it had also – in contrast to its declared position at the outset – had to concede that the Union could develop a defence policy, which might some time in the future include a defence responsibility. In addition, the extent to which the 'intergovernmental' JHA and CFSP pillars were in fact detached from the institutional and decision-making dynamics of the EC pillar is also questionable.[4] On close examination of the Treaty, many Eurosceptics argued that the Maastricht pillars were less intergovernmental than the government had a vested interest in portraying.

Even with the deletion of the federal goal and the government's own claim to have turned the tide of supranationalism through the creation of the pillared structure, the intergovernmental nature of the TEU should not be exaggerated. The EC's explicit competence had been extended in areas which ranged from education, culture, public health, and trans-European networks, to research and development and industrial policy. Although there was now a subsidiarity clause in the Treaty to the effect that action would only be taken in so far as the objectives could not be achieved at the national level, the success of the British government in limiting extension of competences was therefore minimal; for example it did prevent the creation of an energy chapter. The fact was that, despite earlier misgivings, the government had now accepted that these issues were better handled at the Community level rather than at the national level, with the European Union becoming more and not less embedded in domestic decision-making processes. The government had, however, preserved its veto in some sensitive areas in Council by limiting the extension of majority voting.

Reflecting on the common themes which explain Britain's policies at the IGCs of 1990 to 1991, and her success and failure in achieving them, the first and most obvious comment is that the British position, and indeed the Conference itself, was 'impregnated by contingency'.[5] As the Introduction highlighted, the negotiations took place over a 12-month period in which governments were confronted with the invasion of Kuwait, civil war in Yugoslavia, the military coup in Moscow and the collapse of the Soviet Union. The attention of governments and nego-tiators was not always – or even principally – on the negotiations at any one time, and the process of bargaining often reflected this overload. The scale of the overload together with the artificial deadline of December 1991 for conclusion of the negotiations were exacerbating factors which acted as a powerful incentive to seek a solution.

The Treaty was not the sanitized product of 12 Member States rationally negotiating over an agreed set of objectives. Moreover, all participants often adopted inappropriate negotiating strategies and misinterpreted bargaining moves. London, initially at least, was guilty of misreading the determination of its partners to proceed to EMU, and its miscalculation over the commitment of the 11 to the Social Partners Agreement brought the negotiations to the brink of collapse at the Maastricht European Council.

A key consideration for Britain, however, was that, notwithstanding the day-to-day problems of interpreting the position of its negotiating partners, the government found itself surrounded by Member States which were considerably more positive about taking the European integration process forward than it was, and as a consequence more able to explicitly trade across issues. The British relationship with the integration process had always been a troubled one, and this background history set the broad parameters of Major's policy. In addition to this, however, during the final years of Mrs Thatcher's period in office her anti-European views meant that her influence over the European agenda increasingly slipped away from Britain, leaving her more isolated and mistrusted than ever before.

But Thatcher's legacy affected not just Major's external scope for manoeuvre. Thatcher had been a hugely divisive national figure. In particular, the downfall of Thatcher marked a loss in ideological direction of the Conservative Party, possibly leaving it more divided than at any other time since the policy of German appeasement and certainly the tariff reform crisis of 1906. John Major's key priority in 1990 to 1991 was thus the management of an extremely volatile Conservative Party. Given also his conviction that success in the negotiation of the Treaty was a key element of his electoral strategy, this is the most immediate explanation of why Britain's negotiating stance at Maastricht developed as it did.

The first aspect of Major's anxiety to manage his domestic audience was his sensitivity to the views of Conservative backbenchers. He did after all expect to be reliant on them for the Treaty's ratification. It was noticeable that 'almost unrelenting attention' was paid to the concerns of the Parliamentary party, and to influential factions like the European Reform Group, in the run up to the Luxembourg and Maastricht European Council meetings.[6] As the Introduction indicated, a number of institutional changes under Mrs Thatcher had strengthened the autonomy of back-bench MPs from the party leader and their leverage power, and at no point could the Prime Minister take their views for granted. At the same time, however, two points must be noted.

First, the government had a considerable array of weapons in its armoury with which to influence MPs and these extended far beyond MPs' instinct for self-preservation and re-election. These weapons of influence ranged from the control of the parliamentary agenda to the deployment of the Whips and hints of rewards for loyalty from party managers. Second, back-bench influence was limited by a policy of withholding information. MPs were denied detailed knowledge of the draft treaties as they were not placed in the House of Commons library, so they had neither the ability to make an independent judgement on progress in the IGC, nor the technical expertise to challenge the government's position. Commons committees played no serious role in monitoring progress or extracting information from the government, though it is arguable that they might have done if either the Foreign Affairs or Defence committees had been more strongly led. Committee working practices could also have been more effectively organized to monitor progress in the year-long negotiations which covered several parliamentary recesses.

Fortunately for the government, Eurosceptics in Parliament failed to develop an independent system to judge progress in the IGCs, although they had more than enough funds to do so. Nor did British opponents of Maastricht seek transnational alliances with other like-minded groups in other Member States, something which only developed in the aftermath of the signature of the Maastricht Treaty to strengthen their negotiating powers.

The government withheld a full parliamentary debate on the IGCs until November 1991. It was through Whips' eyes that John Major saw the debate as an opportunity to muster support from his own party rather than as a matter of principle. Even then the debate was only held when the parameters of the possible agreement and scope for compromise were clear. In language which was carefully crafted to appeal to backbenchers, moreover, Major only made specific commitments to the House on those elements of the Treaty on which there was agreement (the pillared structure, the principle of foreign and security policy and the commitment to NATO), or where the issue was never in doubt (removal of the term 'federal vocation' and opposition to the wholesale introduction of majority voting in foreign and defence policy). Where the outcome was uncertain, commitments were studiously avoided (for example on the applicability of the co-decision procedure), or made in general terms leaving as wide a margin as possible for the Prime Minister to seek a compromise (social policy).

The bottom line was that despite the government's various means of influencing the behaviour of backbenchers, Major could at no time take the support of the parliamentary party for granted. There were four reasons for this. First, the IGCs were an iterative process of bargaining in which participants continually had to reassess their preferences and adjust to the flow of proposals and shifting coalitions. Second, the government had to react to the unfolding environment at both the European and domestic levels, and respond to both simultaneously. These two considerations therefore relate to the particular nature of IGCs, and underline the point that treaty negotiations of this sort would have been a difficult process for any British government to handle.

The remaining factors, however, are contingent, and explain the specific problems which Major faced. Thus the third consideration was that using the disciplines of party management as a substitute for an open debate was only a temporary alternative for building a secure political base for negotiation of the Treaty and its subsequent ratification. Many Conservatives did not develop a strong belief in the Treaty and the majority supported the government for wholly manufactured and rather transient reasons.[7] In particular, the unreconciled Friends of Bruges Group were eventually discounted but remained potentially dangerous for they were 'a stubborn set of individuals resisting blandishments and threats alike'.[8] The possibility of them joining forces with the 50 MPs standing down at the next election, perhaps led by Margaret Thatcher or a politician of Cabinet rank, loomed throughout the IGC and presented a continuous threat to the government's handling of the negotiations.

Fourth, as Chapter 1 argued, John Major did not have and indeed never had a strong base in the party because of a lack of a firm set of beliefs, and he felt personally threatened by the very presence of Mrs Thatcher on the backbenches. Reflective of John Major's own insecurity was his perception that he needed a 'big idea' that highlighted the difference between him and Mrs Thatcher even though many considered 'politics and not ideas as his game'.[9] This situation was further complicated by a deteriorating relationship with Mrs Thatcher which, by the end of the negotiations, was very tense. At the practical level Major's strategy was to rely on the 'party faithful' and a small number of Major 'loyalists' who would follow his policy lead if it were decisive. In addition, he could hope for support from neo-liberal backbenchers, so long as he could limit the effect of any social policy amendments and deliver the single currency opt out and present the remainder of the Treaty as lacking real substance. He could also rely on the left wing of the party if he could reach an agreement that kept the United Kingdom at the heart of Europe.

Against this backdrop, the most important problem for Major was the disagreement within Cabinet. The Prime Minister invested considerable effort into building up support from Cabinet colleagues, especially those Thatcherite ministers who were the most reluctant to engage in the negotiations. Where the Cabinet was genuinely united, such as on the EP and CFSP dossiers, the Prime Minister and Foreign Secretary – what Hill has termed 'the foreign policy executive'[10] – had wide scope to act as they saw fit. But once disagreement surfaced in the Cabinet, the maintenance of a united front became Major's priority, with far-reaching ramifications for the policy he could pursue at the negotiating table.

These ramifications were most evident in the social policy dossier, where one of Major's 'Thatcherite' ministers, Michael Howard, effectively operated a veto on whether the Prime Minister could accept the Lubbers compromise at the Maastricht European Council. Indeed, these pressures brought the negotiations to the brink of failure. Thus, the political imperative of avoiding damaging splits prior to the general election overrode all issues, including Major's general preference for reaching agreement at the Maastricht European Council.

The evidence of the Maastricht negotiations thus confirms the argument 'that the first business of a government is to ensure its own survival'[11] and that where a government is facing 'the alternatives of cooperation in the EEC [*sic*] on the one hand and domestic crisis on the other [it] most naturally and most often bows to domestic pressure'.[12] At certain key moments the 1990 to 1991 negotiations were not about what might be negotiated between the Heads of Government, but about what could be accepted in the Cabinet. Ultimately, when it came to a choice, the government compromised with domestic opposition more than they were willing to do so with foreign governments.

As to the question of why certain issues, such as EP and CFSP, failed to prompt Cabinet-level splits, while others, like social policy and to a lesser extent EMU did, part of the answer at least is that knowledge is power. Where the issues were not understood by ministers, the Prime Minister and Foreign Secretary played the leading roles. For the most part the issues under discussion in the IGCs were highly technical, with the bargaining conducted in diplomatic language whose meaning was not self-evident outside the small circle of officials dealing with it, despite the ample opportunity in Cabinet committees to debate the issue.[13] This limited not only the ability of ministers to understand detailed negotiating briefs outside their own departmental responsibilities and expertise, but also their ability to contribute significantly to the debate concerning the specifics of the negotiating position.[14]

The Treaty negotiations were, moreover, one among many issues demanding attention from ministers, with the replacement of the

Community Charge and the departmental implications of the Citizen's Charter tending to dominate their time.[15] Ken Clarke, the then Education Secretary, later candidly noted that he was not interested in the 'diplomatic minutiae' of the Maastricht Treaty and, indeed, he had not even read it.[16] Even those Cabinet ministers with departmental responsibilities directly at stake in the IGCs found that their attention was not always focussed on both the detail of the debates and the over-all package of measures which would result. The Chancellor spent much of his time wrestling with the Community Charge and then craft-ing an election-winning budget. Even Michael Howard felt that his overriding priority was to prevent compromises on social policy and so concentrated narrowly on this aspect of the negotiations.

In these circumstances, a key factor in determining whether minis-ters would take issue with the Prime Minister and Foreign Secretary was contact with permanent officials who possessed detailed knowl-edge and access to the unfolding negotiating briefs. On foreign and security policy, the technical expertise resided in the MoD and the FCO, with only a watching brief by other departments and ministerial colleagues. On this issue the Foreign Secretary and the Defence Secretary, Tom King, shared the same personal preferences for accommodation and compromise. As a consequence, the foreign policy executive had quite a wide margin of manoeuvre with little or no interference from other Cabinet ministers.

The EP was of most direct concern to the FCO. As a consequence, the issue remained the preserve of diplomats and the Foreign Secretary and thus escaped the process of internal bargaining. Hence, despite being personally opposed to making concessions on the EP and the ample opportunity to discuss the issue in the ministerial sub-committee on European questions, Michael Howard and Peter Lilley felt unable to intervene actively in the discussions – though these ministers were known to be uneasy about the proposals.[17] On social policy, however, Howard and Lilley occupied the two economic ministries which would bear the full impact of any agreement reached. Both were therefore in important positions in the policy-making process, with access to departmental expertise and the resources to influence negotiating objectives directly.

On EMU, it was the Treasury and FCO which were pre-eminent in the negotiations. Here, however, the Prime Minister succeeded in dominating the discussions due to three key factors. The first of these was that he had himself just left the Treasury and had been principally responsible for the central British policy of the hard ECU in his capacity as Chancellor. Secondly, John Major's relationship with Norman Lamont deteriorated throughout 1991. At times, as Seldon notes, the Prime Minister doubted Lamont's judgement, and anyway Major had a very close relationship with Nigel Wicks, the personal representative undertaking the day-to-day work in the IGC-EMU. Thirdly, Norman Lamont, Major's successor as Chancellor, failed to play a leading role in the discussion of EMU as it developed during the course of 1990 and 1991. Lamont always appeared uncomfortable and rather bored by ECOFIN meetings and did not mind expressing his irritation with other ministers, in striking contrast to Hurd who relished the challenge of IGC-PU negotiations and the clubable atmosphere of foreign ministers meetings.

As well as access to detailed knowledge, as the above comment suggests there were two further factors in determining whether ministers would take issue with the foreign policy executive. The first of these was interdepartmental coordination. An important sub-text in the CFSP dossier, for instance, was the shared departmental interest of the FCO and MoD in external policy, and the need to resist Treasury pressure for defence cuts. This gave officials a shared perception of the problems, a unity of purpose concerning objectives and a preference for seeking compromises where possible. As one Cabinet minister noted 'the Foreign Office was the past master of selling the policy of surrender'.[18] One Department of Employment official ruefully commented that unlike the FCO, which gained a new lease of life from an EU foreign and security policy, his department had nothing to gain and everything to fear from a social policy agreement at Maastricht. At the same time, it is worth noting that poor communication between the Department of Employment and the FCO hampered the prospects of a negotiated solution to the social policy dossier.

The importance of coordination was made all the greater by the fact that the negotiations took place in several forums, with CFSP issues being discussed, for instance, not only in the IGC-PU but also in NATO and WEU. Similarly, EMU was discussed not only by the Heads of Government in the European Council meetings but also by finance ministers at a series of ECOFIN meetings and by Bank officials in various committees. Social policy too was discussed not just by government ministers, but also by business and trade union representatives in the UNICE-ETUC talks. What is clear is that good policy coordination may be a necessary but not a sufficient condition for effective bargaining. Where there was bad coordination the chances of securing a satisfactory outcome were severely limited. However, given the absence of positive goals in many dossiers, good – often excellent – coordination did not always deliver British objectives.

The second key factor determining whether ministers would take issue with the Prime Minister was the personality of individual ministers – and indeed of the Prime Minister and Foreign Secretary themselves. Major's instincts were those of a manager seeking consensus, while the patrician Hurd was known to favour compromise over confrontation. As an illustration of how personality mattered, it is interesting to note that in the JHA dossier, the Home Secretary Ken Baker opposed many aspects of the JHA negotiations and held a number of meetings with the Foreign Secretary and the Prime Minister to express his concern.[19] Baker even telephoned officials at Maastricht, and while opposed to a number of decisions taken by the Prime Minister did not seek to overturn them.[20] That Ken Baker was unsuccessful in putting the 'intellectual backbone' into John Major was a reflection of the Prime Minister's willingness to discount Baker's advice.[21]

What it also suggests, however, is that the background context of existing perceptions about an issue was a key element in determining the credibility of potentially dissenting ministers. Where issues touched on firmly held convictions and had potentially adverse effects on existing images, dissenting ministers had greater scope to garner back-bench support and the Prime Minister was forced to be cautious. Where there was no settled image, or where settled images were apparently unchallenged, the Prime Minister and his Foreign Secretary had greater leeway to define the problem and take the initiative.[22]

Thus the social policy dossier occasioned problems because it challenged entrenched Thatcherite conceptions concerning the role of the market and the state and the notion of 'social partnership' and the 'social market'. Conversely, in the CFSP dossier, the government managed to make compromises precisely because it was successful in appearing to endorse Atlantic structures, securing a strengthening of the Alliance, and also a leading role for British forces within it. The creation of a Rapid Reaction Corps, and the development of WEU, were sold to Conservative backbenchers as simple incremental adjustments to NATO. Few outside a small circle of key policy-makers understood how closely the NATO and IGC debates were linked and the extent of the concessions made.

A closely related factor in determining whether dissent would be credible was the probable impact of the agreements reached. On social policy, there was no doubt that the Social Chapter would result in the imposition of specific, and from the government's perspective, very unpalatable employment laws. The same threat of real and lasting ramifications at home was true of EMU. On CFSP by contrast, the debates were largely abstract, and by the end of the IGC-PU the defence debates in particular were divorced from the substantive issues of the size, shape and purpose of forces on the ground.

At the end of the day, Major's sensitivity to the attitudes of back-benchers and his preoccupation with maintaining a united front in the Cabinet were therefore interlinked, since the influence of ministers was determined by the extent of back-bench support they could attract. The resignation of a potential leader of the Eurosceptics was accordingly a far more serious prospect than the resignation of a minister without factional support and incapable of launching a challenge for the political and ideological leadership of the party.

It was indeed something of an irony that the greatest problems for John Major in terms of determining his policy at the IGCs came from the Conservative Party rather than the Labour Party. Indeed, Labour on the IGCs was the dog that did not bark in the night. The central importance of Conservative Party divisions during 1990 and 1991 was partly a reflection of this absence of opposition from Labour. In addition, however, the avowedly pro-European stance of the Labour Party limited the possibilities for Conservative Eurosceptics to vote with the opposition parties on the EMU and EP dossiers, where government control was greater than on social policy. The parliamentary debates were also poorly choreographed by the Labour front bench. For example in the November parliamentary debate Neil Kinnock blunted his own attack on government policy by unparliamentary comments in response to heckling from Conservative backbenchers. Nor was the shadow Foreign Secretary Gerald Kaufman a particularly effective performer on the floor of the House of Commons. Kaufman's self-perception was that he could beat Hurd on debating points but always lost the argument.[23]

However, with hindsight one could make a good case that the Labour front bench played a shrewd game during the negotiations, using them to educate MPs and party activists, while retaining a low profile and keeping its powder dry for the ratification process. This argument is supported by the lack of public response to the one issue on which Labour did attempt to voice a line distinct from that of the government, social policy. Indeed, as a consequence of the failure of governments of all political hue to educate the electorate concerning

EC membership, the wider public showed little interest in the issues discussed in the IGC and let the government take the lead in defining British interests.[24]

This lack of public interest was compounded by the relative quiescence of the press on the subject of the negotiations. In general, the majority of correspondents relied heavily on the national delegation, and, even among reputed international newspapers, few gave a complete picture of the many components of the summit proceedings, describing different approaches of the delegations to the issues.[25] Thus while there was a clear anti-European/Anglo-Saxon concentration in the majority of newspapers, particularly those owned by Conrad Black and Rupert Murdoch, the press served Eurosceptic objectives poorly in the quality of its reporting from Brussels and continental capitals. Part of the explanation lies in the weight of other news items both in Europe and elsewhere. Coverage of the 1990 to 1991 IGCs was crowded out by more newsworthy stories which included the Gulf war, followed by the Kurdish safe-havens initiative and then the outbreak of fighting in Yugoslavia followed by the coup in the Soviet Union. Part of the explanation also lies in the complexity of the issues which were unintelligible not only to MPs but also to the general public.

A further aspect of this low level of public or press involvement in the substance of the IGC debates was the limited opportunity for extra-parliamentary groups to influence the government. A case in point is the Bruges Group which operated half inside and half outside the parliamentary Conservative Party. Despite being one of the best-resourced political groups on the right wing, its influence in concrete terms was minimal. One aspect of this was its failure to capture public attention with its warnings about the threat posed by the IGC to British sovereignty. With hindsight the focus on sovereignty was probably an ill-considered strategy since the Group's warnings were without focus and failed to give specific instances of cause for public concern. This failure was exacerbated by the Bruges Group's failure to coordinate the various Eurosceptic groupings in and outside Westminster. The partial involvement of Mrs Thatcher, who herself felt shut out from the policy-making process, made her contribution somewhat erratic.

It was only in the social policy dossier, where the CBI's participation in the UNICE-ETUC negotiations resulted in the Social Partners Agreement, that a non-government agency had a significant impact on the government's negotiating position. Thus despite the government's ultimate control of the agenda at home, its resources and ability to influence economic interest groups with transnational interests and direct access to European decision-making processes were limited.

CONCLUSION

In seeking to explain Britain's policy and achievements in the negotiation of the Maastricht Treaty, a number of points are evident. The first is that one can only understand the actions of the Major government by placing those actions in the context of Britain's troubled relationship with Europe and the process of European integration. The UK has never grasped the nettle of the costs and benefits of closer European integration, and this shaped the way the process could be portrayed in the domestic arena. In addition, the weight of previous policy imposed important constraints on British actions in key areas, especially social policy and foreign and security policy issues.

The second point is that Major was under considerable external pressure to participate in a significant deepening and widening of the European integration process. At the same time, however, domestic considerations dominated government thinking. The most important force in shaping this domestic environment was the divisive legacy of Thatcherism for the Conservative Party, both in terms of ideology and party management. While the government thus had a broad commitment to certain policy preferences prior to the IGCs, this broad strategy, and more especially the detailed proposals and concessions made in the IGC, was always subject to pragmatic political judgements based on party management criteria and considerations of electoral advantage. And the ultimate price of these domestic considerations proved to be the expedients of an opt out on social policy and EMU, with Britain leading the way to the very two-speed Europe which she had set out to oppose.

NOTES

1. This phrase was used by No. 10's Press Officer Gus O'Donnell in a press briefing immediately after the European Council, and the phrase often attributed to John Major was subsequently reported to have caused him some irritation. See Seldon, *Major*, op. cit., p. 248; Hogg and Hill, *Too Close to Call*, op. cit., p. 157.
2. Sarah Lambert and Andrew Marshall, 'Words That Set in Store the Aims of Europe', *Independent*, 12 December 1991.
3. These six areas are subject to co-decision, but all except culture are settled by QMV procedure in the Council of Ministers. It was Major who insisted on unanimity for research and development and Kohl insisted on it for culture.
4. For a further discussion see Walter Sweeney, 'Falsehood that Maastricht's "Pillars" Can Be Kept Separate', in Ian Duncan Smith, Bernard Jenkin, Barry Legg and Walter Sweeney, *Game Set and Match?*, Conservative Way Forward, Occasional Paper No. 2, 1993, pp. 49–55.
5. Dyson, *Elusive Union*, op. cit.
6. Author's interview with a Cabinet minster.
7. One Tory minister remarked that a third of all ministers wanted the Maastricht process to fail. 'Down but Not Yet Out', *Economist*, 31 July 1993, p. 20.
8. One Cabinet minister described them as 'predictable and unmanageable'. The quote is from Dunleavy, 'The Political Parties', in Patrick Dunleavy, Andrew Gamble, Ian Holliday and Gillian Peele (eds), *Developments in British Politics 4*, London, Macmillan, 1993, pp. 123–53, p.133.
9. Nigel Lawson quoted in Seldon, *Major*, op. cit., p. 83.
10. Christopher Hill, *Cabinet Decisions on Foreign Policy: the British Experience October 1938–June 1941*, Cambridge, Cambridge University Press, 1991, p. xviii.
11. In the more journalistic phrase of *The Times*, 'a politician is first and foremost always a politician'. 'The Maastricht Calculus', *The Times*, 5 December 1991.
12. Donald Puchala, 'Domestic Politics and Regional Harmonization in the European Communities', *World Politics*, vol. 27, no. 4, July 1975, pp. 496--520, p. 507.
13. Robin Oakley 'Looking for Clues in Euro-speak', *The Times*, 14 November 1991. As noted, one consequence of this lack of a clear line on the EP from ministers was that it made it extremely difficult for officials to negotiate in Brussels.
14. Author's interviews. For recent confirmation see R. A. W. Rhodes and Patrick Dunleavy, 'From Prime Ministerial Power to Core Executive', in *Prime Minister, Cabinet and Core Executive*, op .cit., pp. 11–37, p. 21.
15. Wallace, *The Foreign Policy Process in Britain*, op. cit., p. 17.
16. See Andy McSmith, *Ken Clarke: a Political Biography*, London, Verso, 1994, p. 230; see also Malcolm Balen, *Ken Clarke*, London, Fourth Estate, 1994, p. 93 & p. 252. Nicholas Budgen admitted that the Treaty

had been 'taken on trust' and that few MPs had read it, and that the Danish referendum might encourage a few more to have a look at it. *Daily Telegraph*, 5 June 1992.

17. Author's interview with Timothy Collins.
18. Author's interview with Ken Baker.
19. Ken Baker, *Turbulent Years*, op. cit., pp. 442–3. The TEU includes a commitment to removing border controls, an issue on which the Home Office was given legal advice at the time of the IGC-PU that the British exemptions secured in the Single European Act would not absolve the government.
20. Author's interview with Ken Baker.
21. Author's interview with a Cabinet minister. As a former Home Secretary, Hurd was of course very familiar with the issues involved.
22. This argument relies on Hill, *Cabinet Decisions on Foreign Policy*, op. cit., p. 233.
23. In fairness, Hurd's contribution to the parliamentary debate was one of the most effective and amusing that he made in his 20 years in the House of Commons.
24. See Simon Heffer on the inability of the public to get involved in the EC debate, *Spectator*, November 1991, quoted in K. Baker (ed.), *The Faber Book of Conservatism*, London, Faber and Faber, 1993.
25. Kurt Becker, 'The Role of the Media', in Cesare Merlini (ed.), *Economic Summits and Western Decision-Making*, Beckenham, Croom Helm/EIPA, 1984, pp. 153–66, p. 165.

7 Conclusion

While the final balance-sheet of British success and failure in the negotiations of 1990 to 1991 showed mixed results, the final form of the Treaty on European Union was nevertheless shaped by British policies in several key areas. Thanks to Britain's resistance, the new European Union had neither a defence competence nor majority voting in foreign policy. Similarly, the Union was denied enhanced social provisions. It was only on EMU and the EP, where the principle of co-decision was agreed, that Britain failed to play a leading role in shaping the eventual outcome.

Equally significantly, Britain's role in the shaping of the final Treaty had far-reaching consequences for the way in which policy would be made in the new European Union. Hitherto, the 'Community method' had prevailed, with all Member States signing up to the same agreed objectives. Now, thanks to the British opt outs on EMU and social issues, the way had been opened to selective participation by Member States in policy areas of their choosing. Ironically, this idea of a two-speed Europe was something to which all British governments had been opposed.

Prior to the IGCs, John Major and Douglas Hurd had rejected a multi-speed Europe as divisive and liable to lead to the permanent marginalization of those Member States who chose not to participate in certain areas. Although also opposed to a multi-speed Europe, Mrs Thatcher had taken a different line, contending not only that such a Europe would allow other Member States to forge ahead with integration measures over which Britain would have no influence or control but also that it would create an irresistible momentum which would ultimately force Britain to participate in those measures after all. She therefore advised that the government should exercise its veto rather than follow a course of partial involvement.[1] Arguably, however, the difference between the two Prime Ministers was that John Major was faced with the reality of exercising the British veto and through political expediency took a short-term view whereas Mrs Thatcher was not. Major was willing to settle for determining the terms and conditions of Britain's own self-exclusion from particular policy issues and at that time appeared prepared to put up with the longer-term implications of his decision.

Given this difference, it is interesting to consider whether Major's stance was wholly tactical or whether he was also in substance more pro-European than Mrs Thatcher. To some extent, Major and his advisers vastly over-stated the extent to which Mrs Thatcher's style alone had marginalized the British government. The evidence of the Maastricht negotiations suggests that he was on substance more pro-European than Mrs Thatcher, and genuinely believed in the idea of placing Britain at the very heart of Europe at the time he put it forward in the spring of 1991. However, this aspiration steadily evaporated in the absence of a firm domestic base from which to negotiate with other governments and in the face of a clear indication that other Member State governments wanted to move further and faster than Major was able to accept.[2]

Yet the fact that Britain was allowed the expedient of her opt outs illustrates that another, well-established aspect of EC policy-making was alive and flourishing in the new EU. This was the degree of collusion between Heads of Government based on a mutual understanding that they should not create difficulties for colleagues in awkward domestic situations.[3] Certainly Britain's partners did not want her to veto the Treaty, and this was an important incentive behind their offering the opt outs as a solution to her difficulties on EMU and social policy. But the drastic nature of the veto cut both ways. Thus, although the Treaty amendments required unanimity the political reality of the negotiations was that the government could only threaten the British veto on a handful of points. The evidence is that other Heads of Government were acutely conscious of Major's volatile domestic situation – not least because he was only too ready to provide them with evidence of it – and that they were prepared to seek concessions in order to ease this situation and so secure the Treaty.[4]

In terms of the implications of the TEU for the European integration project itself, the course and conduct of the IGCs of 1990 to 1991 touched on a whole range of issues, such as the purpose and identity of the EC/EU and its claims to be legitimate and democratic. It is important to remember, however, that it was only the IGC-EMU which had from the outset a clearly defined objective. In addition, both IGCs had their immediate origins in the momentous and confusing events surrounding the collapse of communism and the reunification of Germany. Thus much of the old baggage of previous debates and controversies reappeared at the conference table in 1990 to 1991, and the outcome of the negotiations can only be understood in their context of the pre-history of the European integration project. And, so far as the IGC-PU was concerned, Jacques Delors was straying from the truth when he declared of the 1990 to 1991 negotiations that everyone else was playing football while the British Prime Minister had decided to play rugby.[5] If everyone else was playing football, they were certainly doing so with a minimal knowledge of the objectives of the game. The essential weakness of the Treaty articles based on the IGC-PU were that they were not a product of a carefully thought-through and logical process. In the absence of any clearly defined objective, the negotiations became genuinely open ended and a vehicle for particular pet projects of individual Member States.

In view of these inauspicious beginnings, the final Treaty made surprisingly large steps in advancing the integration process. This was most obvious in the sphere of EMU, but on the question of enhancing the powers of the EP, too, the introduction of the co-decision procedure marked a significant first step towards resolving the notorious democratic deficit problem. Even on defence, there was agreement that the Union might in future develop a defence responsibility. But the price of this clearer definition of the aims of the European integration project was the abandonment of the Community method and the opening of the way to a multi-speed Europe. The question of whether this strengthens or weakens the project is a moot point. On the face of it, it would seem axiomatic that the ideal of integration is nothing if it is not inclusive, and that enterprises like the single currency need the participation of all to succeed. Yet this needs to be set against the growth in membership of the Union from its original 6 participants to its present 15, and the enthusiasm of the states of Eastern Europe to become involved in the process. If enlargement is indeed to proceed, recognition of the diversity of Member States and an admission that some will be better able or willing to participate in particular areas of integration seems only good sense.

In terms of the implications of the TEU for Britain's relationship with Europe, the argument of this book has been that British attitudes and achievements in the negotiations of 1990 to 1991 were most immediately the product of a highly particular set of external and domestic circumstances. John Major found himself under intense external pressure to assist with, or at least acquiesce in, steps towards closer integration. At the same time, he was preoccupied with a highly unstable situation in the governing Conservative Party following the overthrow of Mrs Thatcher and the need to prepare for a general election in 1992.

Yet, as the foregoing chapters have also indicated, it would be an incomplete explanation to portray Major's policy simply as a product of these very particular circumstances. To conclude that 'John Major was caught in a strait jacket of party controversy' is too glib, for it falsely implies that Major was bound in the same way on each issue and had no room for manoeuvre at all.[6] Moreover, this conclusion fails to take into account the degree of pressure which Britain was under by 1990 from external sources to participate in, or at the very least to stop impeding, steps towards closer European integration. The Prime Minister's actions were embedded in the history of the European integration project and the British relationship with it. And at the centre of this historical relationship were two important British failures. The first was an underestimation of the political momentum in other Member States of the EC to advance the integration process. The second was Britain's failure to resolve the dichotomy between adherence to the doctrine of the absolute sovereignty of the Westminster Parliament and the implications of the integration project. Successive governments of all political persuasions had thus involved Britain ever more deeply in moves towards integration, while at the same time failing to educate backbenchers and the public about how this impacted upon parliamentary sovereignty.

Thus, although it was in fact only on EMU that an opt out had been seriously examined in advance of the Maastricht European Council, the policy of selective involvement on which Britain embarked with the TEU was in a sense the logical product of Britain's long-standing attitudes towards Europe. As so often before, policy-makers failed to recognize the determination of their partners to proceed with further moves towards integration, most obviously on EMU and social policy. And, as so often before, the government shrank from grasping the nettle of engaging its domestic audience in a thoroughgoing debate on sovereignty and integration. The policy of selective involvement was thus not simply an aberration brought about by a peculiar combination of external and domestic circumstances. It should be seen in the context of Britain's European dilemma. The government was unwilling to withdraw from the process altogether, yet at the same time was deeply uncomfortable with the consequences of full participation in the process of integration.

A further consideration raised by the new policy of selective involvement is the question mark it poses concerning the validity of the image of Britain as an 'awkward partner' in Europe, resisting compromise and generally seeking to impede agreement. In fact, it seems that a rather more subtle image of Britain's dealings with its European partners is needed. The shortcomings of the 'awkward partner' school of thought – at least for this period of time – are underlined by the rather narrow assumptions it makes about the domestic impact on Britain's European policy. The argument relies in large part on the operation of the first-past-the-post and adversarial party system.[7] It assumes that the party in opposition automatically opposes government policy and so limits the government's negotiating space. With the Labour Party a recent convert to a pro-European stance, the awkward partner thesis would suggest the government's room for manoeuvre would be small in 1990 to 1991.[8] In fact the Labour Party was relatively quiescent during the negotiations especially on EMU, and it was Major's own party which did most to constrict his scope to negotiate. In 1991 it was the intra-governing party division and the threat the outcome posed to the Conservative Party's ideological self-image which provide the key party explanation of the British government's behaviour.[9] Indeed, one might actually argue that Major's position would have been far more difficult if Labour had taken an actively anti-European position, since this would have allowed Eurosceptics the opportunity of voting with the opposition on occasion.

As regards Britain's political methods of doing business, of refusing to accept linkages between different policy sectors and accepting concessions from others, but refusing to give anything in return, the style was clearly awkward. A key problem was that there were few positive goals that the government wanted to achieve and there was virtually nothing on either IGC agenda to attract the government. It is true the government tabled a number of proposals, for example on foreign policy, but there were two weaknesses to the British position. It soon became obvious that other governments wanted to go further than the British government and a number of the British proposals (notably on JHA issues) were tabled simply so that there should be a minimalist text to counter those put forward by others. Other British proposals, such as increased powers for the ECJ and the Audit Court, concerned minor issues and definitely not things which the government was prepared to pay a price for. However, even though Britain appeared to be out of step on a number of key issues and lacked the political commitment to the process, its awkwardness did fall short of holding the Treaty negotiations to ransom, provided that an acceptable means to accommodate the British government's view could be found.

Finally, while there has often been a distinction between style and substance in Britain's European policy, two conclusions can be drawn from the 1990–1 IGC negotiations. First, as the chapter on EMU has shown, the hard ECU plan was fatally weakened by the personal stance of Mrs Thatcher who was unwilling to accept that the hard ECU might one day lead to a single currency.[10] The technical merits of the hard ECU plan were thus fatally undermined by the diplomatic strategy chosen to accompany this initiative. Second, the change in political style in handling European partners, from that of Margaret Thatcher to John Major – from crude anti-Germanism and confrontation to an attempt to build a stronger relationship with Germany and a more consensual style of bargaining – was not sufficient to obscure the fundamental differences between the British government and its partners on the substance of policy under discussion at the Maastricht IGCs.

The year-long negotiations also raised an important issue concerning the British government's external strategy for handling the IGC negotiations through *rapprochement* with Germany. This *rapprochement* was built on a strong personal relationship between the new British Prime Minister and German Chancellor. It was true that this did ease the way for the EMU and social policy opt outs and that Helmut Kohl was willing to make compromises to take into account many British objections, but the British government never thought Bonn would want to be seen to block a treaty, which, however modest compared to their own aspirations, was in a significant number of areas a move towards closer integration. Ultimately what is clear, however, is that Britain's pro-German diplomatic strategy could not compensate for the fundamental weakness of the Major government, namely that it negotiated without any commitment to closer European integration.

Some journalists, scholars, and even certain politicians, have argued that German support came at a price. This price was the overturning of British objections to recognition of Croatia and Slovenia, a policy to which Germany was deeply committed and which was agreed between foreign ministers within days of the Maastricht European Council on 16–17 December 1991.[11] Douglas Hurd has denied that any such deal took place and the evidence of this book is supportive of his claim.[12] As Chapter 1 has shown, the British government was simply not in a position to offer or accept a deal like this. By the early summer of 1991 it was apparent that London would not be able to pre-commit itself to a single currency and the opt out solution appealed to its partners in its own right – a solution agreed in principle at the Luxembourg Council some six months prior to the recognition issue. As far as the social policy opt out is concerned, the case for linkage might be plausible, since it was a last-minute expedient at the Maastricht European Council. When challenged, Major was willing to bring the negotiations to the brink of collapse over this issue, and, while the German Chancellor was a key player, he was only one – and not even the most antagonistic – of ten other Heads of Government who had to approve the social policy opt out.

Confusion may exist over the linkage question because, at the meeting to discuss recognition of Croatia and Slovenia, the German Foreign Minister (in the presence of officials) pointedly said to Hurd that the German government had been sympathetic to British domestic concerns over the Maastricht Treaty and now expected the British to be sympathetic to Bonn's position. It may well be that the German government thought there was implicit linkage between their acquiescence at Maastricht and the recognition issue, but this was not true for the British government. Indeed, at the meeting to consider recognition, Hurd (with lukewarm support from the French Foreign Minister) was one of the few foreign ministers arguing that EC recognition should be postponed.[13] In part, Hurd acquiesced because he thought Germany would announce recognition anyway and thought it better that France, Britain and Germany had a united policy. In part, Hurd thought there would be little point in a fundamental break with Germany on this issue which, by December 1991, the British government itself saw as inevitable, and essentially a difference of timing rather than of principle. While the evidence suggests there was no deal, the difference between British and German perceptions and confusion surrounding this issue might well go some way towards explaining why the relationship between John Major and Kohl was so transient and volatile, with Maastricht marking the high point.

It is an interesting question – particularly in view of subsequent events in the Conservative Party – to consider whether, in less politically volatile circumstances, even a managerial Prime Minister like John Major who looked at everything through a Whip's eyes might have taken a firmer line either in resisting pressures to compromise from his negotiating partners or forcing his party to accept concessions on the European issue and riding out opposition. It has been argued that Major could only have resolved the issue of Europe by confronting his party, like Peel, with a stark choice. The possible corollary of this, however, might well have been an open split and the possibility that the majority of his backbenchers and some of his

Cabinet might have deserted him.[14] And, in the short term at least, Major's strategy paid off, helping him to secure that ultimate measure of political success, a fourth election victory for his party.

The real problem for Major was that although his close control of information about the negotiations and avoidance of any real parliamentary – or indeed public – debate on most issues during the period 1990 and 1991 certainly paid short-term dividends in terms of controlling a potentially volatile domestic audience, it did so only at the cost of building up even greater suspicion and resentment for the future. The feeling of deception among Eurosceptic backbenchers, built up over 12 months of the IGC negotiations, was an important part of the backlash during the Maastricht ratification debates. And by the time the Maastricht Treaty had been ratified, the opportunity for calm and reasoned public debate about the issue of Europe was gone.

Among the various right-wing groupings, it was only the Friends of Bruges and the European Reform Group which were at all organized during the debates leading to the TEU and there was little co-operation between them. The Maastricht Bill changed that. It took over a year to ratify, 70 parliamentary votes and 61 debates, and was only passed in July 1993, when the government made it a confidence issue.[15] During this time, back-bench resentment was given full rein and ratification finally revealed the depth and bitterness of the fissures in the Conservative Party. By the end of this process, Eurosceptics had become far better organized and financed, and, while the different groupings never merged, there was sufficient overlap of membership and a unity of purpose to have a devastating effect both for the government's European policy and party unity.[16]

There is one final aspect of Britain's relationship with Europe which is often neglected and which deserves further comment here. Evidence from the Maastricht negotiations suggests that IGCs present particular problems for British governments. First, IGCs like those of 1990 to 1991 have a clear (but often arbitrary) deadline for conclusions to be reached. When combined with the intensity of IGC negotiations, this marks the process out as rather different from more routine bargaining. In particular, it telescopes the pressures under which the British government always operates. Second, constitutional or treaty-making negotiations raise the shadow of the future, and in particular the ultimate aim of the integration process, an issue which the British have always shrunk from addressing. Almost inevitably this also involves arguments concerning commitments to rhetorical statements which challenge the British self-perception as practical and pragmatic people. Third and finally, treaty amendments necessitate a parliamentary ratification process, which, given the strongly held views on Europe in British political parties, often challenges the very limits of party loyalty in a way that few other issues can. The British government's insistence on presenting the outcome of IGC negotiations as a 100 per cent success is just another aspect of the refusal to educate the parliamentary elite and the electorate on the process of integration. Perhaps, understandably, the temptation is strong on a matter such as a treaty amendment where unanimity is required, since governments feel vulnerable to the question of why they reached agreement – but arguably this is a reflection of the nature and weakness of the British discourse on European integration. In short, all IGCs will be a difficult process for British governments to manage. Some IGCs, however, are more difficult than others, and, as this book has demonstrated, the domestic circumstances of 1990 to 1991 ensured that negotiations culminating in the Maastricht Treaty were supremely difficult.

Where then does this leave the British relationship with Europe and the prospects for her future participation in the integration project? Despite their post-Maastricht strength and widespread support amongst the general public, it is possible that the Eurosceptics may yet be defeated by the flaws in their own arguments. As one scholar has pointed out, there is an anomaly at the heart of the Eurosceptic claim that the EU is undemocratic, since greater democratization would lead to greater accountability and legitimacy for EU actions and so strengthen it in relation to national parliaments.[17] The problem, however, is that, until an effort is made to resolve the fundamental dichotomy between integration and sovereignty, each new development in the integration project will continue to reopen all the old debates. Perhaps ultimately, therefore, the British relationship with Europe, and the prospects for Britain's future involvement in moves towards closer integration are dependent on the continuing success of the project. Jean Monnet stated, 'there is only one thing you British will never understand: an idea. And there is one thing you are supremely good at grasping: a hard fact.'[18] And the hard facts of economic, social and political success might ultimately prove difficult to resist.

NOTES

1. See Thatcher, *The Downing Street Years*, op. cit., p. 479.
2. Author's interviews. One of the negotiators who had close dealings with John Major said 'having seen him at close quarters ... I think Major had in his own mind strict limits as to how far he would go, I just don't know what they were.'
3. See for instance *Agence Europe*, 5 July 1991.
4. On this see for instance Middlemas, *Orchestrating Europe*, op. cit., p. 189.
5. *Daily Telegraph* Writers, 'Reactions', *Daily Telegraph*, 12 December 1991.
6. Jim Bulpitt, 'Conservative Leaders and the "Euro-Ratchet": Five Doses of Scepticism', *Political Quarterly*, vol. 63, no. 3, 1992, pp. 258–75.
7. See Nigel Ashford, 'The Political Parties', in George, *Britain and the European Community*, pp. 119–48.
8. See for instance Deighton, 'Une maladie imaginaire', op. cit., p. 60
9. These are the two other explanations provided by Ashford under the general heading of political parties and this represents a reformulation rather than refutation of Nigel Ashford's explanation. See Ashford, 'Political Parties', op. cit., p. 119.
10. This point is also made by Stephen George, 'A Reply to Buller', *Politics*, vol. 15, no. 1, 1995, pp. 43–7, p. 44.
11. See for example Seldon's remark, based on a private interview, that 'diplomats close to the process do not dissent that there was an informal understanding'. Seldon, *Major*, op. cit., pp. 249 and 304–5.
12. Author's interview with Douglas Hurd.
13. This was in line with Lord Carrington the EC's special emissary's advice, that recognition should be delayed to extract further concessions from the Croatian government. Hurd was sent to the meeting with an open remit and instructions to report back to the Prime Minister as he saw fit.
14. See for instance Baker, et al., '1846 ... 1906 ... 1996 Conservative splits and European integration', *Political Quarterly*, vol. 64, no. 4, 1993, p. 428, and Seldon, 'The Conservative Party', in Kavanagh and Seldon, *The Major Effect*, op. cit., p. 43.
15. Seldon, *Major*, op. cit., p. 389.
16. Author's interview with Bill Cash MP.
17. Colin Pilkington, *Britain in the European Union*, Manchester, Manchester University Press, 1995, p. 116.
18. Quoted in Uwe Kitzinger, *Diplomacy and Persuasion*, London: Thames and Hudson, 1973.

Select Bibliography

UNPUBLISHED MATERIAL

Blair, Alasdair, 'The UK and the Negotiation of the Maastricht Treaty, 1990–1991', Ph.D. thesis, Leicester University, 1997.

Budden, Philip, 'The Making of the Single European Act: the United Kingdom and the European Community 1979–86', D.Phil. thesis, University of Oxford, 1994.

Marks, Gary, 'European Integration since the 1980s: State-Centric Versus Multi-Level Governance', paper presented at the American Political Science Association Meeting, Chicago, 31 August–3 September, 1995, p. 9.

Mayer, Fritz, 'Bargains within Bargains: Domestic Politics in International Negotiations', Ph.D. diss., Kennedy School of Government, Harvard University, May 1988.

Montero, Carlos J. Closa, 'The Creation of the European Political Union', Ph.D. thesis, Hull University, 1993.

Ponting, Lucy, 'A Creature That Walks without Clothes? EC Responses to the Yugoslavia Crisis, 1991–2', M.Phil. thesis, Oxford, 1993.

Richter, Fabian, 'British and German Attitudes to the European Parliament', undergraduate dissertation, Oxford University, 1995.

PUBLISHED MATERIAL

Select Committee Reports

House of Commons Select Committee on Procedure, *The Scrutiny of European Legislation*, Session 1988/9, House of Commons Paper 368–I and II.

Select Committee on the European Communities, *Economic and Monetary Union and Political Union*, 27th Report, session 1989–90, House of Lords Paper 88–II.

Defence Implications of Recent Events, Tenth Report of the House of Commons Defence Committee, London, Her Majesty's Stationery Office, 1990.

Select Committee on the European Communities, *Political Union: Law-Making Powers and Procedures*, session 1990–91, 17th Report, 1991, House of Lords Paper 80.

Europe after Maastricht, Foreign Affairs Committee, Second Report Vol. II House of Commons, Session 1991–92, 223–II.

Acts of Parliament and Statements

The United Kingdon and the European Communities, Cmd 4715, July 1971.
Statement on the Defence Estimates 1990, Cmd 1022–1, London, HMSO, April 1990.
Statement on the Defence Expenditures: Britain's Defence for the 1990s, Cmd 1559–I, London, HMSO, 1991.
Statement on Defence Estimates, Cmnd 1981, London, HMSO, July 1992.
Industrial Relations in the 1990s, London, HMSO, CM. 1602, 1991.

European Community Institutions

'Draft Treaty Establishing the European Union', *Official Journal*, no. C.77, 19 March 1984.
'Commission of the European Communities', *Community Charter of Fundamental Basic Rights*, COM (89), Brussels, October 1989.
Communication from the Commission Concerning its Action Programme Relating to the Implementation of the Community Charter of Basic Social Rights for Workers, COM (89) 568, Brussels, November 1989.
'Resolution on the IGC in the Context of the Parliament's Strategy on European Union', *Official Journal*, no. C.96, 17 April 1990.
'Commission Opinion of 21 October 1990 on the Proposal for Amendment of the Treaty Establishing the EEC with a View to Political Union', *Bulletin of the European Communities*, supplement 2/91, Luxembourg, pp. 75–82.
Treaty on European Union, Luxembourg, Office for Official Publications of the European Communities, 1992.

Newspapers and Non-academic Journals

Daily Telegraph
Economist
Evening Standard
Financial Times
Guardian
Independent
Marxism Today
New Statesman and Society
Sunday Telegraph
Sunday Times
The Times

Parliamentary Debates

Parliamentary Debates, Sixth Series, House of Commons

Memoirs Biographies and Autobiographies

Anderson, Brian, *John Major: the Making of the Prime Minister*, London, Fourth Estate, 1991.
Baker, Kenneth, *The Turbulent Years: My Life in Politics*, London, Faber and Faber, 1993.
Balen, Malcolm, *Ken Clarke*, London, Fourth Estate, 1994.
Hogg, Sarah, and Hill, Johnathan, *Too Close to Call*, London, Little Brown, 1995.
Howe, Geoffrey, *Conflict of Loyalty*, London, Macmillan, 1994.
Junor, Penny, *The Major Enigma*, London, Michael Joseph, 1993.
Lawson, Nigel, *The View from No. 11*, London, Bantam Press, 1992.
McSmith, Andy, *Ken Clarke: a Political Biography*, London, Verso, 1994.
Ridley, Nicholas, *'My Style of Government': the Thatcher Years*, London, Fontana, 1992.
Seldon, Anthony, *Major: a Political life*, London, Weidenfeld and Nicholson, 1997.
Thatcher, Margaret, *The Downing Street Years*, London, Harper Collins, 1993.
Thatcher, Margaret, *The Path to Power*, London, Harper Collins, 1995.

Secondary Works

Addison, John. T, and Siebert, W. Stanley, 'The Social Charter: Whatever Next?', *British Journal of Industrial Relations*, vol. 30, no. 4, December 1992, pp. 495–513.
Agnail, Martin, 'Labour's Defence Review', *RUSI Journal*, vol. 135, no. 3, Autumn 1990, pp. 1–7.
Aldrich, John, 'A Downsian Spatial Model with Party Activism', *American Political Science Review*, vol. 77, 1983, pp. 974–90.
Allen, David , 'Foreign Policy at the European Level: Beyond the Nation-State?', in Wallace, William, and Paterson, William (eds), *Foreign Policy-Making in Western Europe*, Farnborough, Saxon House, 1978, pp. 147–90.
Allen, David, 'British Foreign Policy and West European Co-operation', in Byrd, Peter (ed.), *Foreign Policy under Thatcher*, Oxford, Philip and Allen, 1988, pp. 35–53.
Andrews, David, 'The Global Origins of the Maastricht Treaty on EMU: Closing the Window of Opportunity', in Rosenthal, Glenda, and Cafruny, Alan (eds), *The State of the European Community: the Maastricht Debates and Beyond*, vol. 2, London, Lynne Rienner/Longman, 1993, pp. 107–42.
Atkinson, Roy, and McWhirter, Norris, *Treason at Maastricht: the Destruction of the Nation-State*, Newcastle, Compuprint, 1994.
Baker, David, Gamble, Andrew, Fountain, Imogen, and Ludlam, Steve, 'Backbench Conservative Attitudes to European Integration', *Political Quarterly*, vol. 66, no. 2, April–June 1995, pp. 221–33.
Baker, David, Gamble, Andrew, and Ludlam, Steve, '1846 … 1906 … 1996 Conservative Splits and European Integration', *Political Quarterly*, vol. 64, no. 4, 1993, pp. 420–34.
Baker, David, Gamble, Andrew, and Ludlam, Steve, 'Whips or Scorpions?

The Maastricht Vote and the Conservative Party', *Parliamentary Affairs*, vol. 46, no. 2, April 1993, pp. 147–66.

Baker, David, Gamble, Andrew, and Ludlam, Steve, 'The Parliamentary Seige of Maastricht 1993: Conservative Divisions and British Ratification', *Parliamentary Affairs*, vol. 47. no. 1, January 1994, pp. 37–60.

Baker, James, 'A New Europe, a New Atlanticism, Architecture for a New Era', *US Mission to the EC*, Public Affairs Office, 12 December 1989.

Baker, Kenneth (ed.), *The Faber Book of Conservatism*, London, Faber and Faber, 1993.

Baldwin Edwards, Martin, and Gough, Ian, 'European Community Social Policy and the UK', in Manning, Nick (ed.), *Social Policy Review 1990–91*, London, Longman, 1991, pp. 147–67.

Barnard, Alan, 'A Social Policy for Europe: Politicians 1 Lawyers 0', *International Journal of Comparative Labour Law and Industrial Relations*, no. 8, 1992, pp. 15–31.

Barnes, John, 'Ideology and Factions', in Seldon, Anthony, and Ball, Stuart (eds), *Conservative Century: the Conservative Party since 1900*, Oxford, Oxford University Press, 1994, pp. 315–45.

Bayliss, John, *British Defence Policy*, London, Macmillan, 1989.

Becker, Kurt, 'The Role of the Media', in Merlini, Cesare (ed.), *Economic Summits and Western Decision-Making*, Beckenham, Croom Helm/EIPA, 1984, pp. 153–66.

Bellany, Ian, *Reviewing British Defence*, Dartmouth, Dartmouth Press, 1994.

Bender, Brian, 'Government Process, Whitehall, Central Government and 1992', *Public Policy and Administration*, vol. 6, no. 1, Spring 1991, pp. 13–20.

Bercusson, Brian, 'Maastricht: a Fundamental Change in European Labour Law', *Industrial Relations Journal*, vol. 23, no. 3, Autumn 1992, pp. 177–91.

Bissell, Paul, 'Thatcherism and the Conservative Party', *Political Studies*, vol. XLI, no. 2, June 1994, pp. 185–203.

Brewster, Chris, and Teague, Paul, *EC Social Policy: Its Impact on the UK*, London, Academic Press in association with Institute of Personnel Management, 1989.

Brittan, Leon, *The Europe We Need*, London, Hamish Hamilton, 1994.

Buller, Jim, 'Britain as an Awkward Partner: Reassessing Britain's Relations with the EU', *Politics*, vol. 15, no. 1, 1995, pp. 33–42.

Bulmer, Simon, 'Domestic Politics and European Community Policy-Making', *Journal of Common Market Studies*, vol. 21, no. 4, 1983, pp. 349–63.

Bulmer, Simon, George, Stephen, and Scott, Andrew (eds), *The UK and EC Membership Evaluated*, London, Pinter, 1992.

Bulpitt, Jim, 'Conservative Statecraft in the Open Polity', in Byrd, Peter (ed.), *British Foreign Policy under Mrs Thatcher*, Oxford, Oxford University Press, 1988, pp. 180–205.

Bulpitt, Jim, 'Conservative Leaders and the "Euro-Ratchet": Five Doses of Scepticism', *Political Quarterly*, vol. 63, no. 3, 1992, pp. 258–75.

Butler, David, Adonis, Andrew, and Travers, Tony, *Failure in British Government: the Politics of the Poll Tax*, Oxford, Oxford University Press, 1994.

Butt Philip, Alan, 'Westminster versus Brussels', in Howarth, Jolyon, and

Maclean, John (eds), *Europeans on Europe*, London, Macmillan, 1992.

Cameron, David, 'The 1992 Initiative: Causes and Consequences', in Sbragia, Alberta (ed.), *Euro Politics*, Washington DC, Brookings Institute, 1992, pp. 23–74.

Camps, Miriam, *The European Common Market*, Princeton, Princeton University Press, 1957.

Carver, Michael, *Tightrope Walking: British Defence Policy since 1945*, London, Hutchinson, 1992.

Cash, William, *Europe: the Crunch*, London, Duckworth, 1991.

Choice and Responsibility, No Turning Back Group, London, Conservative Political Centre, September 1990.

Clarke, Michael, 'The Policy-Making Process', in Smith, Michael, Smith, Steve, and White, Barry, *British Foreign Policy*, London, Unwin Hyman, 1988.

Clarke, Michael, *British External Foreign Policy Making in the 1990s*, London, Macmillan, 1992.

Cloos, Jim, et al. (eds), *Le Traité de Maastricht: genèse, analyse, commentaires*, Brussels, Emile Bruylant, 1993.

Coker, Christopher, 'The Special Relationship in the 1990's', *International Affairs*, vol. 68, no. 3, July 1992, pp. 407–22.

Connolly, Bernard, *The Rotten Heart of Europe*, London, Faber and Faber, 1995.

Corbett, Richard, 'Testing the New Procedures: the EP's First Experiences with Its New Single Act Powers', *Journal of Common Market Studies*, vol. XXVII, no. 4, June 1989.

Corbett, Richard, 'The Intergovernmental Conference on Political Union', *Journal of Common Market Studies*, vol. XXX, no. 3, September 1992, pp. 271–98.

Corbett, Richard, *The Treaty of Maastricht: from Conception to Ratification*, Harlow, Longman, 1993.

Cosgrove, Patrick, *The Lives of Enoch Powell*, London, Bodley Head, 1989.

Davies, A. J., *We, the Nation: the Conservative Party and the Pursuit of Power*, London, Little Brown, 1995.

Defence and Security in the New Europe, London, European Democratic Group, 1991.

Deighton, Anne, 'Say it with Documents: British Policy Overseas 1945–52', *Review of International Studies*, vol. 18, no. 4, 1990, pp. 393–402.

Deighton, Anne, 'Une maladie imaginaire: Englands Europaische Dilemma', in Beutler, Beatrice (ed.), *Reflexions über Europa*, München, Aktuel, 1992, pp. 52–63.

Delors, Jacques, 'European Integration and Security', *Survival*, March–April, vol. XXXII, no. 2, 1991, pp. 99–109.

Dickie, John, *Inside the Foreign Office*, London, Chapmans, 1992.

Dinan, Desmond, *Ever Closer Union?*, London, Macmillan, 1994.

Doutriaux, Yves, *Le Traité sur L'Union Européenne*, Paris, Armand Collin, 1992.

Dudley-Edwards, Ruth, *True Brits: Inside the Foreign Office*, London, BBC Books, 1994.

Duff, Andrew, Pinder, John, and Pryce, Roy (eds), *Maastricht and Beyond*, London, Routledge, 1994.

Dunleavy, Patrick, and Rhodes, R. A. W. (eds), *Cabinet, Core Executive and Prime Minister*, London, Macmillan, 1995.

European Dimensions of Collective Bargaining after Maastricht, Brussels, European Trade Union Institute, 1992, pp. 63–8.

Evans, Peter, Jacobson, Harold, and Putnam, David (eds), *Double Edged Diplomacy: International Bargaining and Domestic Politics*, Berkeley, Calif., University of California Press, 1993.

Fink-Hoojer, Florika, 'The Common Foreign and Security Policy of the European Union', *European Journal of International Law*, vol. 5, no. 2, 1994, pp. 173–98.

Forster, Anthony, 'The United Kingdom', in Anstis, Charles, and Moens, Alexander (eds), *Disconcerted Europe: the Search for a New Security Architecture*, Boulder, Colorado, Westview, 1993, pp. 135–58.

Forster, Anthony, 'Britain and the Negotiation of the Maastricht Treaty: a Critique of Liberal Intergovernmentalism', *Journal of Common Market Studies*, vol. 36, no. 3, September 1998, pp. 347–68

Frankel, James, *The Making of British Foreign Policy: 1945–73*, London, Oxford University Press, 1975.

Freedman, Lawrence, 'The Case of Westland and the Bias to Europe', *International Affairs*, vol. 63, no. 2, 1986, pp. 1–19.

Fursdon, Edward, *The European Defence Community: a History*, London, Macmillan, 1980.

Galbraith, J. K., 'Power and Organisation', in Lukes, Steven (ed.), *Power*, Oxford, Blackwells, 1986, pp. 211–33.

Gambles, Ian, 'Prospects for West European Security Cooperation', *Adelphi Papers*, no. 244, London, Brassey's for IISS, Autumn 1989.

George, Stephen, *Politics and Policy in the EC*, Oxford, Oxford University Press, 1991.

George, Stephen, 'The British Government and the Maastricht Agreements', in Rosenthal and Cafruny, *State of the European Community*, vol. 2, pp. 177–92.

George, Stephen, *An Awkward Partner*, Oxford, Oxford University Press, 2nd ed., 1994.

George, Stephen, 'A Reply to Buller', *Politics*, vol. 15, no. 1, 1995, pp. 43–7.

Geyer, Robert, 'Democratic Socialism and the EC: the British Case', *Journal of European Integration*, vol. XVI, no. 1, pp. 5–28.

Gnesotto, Nicole, 'Défense européenne: pourquoi pas les Douze?', *Politique Étrangère*, vol. 55, no. 4, 1990, pp. 881–3.

Gorman, Teressa, *The Bastards: Dirty Tricks and the Challenge to Europe*, London, Pan Books, 1993.

Grant, Charles, *Delors: Inside the House that Jacques Built*, London, Nicholas Brealey, 1994.

Grant, Wyn, *Pressure Groups, Politics and Democracy in Britain*, London, Philip Allan, 1989.

Greenwood, David, 'Expenditure and Management', in Byrd, Peter (ed.), *British Defence Policy: Thatcher and Beyond*, London, Philip Allan, 1991, pp. 36–66.

Greenwood, Justin, *Transnational Organisations and European Integration*, London, Sage, 1992.

Gucht, Karel de, and Keukeleire, Stephen, 'The European Security Architecture: the Role of the European Community in Shaping a New European Geopolitical Landscape', *Studia Diplomatica*, vol. XLIV, no. 6, 1992, pp. 29–90.

Guy Peters, B., 'Bureaucratic Politics and the Institutions of the European Community', in Sbragia, Alberta (ed.), *Euro Politics*, Washington DC, Brookings Institute, 1992, pp. 75–122.

Hall, Mark, 'Industrial Relations and the Social Dimension', in Hyman, R., and Ferner, A. (eds), *New Frontiers in Industrial Relations*, Oxford, Blackwells, 1994, pp. 281–311.

Hansenne, Alan, 'Does Europe Want Flexibility through Deregulation', *Social and Labour Bulletin*, no. 4, pp. 1–8.

Hartley, Anthony, 'America and Britain: Is the Relationship Still Special?', London, Centre for Policy Studies, no. 137, 1994.

Hartley, Keith, 'The Defence Budget', *Defence Implications of Recent Events*, House of Commons Paper 320, Session 1989–90, London, Her Majesty's Stationery Office, 1990, pp. 125–8.

Hartley, Keith, Hussain, Farooq, Smith, Ron, 'The UK Defence Industrial Base', *Political Quarterly*, vol. 58, no. 1, January–March 1987, pp. 62–72.

Hartog, Arthur den, 'Greece and European Political Union', in Laursen, Finn, and van Hoonacker, Sophie (eds), *The Intergovernmental Conference on Political Union*, Maastricht, European Institute of Public Administration, 1992, pp. 79–97.

Hayward, J. E. S., *The State and the Market Economy*, Hemel Hemstead, Harvester Wheatsheaf, 1983.

Heclo, Hugh, and Wildavsky, Aron, *The Private Government of Public Money: Community and Policy inside British Politics*, London, Macmillan, 1974.

Hennessy, Peter, *Cabinet*, Oxford, Oxford University Press, 1986.

Hennessy, Peter, *Whitehall*, London, Fontana, 1988.

Heseltine, Michael, *Where There's a Will*, London, Hutchinson, 1987.

Heseltine, Michael, *The Challenge of Europe: Can Britain Win?*, London, Wiedenfeld and Nicholson, 1989.

Heseltine, Michael, *The Democratic Deficit: the Balance in Europe for Britain to Redress*, London, Centre for Policy Studies Paper No. 10, 1989.

Heywood, Paul, 'British Politics in the 1990s: the Return of Consensus', *Talking Politics*, vol. 4, no. 2, Winter 1991–2, pp. 74–5.

Hill, Christopher, 'Britain: a Convenient Schizophrenia', in Hill, Christopher (ed.), *National Foreign Policies and European Political Co-operation*, London, Allen and Unwin/RIIA, 1983.

Hill, Christopher, *Cabinet Decisions on Foreign Policy: the British Experience October 1938–June 1941*, Cambridge, Cambridge University Press, 1991.

Hill, Christopher, 'The European Community: Towards a Common Foreign and Security Policy', *The World Today*, vol. 47, no. 11, 1991, pp. 189–93.

Hill, Christopher, 'Foreign Policy', in Catterall, Peter (ed.), *Contemporary Britain: an Annual Review, 1992*, Aldershot, Dartmouth, pp. 132–44.

Hoffmann, Stanley, 'The European Process at Atlantic Cross-Purposes', *Journal of Common Market Studies*, April 1964, pp. 85–101.

Hoffmann, Stanley, 'Obstinate or Obsolete? "The Fate of the Nation State and the Case of Western Europe"', *Daedalus*, vol. 95, no. 3, 1966, pp. 882–97.

Hoffmann, Stanley, 'Reflections on the Nation State in Western Europe Today', *Journal of Common Market Studies*, vol. XXI, nos 1 & 2, September/December 1982, pp. 21–38.

Holland, Martin, 'Electoral Status and Candidate Selection: Data and Findings from the 1989 British Direct Elections to the EP', *Political Science*, vol. 38, no. 2, 1991, pp. 157–71.

Horne, Alistair, *Macmillan: 1957–86*, London, Macmillan, 1989.

Howe, Geoffrey, 'Sovereignty and Independence: Britain's Place in the World', *International Affairs*, vol. 66, 1990, pp. 675–95.

Howe, Geoffrey, *Britain and the European Community: a Twenty Year Balance Sheet*, occasional paper, Cambridge, Tory Reform Group, Elitian, January 1994.

Huelshoff, Michael, 'Domestic Politics and Dynamic Issue Linkage: a Reformulation of Integration Theory', *International Studies Quarterly*, vol. 38, 1994, pp. 255–79.

James, Simon, *British Cabinet Government*, London, Routledge, 1992.

Judge, David, 'Incomplete Sovereignty: the British House of Commons and the Internal Market', *Parliamentary Affairs*, vol. 57, no. 3, 1988, pp. 321–8.

Kavanagh, Dennis, and Seldon, Anthony (eds), *The Major Effect*, London, Macmillan, 1994.

Keohane, Dan, 'The Approach of British Political Parties to a Defence Role for the European Community', *Government and Opposition*, vol. 27, no. 3, Summer 1992, pp. 299–310.

Keohane, Robert, and Hoffmann, Stanley (eds), *The New European Community*, Boulder, Colorado, Westview, 1991.

King, Anthony, 'The Rise of the Career Politician – and Its Consequences', *British Journal of Political Science*, vol. 11, 1981, pp. 249–85.

Kinnock, Neil, 'International Security in a Changing World: the Labour Party Perspective', *RUSI Journal*, vol. 136, no. 2, Summer 1991, pp. 1–5.

Kitzinger, Uwe, *Diplomacy and Persuasion*, London, Thames and Hudson, 1973.

Laffan, Brigid, *Integration and Co-operation in Europe*, London, Routledge, 1992.

Lange, Peter, 'Maastricht and the Social Protocol: why did they do it?', *Politics and Society*, vol. 21, no. 1, March 1993, pp. 5–36.

Laurent, Pierre-Henri (ed.), *The European Community to Maastricht and Beyond*, Annals of the American Academy of Political Science, September 1993, pp. 91–106.

Laursen, Finn, and van Hoonacker, Sophie (eds), *The Intergovernmental Conference on Political Union*, Maastricht, European Institute of Public Administration, 1992.

Layton Henry, Zig (ed.), *Conservative Party Politics*, London, Macmillan, 1980.

Lea, David, *The UK Government's View of EC Social Policy*, Speech to the Annual Conference of the Institute of Personnel Management, 1987.

Lee, Michael, 'The Ethos of the Cabinet Office: a Comment on the Testimony of Officials', in *Public Administration*, vol. 68, Summer 1990, pp. 235–42.

Lerner, David, 'Reflections on France in the World Arena', in Lerner, David, and Aron, Raymond (eds), *France Defeats EDC*, London, Thames and Hudson, 1957.

Letwin, Shirley, *Anatomy of Thatcherism*, London, Fontana, 1992.

Lindberg, Leon, *The Political Dynamics of European Integration*, Stanford, Calif., Princeton University Press, 1968.

Lindberg, Leon, and Sheingold, Stuart, *Europe's Would-be Polity: Patterns of Change in the European Community*, Englewood Cliffs, Prentice-Hall, 1970.

Lindblom, Charles, *Politics and Markets*, New York, Basic Books, 1964.

Lingle, Christopher, 'The EC Social Charter, Social Democracy, and Post-1992 Europe', *West European Politics*, vol. 14, no. 1, January 1991, pp. 129–38.

Lodge, Juliet (ed.), *The European Community and the Challenge of the Future*, London, Pinter, 1989.

Lord, Christoper, 'Sovereign or Confused? The "Great Debate" about British Entry to the European Community 20 Years on', *Journal of Common Market Studies*, vol. XXX, no. 4, December 1992, pp. 419–36.

Lord, Christopher, *British Entry to the European Community under the Heath Government of 1970–74*, Aldershot, Dartmouth, 1993.

Ludlam, Steve, 'Major Shuffling to the Left', *Politics Review*, vol. 5, no. 3, 1993, pp. 31–3.

Malcolm, Noel, *Sense on Sovereignty*, London, Centre for Policy Studies, 1991.

Mazey, Sonia, and Lintner, Valeiro (eds), *The European Community: Economic and Political Aspects*, London, McGraw-Hill, 1991.

Mazey, Sonia, and Richardson, Jeremy (eds), *Lobbying in the European Community*, Oxford, Oxford University Press, 1993.

Mazey, Sonia, and Richardson, Jeremy, 'Policy Coordination in Brussels: Environmental and Regional Policy', *Regional Politics*, vol. 4, no. 2, Spring 1994, pp. 22–44.

McShane, Dennis, 'Europe's Next Challenge to Britain', *Political Quarterly*, vol. 66, no. 1, Jan–Mar. 1995, pp. 23–35.

Menon, Anand, 'From Independence to Cooperation: France, NATO and European Security', *International Affairs*, no. 71, no. 1, 1995, pp. 19–34.

Menon, Anand, and Kassim, Hussein (eds), *The European Community and National Industrial Policy*, London, Routledge, 1997.

Merlini, Cesare (ed.), *European Summits and Western Decision-Making*, Beckenham, Croom Helm, 1984.

Meyer, Robert, 'Key Year for Social Europe', *Industrial Relations Europe: 1992 Supplement*, newsletter, vol. 19, February 1991.

Middlemas, Keith, *Orchestrating Europe: the Informal Politics of the European Union*, London, Fontana, 1995.

Milward, Alan, *The European Rescue of the Nation State*, London, Routledge, 1992.

Milward, Alan, *The Frontier of National Sovereignty: History and Theory 1945–92*, London, Routledge, 1992.

Milward, Alan, *The Reconstruction of Western Europe*, London, Routledge, 1992.

Minogue, Kenneth, 'Is National Sovereignty a Big Bad Wolf?', in Haseler, Steven, Regan, David, Minogue, Kenneth, and Deakins, Edward (eds), *Is*

National Sovereignty a Big Bad Wolf?, Occasional Paper no. 6, London, Bruges Group, 1990, pp. 19–25.

Moravcsik, Andrew, 'Negotiating the Single European Act: National Interests and Conventional Statecraft in the European Community', *International Organisation*, vol. 45, Winter 1991, pp. 19–56.

Moravcsik, Andrew, 'Liberalism and International Relations Theory', *Working Paper*, no. 96, Harvard University, Centre for International Affairs, 1992.

Moravcsik, Andrew, 'Preferences and Power in the European Community: a Liberal Intergovernmentalist Approach', *Journal of Common Market Studies*, vol. 34, no. 4, December 1993, pp. 473–524.

Neunreither, Karl-Heinz, 'The Democratic Deficit of the European Union', *Government and Opposition*, vol. 29, no. 3, Summer 1994, pp. 299–314.

Newton-Dunn, Bill, *A Conservative Agenda for the European Community*, Wandsworth, Conservatives in Europe, 1990.

Nielsen, R., and Szyszczak, E., *The Social Dimension of the European Community*, Copenhagen Handelshojskolens, Forlag, 1991.

Norton, Philip, '"The Lady's Not For Turning" but what about the rest? Margaret Thatcher and the Conservative Party', *Parliamentary Affairs*, vol. 43, no. 1, January 1990, pp. 41–58.

Norton, Philip, 'Factions and Tendencies in the Conservative Party', in Margetts, Helen, and Smyth, G. (eds), *Turning Japanese?*, London, Lawrence and Wishart, 1994.

Nugent, Neil, *The Government and Politics of the European Community*, London, Macmillan, 2nd ed., 1991.

Nuttall, Simon, *European Political Cooperation*, Oxford, Clarendon, 1992.

Obradovic, Daniel, 'Prosepcts for Corporatist Decision-making in the European Union', *Journal of European Public Policy*, vol. 2, no. 2, 1995, pp. 261–83.

O'Hagan, Charles, 'The European Commission's Social Action Programme', London, European Democratic Group, 1990.

O'Keefe, David, 'Legal Issues of the Maastricht Treaty', UK Association for European Law, London, Chancery Law Publishing, 1994.

Padoa-Schioppa, Tommaso, et al., *Efficiency, Stability and Equity: a Strategy for the Evolution of the Economic System of the European Community*, Oxford, Oxford University Press, 1987.

Pauly, Louis W., 'The Politics of European Monetary Union: National Strategies, International Implications', *International Journal*, vol. 47, 1991–2, pp. 93–111.

Pilkington, Colin, *Britain in the European Union*, Manchester, Manchester University Press, 1995.

Pinder, John, 'The Rule of Law and Representative Government: the Significance of the Intergovernmental Conferences', *Government and Opposition*, vol. 26, no. 2, 1994, pp. 199–214.

Poos, Jim, Reinesche, G., and Vinges, D. (eds), *Le Traité de Maastricht*, Bruxelles, Emile Brylant, 1993.

Prout, Christopher, *Federalism, Integration, Sovereignty, Union and All That*, London, Conservatives in Europe, 1990.

Puchala, Donald, 'Of Blind Men, Elephants, and International Integration',

Journal of Common Market Studies, vol. 10, no. 3, 1972, pp. 267–84.

Ranelagh, James, *Thatcher's People*, London, Fontana, 1992.

Reynolds, David, 'A Special Relationship? America, Britain and the International Order since the Second Cold War', *International Affairs*, vol. 62, no. 1, 1985, pp. 1–20.

Reynolds, David, *Britannia Overruled*, London, Longman, 1991.

Rhodes, Martin, 'The Social Dimension of the Single European Market: National Versus Transnational Regulation', *European Journal of Political Research*, vol. 19, nos 2 and 3, 1991, pp. 245–80.

Rhodes, Martin, 'Labour Market Regulation in Post-1992 Europe', *Journal of Common Market Studies*, vol. XXX, no. 1, March 1992, pp. 23–49.

Richardson, Jeremy, and Jordan, Grant, *British Politics and the Policy Process*, London, Unwin Hymans, 1987.

Richardson, Louise, 'British State Strategies', in Keohane, Robert, Hoffmann, Stanley, and Nye, Joe (eds), *After the Cold War*, Boston, Mass., Harvard University Press, 1994, pp. 148–69.

Ridell, Peter, 'The Conservatives after 1992', *Political Quarterly*, vol. 63, no. 4, 1992, pp. 422–31.

Roberts, Ben, Gould, Julius, and Robertson, Patrick, *The Bruges Group Looks at the Charter of Fundamental Rights*, Study Paper 1, London, Bruges Group, 25 October 1989.

Rosamond, Ben, 'The European Community', in Spears, Martin, Spears, Joanna (eds), *The Changing Labour Party*, London, 1992, pp. 171–84.

Rosenthal, Glenda, and Cafruny, Alan (eds), *The State of the European Community: the Maastricht Debates and Beyond*, vol. 2, London, Lynne Rienner/Longman, 1993.

Salmon, Trevor, 'The Growing Pains of European Adolescence: Groping for a European Pillar', *Journal of European Integration*, vol. XVI, nos 2–3, Winter 1993, pp. 209–23.

Sandholtz, Wayne, 'Monetary Bargains: the Treaty on EMU', in Rosenthal and Cafruny, *State of the European Community*.

Sandholtz, Wayne, and Zysman, John, '1992: Recasting the European Bargain', *World Politics*, vol. 42, no. 1, 1989, pp. 95–128.

Schmuck, Otto, and Wessels, Wolfgang (eds), *Das Europäische Parlament im dynamischen Integration prozess*, Bonn, Europa Union Verlag, 1989.

Schoutheete, Philippe de, 'The European Community and its Sub-Systems', in Wallace, William, *Dynamics of European Integration*, London, RIIA/Pinter, 1990, pp. 106–24.

Schoutheete, Philippe de, 'The Treaty of Maastricht and Its Significance for Third Countries', *Österreichische Zeitschrift für Politikwissenschaft*, 1992/3, pp. 247–97.

Schoutheete, Philippe de, 'Reflexions sur le Traité de Maastricht', *Annales de Droit de Louvain*, vol. 1, 1993, pp. 73–90.

Schoutheete, Philippe de, 'The Creation of the Common Foreign and Security Policy: the Reform Debate during the IGC on Political Union', in Regelsberger, Elfrieda, Schoutheete, Philippe de, and Wessels, Wolfgang (eds), *Foreign Policy of the European Union: From EPC to CFSP and Beyond*, London, Lynne Rienner, 1997.

Seldon, Anthony, 'The Cabinet Office and Coordination 1979–87', *Public*

Administration, vol. 68, no. 1, Spring 1990, pp. 103–21.

Shepsle, Ken, 'Congress Is a "They", Not an "It": Legislative Intent as Oxymoron', *International Review of Law and Economics*, vol. 12, no. 2, 1992, pp. 239–56.

Shlaim, Avi, *The Foreign Secretary and the Making of Foreign Policy in Britain since 1945*, Newton Abbot, David and Charles, 1977.

Spicer, Michael, *A Treaty Too Far*, London, Fourth Estate, 1992.

Tarnoff, Peter, 'America's New Special Relationships', *Foreign Affairs*, vol. 69, no. 3, 1990, pp. 67–80.

Taylor, Robert, 'Mrs Thatcher's Impact on the TUC', *Contemporary Record*, vol. 2, no. 6, Summer 1989, pp. 23–6.

Taylor, Trevor, *Reshaping European Defence*, London, RIIA, 1994.

Teague, Paul, '"Constitution or Regime", The Social Dimension to the 1992 Project', *British Journal of Industrial Relations*, vol. 27, no. 3, 1989, pp. 310–29.

Teasdale, Anthony, 'The Life and Death of the Luxembourg Compromise', *Journal of Common Market Studies*, vol. 31, no. 4, December 1993, pp. 567–79.

Thomas, Stafford T., 'Assessing MEP Influence on British EC Policy', *Government and Opposition*, vol. 27, no. 1, 1993, pp. 3–18.

Thompson, Helen, 'The UK and the Exchange Rate Mechanism, 1978–90', in Brivati, Brian and Jones, Harriet (eds), *From Reconstruction to Integration: Britain and Europe since 1945*, Leicester, Leicester University Press, 1992, pp. 227–40.

Towers, Brian, 'Two Speed Ahead: Social Europe and the UK after Maastricht', *Industrial Relations Journal*, vol. 23, no. 2, pp. 83–9.

Tranholm-Mikkelson, Jeppe, 'Neo-Functionalism: Obstinate or Obsolete? A Reappraisal in the Light of the New Dynamism of the EC', *Millennium*, vol. 20, 1991, pp. 1–22.

Tsakaloyannis, Panos (ed.), *The Reactivation of WEU and Its Institutional Implications*, Maastricht, European Institute of Public Administration, 1985.

Tsebelis, Georges, 'The Power of the European Parliament as a Conditional Agenda Setter', *American Political Science Review*, vol. 88, 1994, pp. 128–42.

Tsoukalis, Loukas, *The New European Economy*, Oxford, Oxford University Press, 2nd ed., 1993.

Tugendhat, Christopher, and Wallace, William, *Options for British Foreign Policy in the 1990s*, London, Pinter, 1988.

Wallace, Helen, *The Challenge of Diversity*, London, Routledge for RIIA, 1985.

Wallace, Helen, 'Negotiation and Coalition Formation in the European Community', *Government and Opposition*, vol. 20, no. 4, 1985, pp. 453–72.

Wallace, Helen, 'The Presidency of the EC', in O'Nuallain, Colm (ed.), *The Presidency of the European Council of Ministers*, London, Croom Helm, 1985.

Wallace, Helen, 'European Governance in Turbulent Times', *Journal of Common Market Studies,* vol. 31, no. 3, 1993, pp. 293–303.

Wallace, Helen, 'Britain out on a Limb?', *Political Quarterly*, vol. 166, no. 1, 1995, pp. 46–58.

Wallace, Helen, and Wallace, William, *Flying Together in a Larger and More Diverse European Union*, The Hague, Netherlands Scientific Council for Government Policy, W. 87, June 1995.

Wallace, Helen, Wallace, William, and Webb, Carol (eds), *Policy Making in the European Communities*, Chichester, John Wiley, 2nd ed., 1983.

Wallace, William, *Foreign Policy and the Political Process*, London, Macmillan, 1971.

Wallace, William, 'Europe as a Confederation: the Community and the Nation State', *Journal of Common Market Studies*, vol. XXI, nos 1 & 2, 1982, pp. 57–68.

Wallace, William, 'European Defence Co-operation: the Reopening Debate', *Survival*, November–December 1984, vol. XXVI, no. 6, pp. 251–61.

Wallace, William, 'What Price Independence? Sovereignty and Interdependence in British Politics', *International Affairs*, vol. 62, no. 3, 1986, pp. 367–89.

Wallace, William, *Dynamics of European Integration*, London, RIIA/Pinter, 1990.

Wallace, William, *The Transformation of Western Europe*, London, RIIA/Pinter, 1990.

Wallace, William, 'Foreign Policy and National Identity in the United Kingdom', *International Affairs*, vol. 67, 1991, pp. 651–80.

Wallace, William, 'British Foreign Policy after the Cold War', *International Affairs*, vol. 68, no. 3, July 1992, pp. 423–42.

Wallace William, and Smith, Julie, 'Democracy or Technocracy? European Integration and the Problem of Popular Consent', *West European Politics*, vol. 8, no. 3, July 1995, pp. 137–57.

Watkins, Alan, *A Conservative Coup: the Fall of Margaret Thatcher*, London, Duckworth, 1991.

Watson, Philippa, 'Social Policy after Maastricht', *Common Market Law Review*, vol. 30, 1993, pp. 481–513.

Welsh, Michael, *Labour Market Policy in the European Community: the British Presidency of 1986*, Discussion paper No. 4, London, RIIA, 1986.

Wester, Robert, 'The Netherlands and European Political Union', in Laursen and Hoonacker, *The IGC-PU*, op. cit., pp. 163–76.

Wester, Robert, 'The United Kingdom', in Laursen and Hoonacker, *The IGC-PU*, op. cit., pp. 189–204.

Westlake, Martin, *The New European Parliament*, London, Pinter, 1994.

Westlake, Martin, *The Parliament and the Commission: Partners and Rivals in the European Policy-Making Process*, London, Butterworths, 1994.

Weyland Joseph, and Eyskens, Marc, 'Les conferences intergovernmentale avant le conseil Européen de Maastricht', paper presented to the Insitut d'Etudes Européennes, 8 November 1991, Université Libre de Bruxelles, D/1991/2672/24.

Whiteley, Paul, Seyd, Patrick, Richardson, Jeremy, and Bissell, Paul, 'Thatcherism and the Conservative Party', *Political Studies*, vol. 42, no. 2, June 1994, pp. 185–203.

Wild, Alan, Human Resources Director, Grand Metropolitan, *The Impact of Multinational Enterprises Operating in Europe – Legitimate Paranoia?*, CBI Presentation, 18 May 1992.

Williams, Shirley, 'Sovereignty and Accountability in the European Community', *The New European Community*, in Keohane, Robert O., and Hoffmann, Stanley (eds), *The New European Community: Decision-making and Institutional Change*, Boulder, Col., Westview, 1991, pp. 155–76.

Wincott, Daniel, 'The Conservative Party and Europe', *Politics Review*, vol. 1, no. 4, 1992, pp. 12–16.

Wincott, Daniel, 'Much Ado about Nothing', in Brivati, Brian, and Jones, Harriet (eds), *From Reconstruction to Integration: Britain and Europe since 1945*, Leicester, Leicester University Press, 1993, pp. 207–15.

Wincott, Daniel, 'Institutional Interaction and European Integration: Towards an Everyday Critique of Liberal Intergovernmentalism', *Journal of Common Market Studies*, vol. 33, no. 4, December 1995, pp. 597–609.

Winham, Graham, 'Negotiation as a Management Process', *World Politics*, vol. 20, no. 1, October 1969, pp. 87–114.

Young, John, *Britain and European Unity, 1945–1992*, London, Macmillan, 1993.

Young, John, *Britain and the European Community, 1945-92*, London, Macmillan, 1993.

Appendix 1 List of Interviewees

Sixty-five politicians, officials and practitioners agreed to be interviewed during the research conducted for this book. This is not an exhaustive list of people interviewed and only includes those who agreed to be identified. In the text where an anonymous reference is made to author's interviews with specific departments it should not therefore be assumed the source of the information is limited to interviewees in this appendix. Neither is this list intended to give a full account of the careers of those persons referred to in the book, but rather an indication of the positions held between 1990 and 1991.

Baker, Kenneth	Secretary of State at the Home Office, 1990-2.
Bullard, Sir Julian	Political Director European Political Cooperation, Foreign and Commonwealth Office, 1985–8.
Bussmann, Herman	Deputy Head of Section, EPC, Auswärtiges Amt.
Cameron, Frazer	Political Directorate, European Commission.
Capella, Christopher	Grade 5, European Section, Department of Employment.
Cash, Bill	Conservative MP for Stafford and Chairman of the Conservative Backbench European Affairs Committee 1990–1 and Member of the Select Committee on European legislation.
Collins, Timothy	Special Advisor to Secretary of State for Employment Rt Hon. Michael Howard QC MP, Department of Employment.
Corbett, Richard	Secretariat, European Socialist Group, European Parliament.
Cowper-Coles, Sherard	Assistant, Security Policy Department, Foreign and Commonwealth Office.
Crockett, Andrew	Executive Director, International Division and Audit Division, Bank of England, 1989–93.
Dankert, Piet	Dutch Secretary of State for European Affairs.
France, Deborah	Head of International Social Affairs, Confederation of British Industry.
Fraser, Maurice	Special Advisor to Rt Hon. Douglas Hurd, MP, Foreign Secretary, 1989–95.
Fitzmaurice, John	Chef d'Unité, Direction E, Relations with the

European Parliament, European Commission.

Gardiner, Sir George — Conservative MP for Reigate and Chairman of the Conservative Foreign and Commonwealth Affairs Backbench Committee, 1988–91.

Garel-Jones, Tristan — Conservative MP for Watford, Minister of State at the Foreign and Commonwealth Office with responsibility for Europe, 1990–3.

Gorman, Teresa — Conservative MP for Billericay and founding Chairman of The Alliance for Small Firms and Self Employed People.

Goulden, Sir John — Assistant Under-Secretary of State (Defence), Foreign and Commonwealth Office, 1988–92.

Hadley, David — Deputy Secretary and Head of European Secretariat, Cabinet Office, 1989–93.

Howard, Michael — Secretary of State for Employment, 1990–3.

Hurd, Douglas — Foreign Secretary, 1989–95.

Jargow, Hans von — Head of Section, European Political Cooperation, Auswärtiges Amt, Bonn.

Jay, Michael — Assistant Under-Secretary of State for European Community Affairs, Foreign and Commonwealth Office.

Jochems, Maurits — Head, Defence Planning Policy Section, NATO.

Kerr, Sir John — British Permanent Representative to the European Community (1990–5), United Kingdom Permanent Representative to the European Communities and Britain's Personal Representative for the IGC-PU.

Lamont, Norman — Chancellor of the Exchequer, 1990–3.

Lea, David — Deputy Secretary General, Trades Union Congress.

Lunn, Simon — Deputy Secretary General, North Atlantic Assembly.

Maesschalck, René de — NATO/WEU Policy Planning Section, Belgian Ministry of Defence.

Maganza, Georgio — Conseiller Juridique, Legal Service of the Council of Ministers.

Mather, Graham — Director, European Policy Forum.

Mauch, Hans — European Desk, Auswärtiges Amt, Bonn.

Nivern, Robert — Grade 5, Industrial Relations and European

	Directorate and Head, International Division (European Communities) Department of Employment.
Parmentier, Guillaume	International Secretariat, NATO.
Poettering, Hans-Georg	Christian Democrat MEP (Germany) and Chairman of the Armament and Disarmament Committee, European Parliament.
Prout, Sir Christopher	MEP for Shropshire and Stafford, Chairman of the European Democratic Group and Leader of the British Section, 1989–94.
Schoutheete de Tervarent, Philippe de	Belgian Ambassador to the European Communities, Belgian Permanent Representation to the European Communities and Belgian Personal Representative.
Schumacher, Rolf	WEU Liaison, Auswärtiges Amt.
Shea, Jamie	Defence Policy Planning Section, International Secretariat, NATO.
Sheinwald, Nigel	Deputy Head of the European Community Department (Internal), Foreign and Commonwealth Office, 1991.
Solinge, Alain van	Chef d'Unité, Direction B, Institutional Questions, Legal Service of the European Commission.
Spence, David	German Unification Task Force, European Commission.
Taylor, Christopher	International Affairs Division, Bank of England.
Teasdale, Anthony	Special Advisor to Rt Hon. Sir Geoffrey Howe MP, Foreign Secretary 1986–90.
Tibbles, Richard	Secretariat of the Western European Union.
Welsh, Michael	MEP for Lancashire Central, 1979–4, and Chair of the Committee for Social Affairs and Employment, 1984–7; Chairman of Positive Europe Group since 1988.
Westlake, Martin	Head of Section with responsibility for European Parliament Affairs, European Commission.
Williams, Nicholas	Defence Policy Planning Section, International Secretariat, NATO, MoD secondment.
Williamson, David	Secretary General of the European Commission.
Wright, Steven	Counsellor (External Relations), Office of the United Kingdom Permanent Representative to the European Communities.

Appendix 2 Chronology of Key Events 1989–91

1989

9 November	Opening of East German borders and removal of travel restrictions.
18 November	Special EC Summit Paris. Mrs Thatcher argues for preservation of NATO and the Warsaw Pact.
20 November	The European Commission presents its Social Action Programme of 47 measures to implement the legally binding aspects of the Social Charter.
22 November	Kohl and Mitterrand appear together at an emergency European Parliament debate in Strasbourg and call for closer European integration.
5 December	Mrs Thatcher defeats by a substantial majority the first challenge to her leadership since being elected Party Leader in February 1975.
8–9 December	Strasbourg European Council. A decision is made to convene an IGC on Economic and Monetary Union, to commence after the West German general election on 9 December 1990.
13 December	In Berlin US Secretary of State James Baker calls for a new Transatlantic declaration between the EC and US.

1990

14 March	Adoption of the Martin Report by the European Parliament.
18 March	First 'free' election in the German Democratic Republic with 'The Alliance for Germany' winning 48% of the vote.
19 April	Kohl-Mitterrand letter to Irish Presidency calls for the Summit to decide on convening an IGC on Political Union to transform the EC into a European Union.
19 April	Joint Bush-Mitterrand declaration calling for a NATO summit by the end of the year.

28 April	Extraordinary European Council, Dublin, to consider launching Political Union IGC.
7–8 June	NATO foreign ministers publish the Turnberry Declaration to improve relations with the Warsaw Pact.
25–26 June	Dublin European Council formally approves an Intergovernmental Conference on Political Union to run in parallel with the EMU negotiations and to conclude in December 1991 to allow political and economic union to take place by 1 January 1993.
5–6 July	Atlantic Alliance Heads of Government meeting, London, which rejects the extension of NATO out of area, but launches a review of NATO force structures and strategy. President Mitterrand announces all French troops will be withdrawn from Germany by 1994.
14 July	Nicholas Ridley, Secretary of State for Trade and Industry, resigns two days after attacking Germany and France for their role in launching a plan for European Union.
15 July	Proceedings at a confidential Chequers seminar which took place on 24 March on Germany made public by the *Independent on Sunday.*
2 August	Iraqi invasion and annexation of Kuwait.
17 September	A Labour MEPs' report 'The New Europe' calls for the EC to be given greater power over key issues.
3 October	German unification as the German Democratic Republic ceases to exist when its five Länder become part of the Federal Republic of Germany.
6–7 October	France and Germany call for the EC to develop a foreign and defence policy-making role at an informal (gymnich) meeting of the EC foreign ministers in Asolo.
8 October	Britain joins the Exchange Rate Mechanism.
21 October	Commission opinion on European Political Union containing proposals for an EC competence in foreign and defence.
27–28 October	Rome European Council convened to consider aid to the Soviet Union and Gulf crisis in fact concentrates on the EMU and Political Union negotiations to commence on 14 December.
14 November	Leadership challenge to Mrs Thatcher announced by Michael Heseltine.
19 November	Heads of Government attend the Paris CSCE meeting.
22 November	Mrs Thatcher withdraws from the second round of the

	leadership election and announces she will resign as Prime Minister once another leader is elected.
27 November	John Major is elected leader at the end of the second round of the elections after the withdrawal of Michael Heseltine and Douglas Hurd.
2 December	Helmut Kohl returned as Federal Chancellor after the first 'All German' Elections.
5 December	Douglas Hurd says Britain is prepared to consider a formal role for the EC in key areas of security but not defence.
10 December	WEU foreign and defence ministers in Paris focus on the implications of the Gulf crisis.
14–15 December	European Council Rome Summit formally opens the IGCs on Political Union and EMU on 15 December.
20 December	John Major makes his first trip to Washington to meet President George Bush.

1991

6 January	Mrs Thatcher becomes the Honorary President of the Bruges Group.
16 January	Allied Forces launch Operation Desert Storm to recapture Kuwait.
22 January	John Major says that the EC response to the Gulf crisis shows that the EC is not ready for a common foreign and security policy. These sentiments are echoed by Neil Kinnock at the Royal United Services Institute (RUSI) the following day.
19 February	Douglas Hurd at the Winston Churchill Memorial Lecture in Luxembourg outlines acceptable steps towards a common European foreign and security policy.
28 February	Government White Paper *Developments in the European Community* outlines a more positive approach to Europe.
1 March	Formal end of hostilities in the Gulf.
7 March	Jacques Delors at the Alistair Buchan Lecture at the International Institute for Strategic Studies, London, outlines proposals for a common European defence policy.
11 March	At the Anglo-German summit in Bonn, John Major outlines a new positive view of closer European with Britain 'at the very heart of Europe' and hints at a change towards the social market.

26 March	Foreign ministers of the EC meet informally at Senningen to discuss foreign and security policy.
8 April	At a Special European Council meeting, Luxembourg, John Major launches his 'safe-havens' plan for Kurds inside Iraq. A WEU foreign ministers meeting is held in parallel to the Luxembourg European Council.
12 April	Publication of the first Luxembourg draft treaty. Britain dissents and Delors describes it as a betrayal of the Treaty of Rome.
26 April	Foreign ministers of the EC had an informal (gymnich) meeting at Mondorf-les-Bains, Luxembourg, to take stock of the IGC-PU.
22 May	Commission proposal on amendments to the Luxembourg draft treaty.
28–29 May	NATO defence ministers (Defence Policy Committee) meeting, Brussels, which endorses a new Rapid Reaction Force under permanent British command.
2–3 June	Informal (gymnich) meeting of the foreign ministers at Dresden rejects the Luxembourg Treaty structure.
6–7 June	Copenhagen North Atlantic Council acknowledges the security aspirations of the EC Member States to do more in the realm of defence.
12 June	Douglas Hurd gives evidence to the House of Commons Foreign Affairs Committee on progress in the IGC.
17 June	On an American speaking tour Mrs Thatcher attacks monetary union and the idea of WEU as a bridge between NATO and the EU.
20 June	Second Luxembourg draft which includes a reference to the federal goal of European Integration.
27 June	John Major signals willingness to accept some form of reference to federalism provided the term is satisfactorily defined.
25 June	Croatia and Slovenia declare independence from Yugoslavia.
27 June	Vianden WEU Council meeting reaffirms European solidarity with the Atlantic Alliance.
28–29 June	European Council, Luxembourg, takes stock of the progress in the negotiations, but postpones decisions until the Maastricht European Council in December.
1 July	The Warsaw Treaty Organisation formally disbands itself.
5 July	EC foreign ministers meet in extraordinary session and

	dispatch the Troika to Yugoslavia, as well as suspending financial aid and imposing an arms embargo.
5 July	House of Lords report entitled *Political Union: Power and Legislative Procedure*.
19 August	Military coup attempt to remove Michail Gorbachev.
20 August	Employment Select Committee report says the individual Member States will ensure most of the Social Charter will not be implemented.
21 August	Failure of Moscow coup attempt and Gorbachev reinstated as President of the Soviet Union.
27 August	Extraordinary meeting of foreign ministers to consider the repercussions of the Soviet coup.
24 September	New Dutch draft treaty calls for a dramatic new powers for the EP and a common foreign and security policy, and explicitly refers to a federal goal.
26 September	Conservative MEPs urge Major to concede greater powers to the EP.
26 September	The first IGC meeting of the personal representatives since 25 July (a break of 43 days).
30 September	At a meeting of the EC foreign ministers in Brussels, a majority of governments demand a withdrawal of the Dutch draft treaty which is replaced by the second Luxembourg draft. In Dutch diplomatic circles this is referred to as 'Black Monday'.
4 October	Anglo-Italian Declaration on European Security and defence proposes European defence centred on WEU remain autonomous from the EC.
5–6 October	Informal (gymnich) meeting of foreign ministers at Haarzuilen focussed on foreign and security policy.
6 October	Franco-German security and defence initiative which argues that the EC should have a defence role.
29 October	Extraordinary meeting of WEU Council in Bonn. Van Eekelen argues for a gradual approach to a common European defence.
30 October–1 November	Douglas Hurd in Bonn for talks on the Maastricht IGC, joined on last day by John Major.
5 November	Douglas Hurd speech to Atlantic Commission, The Hague, in which he argues that Britain has an awkward but necessary role of asking practical questions.
7–8 November	Atlantic Alliance Rome Summit endorses a new Strategic Concept and confirms NATO as the principal forum for defence discussions.

8 November	Second Dutch draft treaty based on the preceding Luxembourg Presidency document replaces the first draft rejected on 'Black Monday.'
12–13 November	Foreign ministers 'conclave', Noordwijk, Netherlands. Hurd indicates the British government might accept enhanced legislative powers for the European Parliament.
13 November	Election of Sir Norman Fowler as Chairman of the Conservative Backbench European Affairs Committee, replacing Bill Cash.
16–17 November	Foreign ministers meeting, Brussels.
18 November	Anti-federalist Conservative MPs call for a referendum on economic and political union. WEU Council meeting in Bonn discussed the role of WEU and its relationship with the European Union.
20–1 November	Two-day debate in the House of Commons on Maastricht. Mrs Thatcher rejects any European Union Treaty and calls for a referendum.
22 November	Ruud Lubbers, President of the European Council, in London for pre-Maastricht talks.
22 November	Association Agreements signed between the EC and Czechoslovakia, Hungary and Poland.
27 November	John Major in Bonn and Rome for pre-Maastricht talks.
2 December	President Mitterrand in London for pre-Maastricht talks.
2–3 December	EC foreign ministers meeting in Brussels isolated remaining problems prior to the Maastricht European Council.
4 December	Richard Shepherd MP introduces private member's bill to allow a referendum on the Treaty on European Union.
9–11 December	Maastricht European Council concludes the year-long negotiations and Incorporates the EMU and Political Union agreements in one Treaty text.
11 December	Prime Minister's statement to the House of Commons on the Maastricht European Council.
18–19 December	Two-day debate on the European Union Treaty in the House of Commons.

Index

Heseltine, Michael, 26, 27, 31, 108, 137
Howard, Michael, 28, 84, 85, 86–7, 90–1, 92, 166, 167
Howe, Sir Geoffrey, 51, 55–6, 136
Hurd, Douglas, 27, 32, 33–4, 93, 110, 115, 117, 118–19, 120, 121, 138, 141, 142, 146, 147, 167, 168, 169, 174 (note 23), 175, 180–1

IGC-EMU, *see* Intergovernmental Conference on Economic and Monetary Union
IGC-PU, *see* Intergovernmental Conference on Political Union
Institute of Directors (IoD), 83
Intergovernmental Conference on Economic and Monetary Union
British achievements in, 160, 161
and British opt out, 58, 60, 61–3, 64–5, 67, 68, 69–70, 71–2, 172
and convergence criteria, 49, 58–9, 61, 63, 65, 66, 67, 69
draft treaties for: Luxembourg (May 1991), 14; Dutch (September 1991), 4; Dutch (October 1991), 14, 65
international context of, 7–8, 162
origins of, 5, 6, 47–50
structure of, 11
Intergovernmental Conference on Political Union
draft treaties for: Luxembourg (17 April 1991), 13, 141; Luxembourg (18 June 1991), 13, 114, 115, 123, 128 (note 69), 141, 142, 143, 145, 146, 149; Dutch (24 September 1991), 8, 14, 115, 147; Dutch (8 November 1991), 15, 89
international context of, 7–8, 162
origins of, 5–6
and pillar concept, 13, 15, 113–14, 120, 122, 132, 151–2, 161–2, 164
structure of, 9–11
IoD (Institute of Directors), 83

Jay, Michael, 57

Justice and Home Affairs (JHA), 13, 15, 132, 149–50, 152, 161, 169

Kaufman, Gerald, 170
Kerr, Sir John, 9, 11, 20 (note 44), 33–4, 57–8, 92, 139
King, Tom, 110, 167
Kinnock, Neil, 90, 119, 170
Kohl, Helmut, 6, 8, 12, 32, 48, 59, 63, 69, 70, 71, 93, 133, 135, 143, 144, 148, 180–1

Labour Party, 28, 83, 89, 90, 107, 116, 136, 143, 148, 170, 179
Lamont, Norman, 11, 27, 31, 33, 66, 68, 69–70, 72, 167, 168
Lawson, Nigel, 49–50, 51, 52, 53
Leigh, Edward, 86
Leigh Pemberton, Robin, 49
Lilley, Peter, 28, 87, 167
Lubbers, Ruud, 15, 63, 70, 91, 92, 93, 166

Maastricht Treaty (Treaty on European Union; TEU), 1, 15
Major, John
achievements in TEU negotiations, 160, 163–6, 167–8, 169, 170, 172, 175, 178, 181–2
and Common Foreign and Security Policy, 107–23
and Economic and Monetary Union, 53–6, 58, 67–8, 70–2
and European Parliament, 141, 143, 144–9, 152
and 'federal vocation', 128 (note 46)
leadership of Conservative Party, 26–9, 38
and social policy, 85–95
Mitterrand, François, 6, 48, 63, 69, 83, 92, 106, 112, 135, 143

No Turning Back Group, 28, 42 (note 61), 86, 91, 137
North Atlantic Treaty Organization (NATO), 37, 105, 106, 107, 108, 109, 110, 111–18, 121–2, 123,